THE
REGULATORS

Watchdog Agencies
and the Public Interest

THE
REGULATORS

LOUIS M. KOHLMEIER, JR.

HARPER & ROW, PUBLISHERS
NEW YORK, EVANSTON, AND LONDON

1817

353
·09
K79ᵣ

Acknowledgment is made to *Radio Spectrum Utilization* and the *Wall Street Journal* for permission to reprint material, and to the Brookings Institution for permission to quote from Corwin D. Edwards' *The Price Discrimination.*

To

Barbara
Daniel
and
Ann

Contents

Preface

This book is essentially about three kinds of law: constitutional law, administrative law and Parkinson's Law. The first is a statement of the original purposes and organization of government; the second is a method to which government increasingly has resorted in pursuit of some of its purposes; the third is a declaration of the predictability of the enlargement and convolution of government in its continuing pursuit.

All three kinds of law are pertinent to federal programs in a number of social and economic areas, and it is partly for this reason that government reorganization and efficiency are perennial topics of discussion in Washington. This book does not attempt to deal with all such programs. It is about those laws, policies and programs that are concerned with people's jobs and wages and with the goods and services the public buys. More specifically, it is about the major independent administrative, or regulatory, agencies Congress has created to regulate or promote private industry for stated public purposes and it is about the relationships of these agencies to other federal laws and programs which also concern what lately has been termed the "consumer interest."

I am not a lawyer and I would contend that that fact offers certain advantages as well as disadvantages to one who undertakes a comprehensive evaluation of government's efforts of many years to regulate and promote private industry for the public good. The obvious disadvantage is that a tremendous volume of sometimes complex administrative law has accumulated over the past three-quarters of a century. The advantages, perhaps equally obvious, lie in the fact that the enlargement of government and the volume of its law necessarily have promoted specialization in the administration and practice of the law. There are more lawyers in Washington than in any other American city, relative to population, and many of them are in the regulatory agencies or practice before them. Almost all are experts in natural gas law, securities law or some other specialty within the area of administrative law. Lawyers in government or private practice are paid to be specialists, not generalists. But specialization inhibits informed comprehension of the total fabric, which is woven of economic and political as well as legal strands.

This book grew out of my experience as a reporter for nearly ten years in Washington. The events and people were principally in and about the regulatory agencies, the Department of Justice and the Supreme Court. The various parts of the book have been reviewed individually by specialists in their areas and their suggestions are gratefully acknowledged. Drafts of the total manuscript, while it was in preparation, were read by only two persons, one in academic life and the other in government. The latter was Webster P. Maxon, executive secretary of the Administrative Conference of the United States. His position and knowledge transcend the dismal detail of particular laws and agencies and I particularly express my appreciation for his assistance on factual and legal matters.

Beyond that, the research and writing of a book, or of this book, require time, perspective and patience in greater quantity than normally are available to a journalist who works with daily events in the setting of daily deadlines. A great amount of time was made available to me by my employer, the *Wall Street Journal,* and I express my gratitude to that good and gracious national daily newspaper and to those who contributed the *Journal's* time and their own patience. I am indebted particularly to Warren Phillips, executive editor of the Journal; Henry Gemmill, a senior editor and former chief of the *Journal's* Washington news bureau; Alan L. Otten, Mr. Gemmill's successor as bureau chief; and to Charles Stabler of the New York staff. I also acknowledge with thanks the encouragement and assistance of George F. Scheer, a gentleman of Chapel Hill, North Carolina, and certainly of Norbert Slepyan and Phyllis Seidel, of Harper & Row.

The book, however, is solely my responsibility. The selection of cases and materials, the evaluation of the agencies, the conclusions and the basic argument of the book all are mine. It is not to be taken as a reflection of the attitude or position of the *Wall Street Journal* or of the members of its staff.

The notes to the book were prepared with the intention of affording assistance to some readers without burdening all. Those who would question or take issue with me are entitled to know the sources of information upon which I have relied. Also, I have attempted to be helpful to those who would want additional information or would desire to pursue their own research. Earlier books which I have found useful are referred to in the notes. Citations are provided for all pertinent Supreme Court decisions; the court's opinions in the bound volumes of the United States Reports are accessible in many law libraries, and they frequently contain very useful and even readable paragraphs on constitutional, legislative and agency history. I have not attempted to cite all regulatory agency decisions because they are too numerous and the most important ones are taken up in United States Reports.

L. M. KOHLMEIER, JR.

Washington, D.C.

PART ONE

We the People —
as Consumers

1
Consumers, Bureaucracies and Big Brother

If the United States of America enters an era of Orwellian splendor in 1984—give or take a few years—it will have traveled a road paved with each generation's good intentions. Federal laws no longer are commands to the few so much as promises to the many, written by Congresses, endorsed by Presidents, held constitutional by Supreme Courts and handed to bureaucracies to fulfill. There are promises of good education for the young, of good medical care for the old, of subsidies for the farmers and racial equality for Negroes, of superhighways and superior broadcasting, and a multitude of other good things for all.

No promises are older or broader than those made to the people as consumers. There have been laws, first state and then federal, to assure a dollar's value for a dollar spent ever since the dollar was called a Continental. From modest beginnings made by states to prevent overcharging by owners of ferries and bridges, grist mills and water companies, the body of consumer law grew as more people stopped producing the food and clothing they themselves consumed and began to purchase factory-made goods from general stores. It continued to grow as still more people left the farms for city mills and factories, as production and consumption became more impersonal and the nation more industrialized. The first major federal consumer law was enacted in 1887, to protect the people from overcharging by the railroads. Federal laws have since kept pace with industrialization and urbanization, and, since the enactment of the Employment Act of 1946, the federal government has been committed as a matter of national policy to full employment and full purchasing power. "Consumers, by definition, include us all," President John F. Kennedy said in addressing Congress.[1]* "Our goal," President Lyndon B. Johnson later said, "must be to assure every American consumer a fair and honest exchange for his hard-

* Notes begin on page 313.

earned dollar."[2] And Richard Nixon, as a campaigner, said, "The consumer must be protected," adding, "but he must also be trained and encouraged to protect himself."

The average family now spends 15 percent of its day-to-day living costs to purchase transportation, in the form of an automobile, subway or bus fares, and airline, train or boat tickets. Together Americans spend more than $51 billion a year on transportation.[3] And the federal government specifically has promised us the widest possible choice among the best and most reasonably priced transportation services and facilities.

Roughly 25 percent of the average family's spending is for food; collectively we spend some $120 billion annually to eat at home and to dine out. Washington's promises of safe and reasonably priced foods—or at least to make the resources available to fulfill them—are perhaps not quite so large as Washington's transportation programs. Federal law nonetheless reaches the price of yogurt in New York City, for instance, and the price of frozen fruit pies in Salt Lake City —"apple, cherry, boysenberry, peach, pumpkin and mince," as Justice Byron R. White of the United States Supreme Court accommodatingly noted.[4]

Another 13 percent of that average family's spending goes for household operation; the nation's consumers together spend more than $6 billion annually for electricity, another $4 billion for natural gas and $6 billion roughly for telephone service. Washington specifically has promised an abundance of the cheapest possible electricity, natural gas and telephone service. There are other laws, and bureaucracies to administer them, that assure us that radio and television stations will be operated "in the public interest," that the stock market will be run in the best interests of the more than twenty million of us who own corporate securities, and that our deposits in commercial banks and savings and loan associations will be safe and secure.

These and more are Washington's promises to the citizen as consumer. The federal government's assurances to the citizen as employee and wage earner are somewhat more recent and less comprehensive. It has not yet legislated a guaranteed annual income, but there is a law and an agency to guarantee employees the right to join unions and to require employers to bargain on wages and conditions of employment with those unions.

Government regulation of industry in the United States is not the equivalent of government ownership of industry in some other countries. The modern nations of the world have adopted three fundamentally different political approaches to mass production and mass consumption. Under Communism, as practiced in the Soviet Union, the state has abolished private property, assumed ownership of the means of production and attempted to distribute equally among the people the output of consumer goods and services. Under Socialism, as practiced in the Scandinavian countries and some other nations of western Europe, the state has nationalized selected industries and institutions, but the people have retained some private property rights as well as the right genuinely to elect a new government. Under the capitalist system, as practiced in the United States, government has left production almost entirely in private hands and has superimposed upon those industrial activities most vital to the public interest the authority of government to regulate commerce. The distinctions between the three systems have changed and blurred, but certainly have not disappeared. Americans enjoy the greatest freedom, and the highest standard of living of any people in the world. The United States is fortunate in having a perhaps unequaled abundance of natural resources and raw materials with which to work. But the competitive free enterprise system, leashed as deemed necessary under the constitutional power to regulate commerce, also has helped.

On the other hand, it is becoming increasingly obvious that all is not well in the consumers' paradise. For example, transportation was, in a large sense, the beginning of both industrialization and government regulation of industry; but now, some three-quarters of a century after that beginning, America's transportation facilities do not offer the people the widest possible choices of services at the lowest possible prices. Washington has promoted the construction of thousands of miles of urban and intercity superhighways, but the more it builds, the more crowded the highways become and the automobile and truck become a less efficient and convenient means of transportation. Government is consequently turning once more to the railroads but finds that passenger train service all over the nation has declined to the point that it may become extinct within five years. Government determines that it must subsidize the development of newer, modern trains but finds that our railroad technology has sunk so low that this nation, the most technologically advanced in the world, must send a delegation to Japan to learn how to build a truly modern passenger train.

It finds that seventy-five years of an agency's efforts to keep railroad and truck freight rates low have ended with freight rates that are too high. There is an element of transportation cost in the price a housewife pays for every one of the six thousand items stocked by a big supermarket and thus high freight rates ultimately are paid for by the consumer. The President's Council of Economic Advisers tells us that regulation of railroad freight rates, by an agency of government to which the council is not related, results in overcharges paid by consumers of some $400 million annually.

There is evidence that government regulation of commercial airline transportation, which began with the purpose of assuring flying consumers the most frequent and the most reasonably priced possible service, now has become government protection of the biggest airlines, meaning overpriced and not-so-frequent airline service. And there is equally good reason to conclude that regulation of the trucking and the ocean shipping transportation industries has also become protection contradictory to the original promises.

Hubert H. Humphrey once summed up the accomplishments and failures of federal transportation laws and agencies: "The massive waste of time, money and energy caused by faulty transportation makes the Federal deficit fade into insignificance." The accumulated federal deficit, at the time of Mr. Humphrey's expansive comment, stood roundly at $300 million.

Government agencies, like people, are not all good or all bad. One agency recently lowered the prices many consumers pay for the natural gas they use. But this same agency also has placed a floor under the prices producers receive for their natural gas and consistently has ruled against price competition among the big companies that transport gas from wells in the Southwest to the nation's cities. If this agency was not wholly to blame, its bad planning still was part of the reason why thirty million people in the Northeast were plunged into darkness on the evening of November 9, 1965, by the most massive electric power failure in history.

Another agency, created years ago to protect the public resource of radio spectrum space, can be reasonably accused of squandering that resource in regulating the commercial television industry. And there are yet other agencies that simply have failed to do all that the law originally expected of them.

It would seem that big business and a mass-production economy have become too much for a constitutional democracy to manage effectively for the benefit of the people. But to conclude that the agencies created to protect the consumer have been captured by the industries they were supposed to regulate is to oversimplify. Industries do have an interest in the agencies and when politics and business mix there is the risk of scandal, but the exercise of power in Washington is never so simple.

If constitutional democracy has failed to master modern industrial economics, the reasons must lie in the meanings given over nearly two hundred years to the Constitution. The Constitution provided in its Preamble for a government to "promote the general welfare." It provided in its substantive parts for private property rights and it checked these rights with a power conferred on the central government to regulate commerce. The Constitution assigned this power to the Congress, as the branch of government closest to the people. In the age of industrialization, Congress could not or would not legislate with finality but rather delegated to many agencies its power to regulate commerce. Each agency was to be expert in the economics of the industry assigned to it. To each agency Congress sooner or later gave a mandate, a sweeping statement of purpose and authority to assure the public interest in a field of private industrial endeavor. To each agency Congress also gave the power to fulfill that mandate by writing rules and making decisions. The agencies' rules and decisions are the law, as much as if Congress had written the final details, as it applies to the obligations and privileges of business. Inasmuch as the agencies were to be experts in economics, a calling distinct from politics, Congress appropriately created walls to shield the agencies from presidential direction and political shenanigans. This rationale of government regulation of business did not spring forth full-blown but, over the years, evolved as Congress adapted constitutional meanings to mass-production economics.

Each agency began small and clear of purpose. With the increase of industrial technology, old purposes have tended to fade and new powers have been needed. If rates and prices are to be controlled, then the number of competitors in an industry also must be regulated. A law nine pages long and an agency of thirty-two civil servants becomes, over the course of more than two hundred amendments, a law four hundred pages long and a bureaucracy of more than twelve hundred. And finally there emerge many large, expert agencies that in an economic sense are industrial planners and that in a political sense are a distinct branch of government.

In law or in practice, the agencies are not a part of any one of the three branches established by the Constitution. Planning is essentially an executive function, but the agencies are by law independent of the President's direction. Making law is a legislative function, but the agencies in practice are largely independent of Congress because Congress has deferred to their expert judgments for the writing of rules with full force of law. And deciding obligations and privileges under law is traditionally a judicial function, but the agencies are generally independent of the courts because the Supreme Court also has deferred often to their expertness. "The courts," Justice Abe Fortas has said, "may be the principal guardians of the liberties of the people. They are not the chief administrators of its economic destiny."[5] In their independence and with their power, the agencies have become something tantamount to a fourth branch of government.

Perhaps the Constitution could survive a fourth branch in which there are deposited pieces of each of the three kinds of power the Founding Fathers determined to separate. The difficulty is that the fourth branch lacks the essential bases of power upon which the three constitutional branches rest. The power of the legislative branch derives fundamentally from the constituencies from which each of its more than five hundred members were elected; the power of the executive rests upon a constituency and consensus of the nation's people at large; the power of the judiciary is grounded in life tenure.

The power of the regulatory agencies does not rest on constituencies of voters, either regional or national, or on life tenure. Theoretically, the agencies' technological proficiency is their source of power and their guarantee of independence, yet Congress has not discovered a way to make experts of political appointees. Their expert knowledge was to be applied with reference to the public interest, but Congress has found no way to communicate effectively with the agencies nor have the agencies themselves found a way to communicate directly with the consumers they were to represent. They are isolated from the President, yet their walls are pierced by political pressures brought sometimes by the White House and sometimes by members of Congress itself.

Thus does each agency develop a constituency of its own, which is the industry it was created to regulate. The arrangement is not as sinister as it may sound, in terms of pay-offs and petty political wrongdoing with which Washington gossip columns are filled. The conflicts of interest are on a far larger scale.

They first are the conflicts among many agencies, each pursuing an independent course that often leads to bigger and better superhighways, or airliners or ships, as ends in themselves. One agency of government promotes the atomic generation of electricity and another sides with the natural gas industry. One promotes the airlines, another railroads and a third highways. One agency promotes small business and another defends big business. And all this without direct reference to the people.

There is a second and perhaps larger conflict. On the one hand, government agencies uniformly become protectors of industry against the rigors of competition, particularly price competition. On the other hand, there is the competitive free enterprise system, as enforced by federal antitrust laws that are almost as old as government regulation of industry.

Ever since the beginning of the Republic, government has had available to it two basic kinds of power with which to abate or abet the workings of the free marketplace to "promote the general Welfare." The first is the authority to regulate the prices and practices of producers; the second is the authority to promote commerce, generally through grants or the direct payment of subsidies to producers, on the theory that the ultimate benefits will accrue to consumers in the form of more and better goods and services. Under the concept of a federal system of governmental powers divided between the states and a central government of limited authority, the pursuit of the general welfare has fallen into roughly three phases.

During the first century of the nation's constitutional existence, the states assumed almost full responsibility for regulating the prices and practices of producers—to the extent that there was a popular demand for regulation—and they held primary responsibility for promoting the construction of highways and the chartering of railroads and banks. The second phase began with the period of industrial expansion following the Civil War and ran to the beginning of the Great Depression of the 1930's. In it, the states still served as laboratories where schemes of government could be tried and tested, but increasingly Washington took on the task of regulating the prices and practices of vital industries and also began more to assume the promotional responsibility. The third phase began with the New Deal. Since the 1930's, Washington has become dominant in both the regulation and the promotion of industry and, within the central government, the responsibility for the general welfare of the nation's consumers increasingly has become the responsibility of the President.

In the first phase, various states regulated not only ferry and bridge tolls but also the prices that grist mills and cotton gins charged farmers, the rates that water companies charged townfolk and, some years later, the rates charged by grain elevators and railroads. Congress' efforts on the consumers' behalf, during this first hundred years, were sporadic and indirect. As early as 1791 Congress engaged in an impressive exercise of power over commerce, by creating the first United States Bank. But the bank, in which the federal government held a stock interest, was a constant irritation to the states' righters and when the charter of the second United States Bank expired in 1836, Congress did not renew it. It also is true that Congress, which very early recognized transportation as a catalyst of national expansion, in 1806 authorized the Cumberland Road, the first national highway. In the decades immediately following, Congress also promoted canal and railroad expansion. But there already were 25,000 miles of railway lines, built by private capital under state charters, when Congress began to promote railroads with land grants. Consequently, the grants went almost exclusively to railroads in the West. Highway construction was supported largely by the states even as late as the beginning of World War II.

Washington thus remained at a geographical and industrial distance from the ordinary consumer during the first hundred years when the nation was expanding. As part of this expansion, Eli Whitney patented his cotton gin in 1791 and the New York Stock Exchange was organized in 1792. Robert Fulton sailed his steamboat, the *Clermont,* from New York City to Albany in 1807. The Baltimore & Ohio Railroad opened thirteen miles of track in 1830 and reached the Ohio River in 1852. These were the innovations of individuals and private capital, aided and, when necessary, regulated by the states. The states to this day still have primary responsibility for controlling the prices and practices of a few industries, such as insurance companies, and lesser responsibility over a few others, such as banking. But following the Civil War, Washington, under the constitutional doctrine of the supremacy of federal law where it conflicts in jurisdiction with state law, began to assume responsibility for regulation and promotion of industry.

Transcontinental railroad service had begun in 1869, when the Union Pacific and the Central Pacific met at Promontory, Utah. Now rails bound together a nation that extended to the Pacific Ocean. They carried settlers west and lumber east and the products of factories, mines and mills everywhere. More than that, the railroads and the men who financed and built them were the symbols of the industrialization that was creating great wealth for a few and discontent among many—discontent that soon would lead to bloody strikes and unionization of workers.

In the years between 1870 and 1886, more than 150 bills and resolutions were introduced in Congress proposing federal regulation of railroads.[6] Despite the political oratory, there is no evidence that consumers nationwide were demanding lower railroad rates. State regulation apparently was satisfactory enough in the East, where railroads were more numerous and where they were generally competing with one another vigorously, even to the extent of mounting frequent rate wars. In any case, travelers and shippers on the eastern seaboard had transportation alternatives in waterways and dirt highways. In the great Mississippi River valley and westward, railroads had more of a transportation monopoly. Rival towns vied for rail service when tracks were being laid westward, the loser fearing it would never grow without a railroad connection; the largest of these struggles was waged between Chicago (the ultimate victor) and St. Louis for dominance as the gateway to the West. State regulation thus became far more stringent in the West than in the East. The legislatures of Illinois, Kansas and other grain belt states reacted swiftly to demands for cheap and equitable rail service brought by farmers, who in 1867 organized themselves under the banner of the National Grange of the Patrons of Husbandry. But these state laws were not enough. Farmer dissatisfaction grew for several reasons: Court actions brought by the railroads whittled down the authority of the state regulators. Railroad tycoons came to have influence with the state commissions. And increasingly the nation's commerce was moving across state lines.

The National Grange, through members of Congress such as Representative John H. Reagan of Texas and other Populists from out of the West, pressed hard for federal regulation all through the 1870's. But the majority of lawmakers in Washington resisted the novel notion of federal incursion. Congress debated the merits of competition and it appointed a committee to study the matter. The farmers, who seem always to have had a particular talent for political action, continued to press and in 1886 were given a new argument for federal regulation when the Supreme Court handed down a decision that, temporarily, cut deeply into the power of the states to keep rail rates low. However, public as well as political sentiment in the 1880's unquestionably was turning against the railroads. Railroad builders in the West, such as bearded James J. Hill, had received vast land grants but made no appropriate showing of gratitude. Railroad corporations all through the nation, through mergers arranged in Wall Street as well as physical expansion, were becoming the biggest of big businesses. And their cause surely was not helped when William H. Vanderbilt of the New York Central in 1883 said, as part of a statement to an inquiring newspaper reporter, "The public be damned."

The Senate passed the original Act to Regulate Commerce by a vote of 43 to 15 and the House by 219 to 41, with a rather large number of lawmakers on each side of the Capitol having absented themselves from voting. President Grover Cleveland signed it into law on February 4, 1887. The Act to Regulate Commerce was a law of broadest significance to the American political system, for it departed radically from the idea of limited governmental authority that reached private action only to punish wrongful acts after they were committed and then only in the occasional context of cases and controversies. The Act to Regulate Commerce substituted for the narrow, case-by-case approach of traditional law a permanent, continuing, day-by-day surveillance of the private conduct of the railroads. Its central purpose was not to punish what had been done but to regulate for the purpose of preventing the occurrence of objectionable deeds in the future. To practice this type of preventive medicine on the railroads, the act created a new agency of government, the Interstate Commerce Commission. This marked the beginning of the second phase of the development of consumer law. Even though the states invented the regulatory commission idea, the ICC was a breakthrough in the art of government in the wholly practical sense that a pervasive and omnipresent central authority was spread from one ocean to the other. The commission was to consist of five men, because its uncommonly large discretionary powers should not be entrusted to fewer. It was to be saved from political skulduggery by the requirement that no more than three should be of the same political party. The President would appoint the commissioners, subject to Senate confirmation, but he would have no authority to veto their decisions or remove them during the terms to which they were appointed. Apparently unable to break totally with the constitutional concept of the executive branch as the administrator of law, Congress directed the commission to report annually to the Secretary of the Interior; this requirement, however, was repealed two years later. Thus was the form of the regulatory commissions established as independent, expert, nonpartisan agencies wherein the worlds of politics and industrial economics would be reconciled.

The ICC was not born full-blown; no agency ever is. Its functions were to require railroads to charge "reasonable" and "just" passenger fares and freight rates, to guard against rates that discriminated against one town or group of customers in favor of another, to force railroads to post their fares and rates for public inspection, and to inquire into the management of railroad companies. The authority of the ICC to make railroad service cheaper and safer grew steadily, through Republican and Democratic presidential administrations alike, from about 1890 until the entry of the United States in World War I, when the government seized the railroads. President Benjamin Harrison, a Republican, in 1891 signed into law a bill giving the ICC broader power to require testimony of witnesses at commission hearings. In 1906 another Republican, Theodore Roosevelt, signed a major law that gave the ICC power to prescribe maximum rates a railroad could charge in the future. And in 1910 a third Republican President, William Howard Taft, signed the Ash

Pan Act, which said that steam locomotives must be equipped with ash pans that could be dumped without the necessity of a worker going under the locomotive; diesel locomotives that pull trains today have no ash pans but the Ash Pan Act still is law. Appropriately, Congress increased the size of the commission from five members to seven in 1906, to nine in 1917 and to eleven in 1920.

By the first decade of the twentieth century, railroads and railroad barons were no longer the single most prominent manifestation of the emergence of big business and the impersonalization of consumer affairs. The basic outlines of the nation's steel, oil, communications and other basic industries, as they exist today, already were emerging. Many states had been regulating telegraph and telephone rates almost since the beginning of those industries, just as they were regulating water supply companies, electric companies and other utilities. Western Union Telegraph Company had been founded back in 1856 and the foundations of the American Telephone & Telegraph Company were laid before the turn of the century. In 1910, President Taft signed the first federal law to regulate the interstate and foreign operations of telegraph, telephone and cable companies. Logically enough, it assigned this task to the Interstate Commerce Commission. And the ICC, for a brief moment, appeared to be the chosen instrument for all federal regulation of commerce.

Whatever might have been, Congress in 1913 began to create new agencies to deal with what it deemed new national economic problems that the states would not or could not solve. Then, and each time since, Congress has used the ICC mold of a multimember commission or board, in theory politically independent and economically expert, whose task is to assure that industry operates in the best interest of the nation's consumers. There are now more than fifty administrative bodies in the federal government that have something to say, directly or indirectly, about consumer affairs in the broadest definition of that term. Some of these lesser bodies are wholly apart from the executive branch of government and some for housekeeping purposes share a roof with one of the cabinet-level departments. Some are of multimember commissions or boards and others, with relatively narrower responsibilities, are headed by a single administrator. Greater or lesser, all these administrative bodies decide private rights or obligations under statutes enacted by

Congress and all exercise their authority under rules of law that were made to preclude presidential direction, political influence and abuse of discretionary power.[7]

But there are conflicts in the exercise of power between these agencies and the three branches of government, and they are conflicts which are not easily seen. Evidence and testimony appear from time to time suggesting that something has gone amiss in government's attempts to adjust old constitutional powers and freedoms to the needs of a mass-production economy. The late Justice Robert H. Jackson said some years ago that the rise of the consumer agencies was "probably the most significant legal trend of the last century" and then he added that the rationalization of the agencies with constitutional purposes is but "a smooth cover which we draw over our confusion as we might use a counterpane to conceal a disordered bed."[8] President Kennedy spoke of "a chaotic patchwork of inconsistent and often obsolete regulation evolved from a history of specific actions addressed to specific problems of specific industries at specific times."[9] Every President of recent history has complained, with justification, that he is charged with more responsibility to the people as wage earners and wage spenders than he has authority to fulfill that responsibility.

Perhaps the only sure conclusion to be drawn is that government, as presently constituted, has made more promises than it can keep. Perhaps we have come upon the discovery that an inflation of promises and laws, no less than of money, is built into the system of representative government. But the promises have been made and government will not repeal them. America will continue to try to find new answers, in the old Constitution or perhaps eventually in a new one, by weighing, as it always has, private rights against government powers, state powers against national powers and, within the national government, legislative and executive and judicial powers against one another. The balance today weighs more in Washington's favor, as against individual and state rights, than once it did. And, inside Washington, the balance weighs more toward executive power. The nation's hopes for material plenty are centered on the President, and gradually the President, by vote of Congress or without it, is acquiring authority commensurate with responsibility. He has a Council of Economic Advisers and a special assistant for consumer affairs. He uses the power of his office to prevent a steel price increase and to settle a railroad strike. He has a Department of Transportation that has assumed some of the authority of a few of the old independent regulatory agencies and all of the responsibility for bringing sense and coordination to the nation's conflicting transportation laws and agencies. He has, in short, begun to do what the branch closest to the people has failed to do: to coordinate the conflicting powers of government, to establish some manner of priority among multiple federal aims and to create order out of chaos.

2

Regulation and the Spirit of the Constitution

Thurman W. Arnold was the last great trust buster in the tradition of Theodore Roosevelt that America has had and possibly ever will have. He was Assistant Attorney General in charge of enforcement of the federal antitrust laws during the latter years of the Franklin D. Roosevelt Administration and his enthusiasm for his job prompted the conservative Chicago *Tribune* at the time to pronounce him an "idiot in a powder mill." Many years later, Arnold reminisced about his New Deal days in an address before a dinner meeting of lawyers at the Hotel Commodore in New York City. He asked his audience not to check up on the accuracy of his recollections because "I am an old man and most of the things that I remember best never really happened."[1]

Thurman Arnold in fact remembered very well and his facetious comment can be applied, without facetiousness, to government regulation of business in a free enterprise society. The thing best remembered about federal regulation that never happened involves the right and the obligation of government to regulate businesses that are natural monopolies and that thus are beyond the reach of the competitive free enterprise system. States always have regulated public utility electric, gas, telephone and water companies, and they still do. But neither state nor federal regulation has been confined to businesses that are natural monopolies nor have they pretended to rest on public utility theory. Rather, regulation has been applied to certain businesses with multiple competitors and it therefore has been a source of great and growing confusion.

The natural confusion over the role of economic regulation in a capitalistic free enterprise system is quite obvious. Government, for instance, regulates industries consisting of large numbers of corporations, yet it does not exercise parallel authority over the pricing and other economic practices of the automobile manufacturing industry, which consists of fewer competitors than most regulated industries. Businessmen are certainly the foremost upholders of the free enterprise faith and they allegedly are the most vocal opponents of government regulation. Yet, free swinging competition, and particularly price-cutting, is not the favorite occupation of many businessmen and sometimes they embrace even in public the notion of government regulation as a substitute for competition. No less an upholder of the faith than the United States Chamber of Commerce not long ago supported an expansion of regulation, in order, it said, to curb "truckers who engage in cutthroat competition, ignoring the regulations of the Interstate Commerce Commission."[2] Economists seem particularly confused by the alternatives of regulation and competition. Many have long suspected that mass-production economies require huge corporations and that the old notion of free-swinging competition among many smaller producers, who of course fragment the market, is outmoded. They thus reject competition but they are divided over whether, in the absence of competition, government regulation is desirable or undesirable.

Among those industries that are not regulated by the federal government, in any comprehensive sense, competition of course is not outmoded even if it also is not as vital a force as once it was. The most impressive evidence of the continuing vitality of competition probably is the rise of discount-house retailing since World War II. Principally by engaging in cutthroat price competition, discount houses have revolutionized department store and drugstore retailing, and consumers have been the beneficiaries. Clearly, the competitive system still has a role in giving builders of better mousetraps free opportunity to try to sell their wares and rewarding the successful sellers with profits; competitors who won't or can't keep up go bankrupt and disappear. The results can be benevolent or harsh on producers but the competitive system is America's traditional method of allocating national resources. Justice Hugo L. Black of the Supreme Court summed up the role of the system very well when he said in 1958 that it "rests on the premise that the unrestrained interaction of competitive forces will yield the best allocation of our economic resources, the lowest prices, the highest quality and the greatest material progress, while at the same time providing an environment conducive to the preservation of our democratic, political and social institutions."[3]

Because it has been around so long, belief in the twin notions of freedom and competition is not easily shaken off. The Constitution did not attempt to assure complete freedom of economic opportunity in the same sense that its Bill of Rights assured freedom of religious choice, of speech and of the press. But neither was the Constitution written in ignorance of economic philosophies. The Founding Fathers were worldly gentlemen. Their work was influenced by the political unrest in France that stirred for a generation before the Bastille fell on July 14, 1789. It also was influenced by the reactions in both France and England against the excesses of government and mercantilism. Adam Smith, the leading spokesman of the reaction against economic mercantilism, had published his *Wealth of Nations* in 1776, the year of America's Declaration of Independence.

The Constitution also of course was framed by practical necessities at home, flowing from the weaknesses of the old Articles of Confederation that had allowed the states to hamper the free flow of domestic and foreign commerce. Thus the writers of the Constitution gave the central government the power to regulate commerce and assigned that power to Congress. The power was checked and balanced with the Bill of Rights, which in the Fifth Amendment said no person shall be deprived of property without due process of law, nor shall private property be taken for public use, without just compensation. It was from these constitutional roots that the competitive free enterprise system, as well as government regulation of business in the interest of consumers, grew.

During the first century of American history, consumer protection relied on free competition among men, money and ideas, except to the extent that the states regulated particular industries. Political reaction to the economic power of the railroads produced in 1887 the first federal agency to regulate an industry, and the rebellion of the Populists against the railroad trust, the meat trust, the sugar trust and the other trusts that loomed large late in the nineteenth century produced, three years later, another law, the Sherman Act. The Sherman Act in a real sense did what the Constitution had failed to do: it wrote the competitive free enterprise system into law.

The Sherman Act, signed into law by President Harrison on July 2, 1890, was this nation's first antitrust law and it was a peculiarly American addition to the body of common and statute law the

United States originally inherited from England. Mr. Justice Black, in his 1958 opinion on the merits of the competitive free enterprise system, termed the Sherman Act "a comprehensive charter of economic liberty." It outlawed, in the sweeping manner of a constitutional clause, "every contract, combination in the form of trust or otherwise, or conspiracy, in restraint of trade or commerce among the states." It was a criminal as well as a civil statute, and now prescribes criminal penalties of fines up to $50,000 and prison sentences of up to one year for "every person who shall monopolize or conspire to monopolize any part of the trade or commerce among the states." It applied to private corporations that monopolized or tried to monopolize commerce in violation of the competitive system.

Congress enacted the first antitrust law and the first regulatory law almost in the same breath. The Sherman Act and the original Act to Regulate Commerce of 1887 did not contradict one another in substance. The purpose of both was to keep prices as low as possible. The purpose of the Act to Regulate Commerce was to provide a continuing surveillance over the fares and rates charged by individual railroads, and the purpose of the Sherman Act was to make sure that railroads, as well as all other types of corporations, did not conspire together to fix fares and rates or to monopolize an industry.

That was the division of labor that Congress had in mind and, for some years, that basically is how it worked. The Act to Regulate Commerce, which became the Interstate Commerce Act, was used to keep railroad charges low. But the Interstate Commerce Commission recognized that its mission also was shared by rate competition among railroads. The ICC, for example, in 1907 made the statement that "competition between railways as well as between other industries is the established policy of the nation."

The Act to Regulate Commerce and the Sherman Act both sprang from the waves of public protest against big business, originating in the Populist and agrarian movements prior to the turn of the century and taking renewed strength from the new urban and labor union resentment that found voice in three political party platforms in the 1912 election. But if regulatory law and antitrust law were, until roughly 1920, on the same track insofar as purpose was concerned, there was from the beginning a fundamental difference in the form of their administration.

The Sherman Act did not provide for constant government surveillance of all private industrial activity nor did it have the purpose of guaranteeing the lowest possible prices in the future for all products of all industries. The act was not unmindful of the future but it sought, like many other criminal laws, to deter future wrongdoing by punishing and making examples of those who were caught in committing or conspiring to commit wrongful acts. In writing the Sherman Act, Congress was not vague, as it was in delegating wide discretionary authority to the independent regulatory agencies; it was quite specific in outlawing price-fixing and conspiracies to fix prices and in banning monopolies and conspiracies to monopolize. The precise definition of a monopoly still is being debated in Washington, but antitrust law clearly outlaws monopolization accomplished through the concentration of economic power under a corporate trust agreement or through the merger of competitors into a single giant corporation.

The Sherman Act, clear of congressional purpose and not intolerably broad in its delegation of the congressional power to regulate commerce, thus could as a matter of the constitutional separation of powers doctrine be delegated for enforcement to the other two branches of government. The Justice Department, a part of the executive branch under the President, brings antitrust suits, and the federal courts, under the direction of the Supreme Court, decide guilt or innocence.

A special antitrust division was established within the Justice Department in 1903 and ever since then the department has been bringing antitrust suits with the single-minded conviction that consumers will best be served by a maximum amount of price competition among the largest possible number of competitors. The department's conviction, in terms of numbers of suits brought, has been stronger during the administrations of some Presidents than others. The Supreme Court has not invariably upheld the department, but most of the time, and almost all the time in recent years, the court has found the businessmen sued to be guilty as charged.

The Supreme Court was equally inclined to side with the interests of the public against private property rights. A milestone decision in 1837 involved bridges across the Charles River connecting Boston with old Charlestown. The first bridge was a wooden span that was opened about 1790. It was a privately owned toll bridge that had been built under a charter granted by the state of Massachusetts. Some years later, Bostonians began to feel they had paid the bridge proprietor enough and the state chartered a second, competitive span. The proprietor of the first bridge sued, claiming that the second bridge charter amounted to a deprivation of his private property in violation of the federal Constitution. Chief Justice Roger B. Taney, who recently had been appointed to the Supreme Court by President Andrew Jackson, wrote the court's opinion in the case of *Charles River Bridge* v. *Warren Bridge*. Property rights are to be "sacredly guarded," he wrote, but the "interest of the public must always be regarded as the main object."[4]

Another major decision in the definition of private property and public rights came in 1876 with a Supreme Court decision that, as a precedent, supported all the regulation of business that has come after. To this day, all the federal regulatory agencies cite the case of *Munn* v. *Illinois* as their original enabling law.[5] The Supreme Court, in that decision and a number of others that followed, held that state Granger laws providing for regulation of railroads and grain elevators did not violate the federal Constitution's guarantee of private property rights. The court said the private property of elevators and railroads was "affected with a public interest" and, so saying, the court was building on Chief Justice Taney's words of forty years earlier. But *Munn* v. *Illinois* also added a new large dimension to the constitutionality of regulation. State regulation of a private enterprise in the beginning had been based on the franchising power of the state or on the monopoly position of an enterprise, franchised or not. In the Charles River Bridge case and other earlier decisions, the Supreme Court had declared regulation to be a constitutional exercise of state power because of the existence of a franchise or a monopoly.

The court's decision in *Munn* v. *Illinois* began on those familiar grounds, but ended up in new constitutional territory. Messrs. Munn and Scott operated grain elevators in Chicago but they had neither the kind of a franchise nor the kind of a monopoly the first Charles River bridge possessed. The court explained its decision by saying the Munn and Scott enterprise held a dominant position because grain elevator sites in Chicago were scarce. In state law cases that came along in the following years, the court abandoned the thought that the states had to show a franchising or near-monopoly justification for rate control statutes.[6] The doctrine that evolved, and that the court applied to state regulation of grain elevators and subsequently to railroads, insurance companies and other enterprises, said public control of private prices is constitutional because the property concerned is clothed with a degree of public interest that affects the community at large.

Thus the court's decisions upholding the constitutionality of state regulation were precedent when Congress in 1887 for the first time exercised with truly national intent its power to regulate interstate commerce. When Congress created the Interstate Commerce Commission, precedent had established that the private property rights of the Fifth Amendment did not bar regulation of private property by the states; the Amendment thus did not bar federal regulation of private property.

Precedent also had established that, when state and federal law collide, state law must fall.[7] Consequently, the ever broadening stream of federal power and the recession of state authority have not been the overriding constitutional issue of the second century of the Republic. It has been how federal power shall be exercised within the constitutional doctrine which divides central government authority among three coequal branches. The Constitution was reasonably specific in apportioning executive, legislative and judicial powers and in providing for the election of the President and members of Congress and the appointment and tenure of federal judges. Its provisions concerning lesser officers of government were considerably less specific. It said such officers were to be appointed by the President with the consent of the Senate but was silent on whether officers, once confirmed, would serve for terms fixed by Congress or would hold office at the pleasure of the President. The right to fire is a key to control of the bureaucracy. Presidents consistently have argued that they cannot see to the efficient execution of the laws unless they can command the loyalty of appointed officers; Congresses have taken the position that democracy is best served by fixed terms which enhance officers' independence of presidential direction.

The controversy was resolved during the nation's first century insofar as the heads of the great departments of the executive branch are concerned. The First Congress, in resolving to create what today is the Department of State, debated whether the secretary should serve for a fixed term or at the President's pleasure. It decided for the latter. But in 1867 another Congress passed, over the veto of President Andrew Johnson, the Tenure of Office Act requiring the President to obtain the consent of the Senate before removing an appointed officer. The act was repealed in 1887 and cabinet officers ever since have owed their undivided loyalty to the President.

But as the nation's commerce and its government grew, the issue arose time and again with regard to other officers and agencies. Congress in 1887 did not repeal its asserted power to fix terms of postmasters and that same year it fixed the terms of members of the Interstate Commerce Commission. Congress' constitutional right to do so was not challenged until President Wilson fired one Frank S. Myers, the postmaster at Portland, Oregon, a year before the expiration of his term and Mr. Myers sued for his job. The Supreme Court in 1926 deemed the case of "great importance" and heard the oral arguments of the executive branch, then represented by the Coolidge Administration, and the legislative branch, represented by the eloquent Senator George Wharton Pepper of Pennsylvania. A divided court ruled that Congress acts unconstitutionally when it treads upon the right of a President to fire an appointed officer.[8] The decision was taken to mean that members of the ICC and other regulatory agencies, as well as postmasters, henceforth would serve at the pleasure of the President.

There is reason to believe that President Coolidge and his immediate successors used the 1926 decision to establish a measure of political control of the regulatory agencies. When President Roosevelt took office in 1933, he quickly and almost openly moved to harness the regulatory agencies as well as the rest of government to New Deal purposes. He fired a conservative member of the Federal Trade Commission, William Ewart Humphrey, because he felt, first, that the commissioner would thwart his purposes and, second, that he had the constitutional right to dismiss regulatory agency members. But the Supreme Court in 1935 read the Constitution anew and reversed itself.

On May 27, 1935, the court handed down two decisions that together re-isolated the regulatory agencies from presidential control and created a new balance of federal powers over the affairs of producers and consumers. In the first, the court declared major portions of the National Industrial Recovery Act unconstitutional.[9] The act, drawn by the New Deal to pull the nation out of the Great Depression, was Congress' most expansive exercise to date of its power to regulate commerce. It directed the National Recovery Administration, within the executive branch, to formulate Codes of Fair Competition to raise prices and wages in some seven hundred industries and suspended the antitrust laws for such industries. The Supreme Court ruled that the Constitution would not permit so unprecedented and undisciplined a delegation of legislative power to the President. In the second decision, the court said Congress had delegated to certain agencies the power to regulate particular industries, that such agencies "cannot be characterized as an arm or eye of the executive" and that the President could not fire FTC member Humphrey or any other regulatory agency commissioner.[10]

With that pair of important decisions, the Supreme Court read the Constitution to mean that Congress may not give to the President power, nor may he seize massive authority, to regulate the nation's commerce. If Congress chose to delegate its power, it must make the delegation to agencies that operate under congressionally prescribed standards and whose members do not serve at the President's pleasure, the court said.

The court has not repudiated this interpretation of constitutional doctrine. Even before the court in the late 1930's took on a less conservative appearance, it upheld the constitutionality of a number of New Deal laws which, by piecemeal delegation to independent regulatory agencies, accomplished much of what the National Industrial Recovery Act attempted in one grand design. For instance, it upheld delegations to the Securities and Exchange Commission, the National Labor Relations Board and the Tennessee Valley Authority.

In more recent years, a Supreme Court of unblemished liberal reputation similarly has used its authority to curtail presidential power and shield the independence of the regulatory agencies. In 1952 it told President Truman he had no constitutional authority to seize the nation's steel mills.[11] The court said the power of Congress to pass a law for the purpose of taking private property was "beyond question" but Congress had not exercised nor delegated that power. In 1958, the court told President Eisenhower he had no constitutional authority to fire a member of a relatively obscure agency, the War Claims Commission, prior to the expiration of the commissioner's fixed term.[12]

Thus has the Constitution been read and reread over nearly two hundred years to gauge the power of the federal government to regulate the nation's commerce and to discipline the exercise of that power within the government. As it turns out, there are in the Bill of Rights no absolute guarantees of freedom of private conduct from government interference. Freedom of private conduct is a relative matter. Freedom of speech, of the press and of religious practice were and are relatively more absolute than freedom to own and manage private property. The power of Congress to regulate commerce is, in an industrial nation dominated by the interstate commerce of big business, almost without bounds and thus did Mr. Justice Fortas write that the courts are not the chief administrators of the economic destiny of the people. But insofar as the Constitution speaks to the manner of the exercise of the power to regulate commerce, the Supreme Court has been true to the purpose described by James Madison of giving to each branch of government "some practical security against invasion of the others. Power is of an encroaching nature and it ought to be effectually restrained from passing the limits assigned to it."[13]

The difficulty is that the Supreme Court exercises an essentially negative and relatively narrow kind of power. As final arbiter of the meanings of the Constitution, it can tell the President or Congress what they may not do. But its jurisdiction extends only to cases and controversies brought before it. In fact, the court's opportunities to address itself to great questions of constitutional law have not been frequent, perhaps because an aggrieved party must possess large moral and financial resources to press a lawsuit against the President or Congress. The court of course can shape history. It indeed has helped to shape the exercise by Congress of the power to regulate commerce; it has shielded the independence of the regulatory agencies and shoehorned a fourth branch of government into the constitutional scheme. But the most activist Supreme Court cannot reach the actions or inactions of the executive or legislative or fourth branches that others will not challenge, any more than the court can force total constitutional conformity upon all states and individuals not parties to the litigation at hand. It can, as Justice Jackson did, merely express its consternation when regulation and competition come into conflict, when the fourth branch seems to violate the spirit of the Constitution. The more ordered world of law must sometimes coexist with the hurly-burly world of politics.

PART TWO

The Politics and Economics
of Regulation

People and Paraphernalia

The art of politics deals with constituencies, pressures, compromise and power. The science of economics deals with facts and figures, money and machines. The independent agencies that regulate business for the benefit of consumers were created to bridge the two worlds, and their constitutional legitimacy now is chiseled in doctrine and law. The Supreme Court has declared, as a matter of constitutional law, that the agency concept was "created with the avowed purpose of lodging functions in a body specifically competent to deal with them by reason of information, experience and careful study of the business and economic conditions of the industry affected."[1]

The rise of these agencies, that are neither solely legislative, executive nor judicial but that incorporate some of each of the three kinds of power, required certain alterations and innovations in political form. Most basic, of course, was the determination that the agencies should be headed by multimember commissions or boards, each member having an equal vote. Each was to be appointed by the President and confirmed by the Senate for a fixed term, from which he could not be removed, usually of five or seven years. The attempt to keep the agencies above politics was made complete with the requirement that no more than a simple majority of the commission or board members could be of the same political party. It is interesting to note that there is no similar requirement in the Constitution for political bipartisanship among the nine justices who sit on the Supreme Court or in the federal court system as a whole.

Because the members of the commissions and boards do not normally have degrees in engineering or economics or formal education or experience in some other appropriate profession, each frequently has on his personal staff a young engineer or lawyer or one of each. Most of the agencies also have on their staffs, as distinct from the personal staff of a commissioner, two or three professional economists. The total staffs of the agencies range in size from eight hundred or so to about twelve hundred. These people, divided among appropriately named bureaus and offices such as a Bureau of Operating Rights, a Rate Bureau and a Safety Bureau, process applications, make studies and investigations and otherwise do the agency's legwork and paper work.

From the outside, the agencies resemble courts. Congress has passed laws directing each regulator who sits on a commission or board to apply his or her expert knowledge of an industry to particular issues strictly on the basis of the public record; private conversations and off-the-record telephone calls are out. The public record consists of facts and figures, testimony for and against, exhibits, staff studies and so forth. It is thus fitting that each agency has a large room equipped with a raised dais and high-backed leather-upholstered chairs where the regulators sit, just as judges sit in their courtrooms. In front of the regulators' dais are a witness chair and tables for private lawyers representing their clients and beyond are seats for spectators. Some agencies, such as the staid, old Interstate Commerce Commission, mimic the courts to the extent that the regulators enter the room at the pound of a clerk's gavel and all the spectators and lawyers rise and remain standing until the regulators take their seats. All in all, it's a rather awkward way to deal with the dynamics of industrial economics, but it's the best accommodation to constitutional form thus far devised.

Each year the agencies collectively issue more than 100,000 rulings, a far greater output than that of all the federal district and appellate courts. Their edicts are essentially of two kinds. The agencies, after making a staff investigation and holding public hearings by congressional authorization, issue rules that apply with the force of law to all concerned. The Federal Communications Commission, for example, has a rule that no individual or company may own more than one television station in any city; the idea was that the public would get better TV programs, or anyway a greater variety of TV, if each large city had a number of competing stations. Rules that apply so sweepingly are, of course, distinctly not the stuff of the courts.

The second and more frequent kind of agency ruling is more in the tradition of court decisions. Here the agencies hand down a decision that applies, in its immediate effect, only to the case or controversy at hand. The case may have arisen in an application filed for a railroad rate increase or for a license to build a television station. Or it may have grown out of a complaint, filed with the agency by an outsider or by the agency's own staff of investigators, where the question for decision is whether a soap company's advertising illegally misleads consumers or whether a stockbroker made false claims in trying to sell stock in a uranium mine to investors. The cases may arise almost anywhere and deal with almost anything.

The agencies dispose of most of their business on a case-by-case basis, rather than writing rules equally applicable to all businessmen concerned, apparently because the case-by-case approach is easier even though it also is more time-consuming. It is difficult to write rules covering varying situations; rules also dictate results of greater uniformity than the agencies may desire. The agencies frequently have been criticized by judges and scholars for failure to make greater use of their rule-making powers, but the critics have had little effect. The failure is, of course, the principal reason for the agencies' tremendous work load of 100,000 decisions annually. The great majority of these decisions, amounting to more than 90 percent of the edicts of some agencies, are arrived at informally—meaning without the benefit of formal public hearings, sworn testimony and the other trappings of the courts. These are decisions on matters that, considering the size of the agencies and the industries they regulate, are relatively minor or are uncontested. The Federal Communications Commission, for example, almost automatically renews thousands of radio station licenses annually; the Civil Aeronautics Board allows airlines to pool their baggage facilities at the Chattanooga airport, and informally acts on dozens of similar matters; the Federal Trade Commission allows hundreds of garment makers to promise they won't discriminate among their customers. Even though most agencies dispose of much of their business by avoiding the red tape of public hearings, they still in recent years have not been able to keep up. And Congress as a result has passed laws under which the commissioners and board members are permitted to delegate some of their relatively minor cases to committees of staff members.

For handling the formal and bigger cases—bigger because hundreds of millions of dollars and thousands of consumers are involved, or because the case is contested, or simply because there are no direct precedents in prior agency or court decisions—some unique paraphernalia have been developed.

One is the rather recent appointment by several of the agencies of a staff member who is given the title of public counsel and whose specific assignment is to argue the consumer's point of view at public hearings. His job is to develop, by whatever means his ingenuity allows, facts and figures and opinions that bear on the consumer interest in, say, a proposed airline fare increase, an application for the discontinuance of a passenger train or for a permit to open a new bank or to build a hydroelectric dam. The theory behind the public counsel is that, even in a big case with lots of lawyers arguing at a public hearing, the lawyers for a company that filed an application and those arguing against the application are representing the selfish interests of their clients, which do not necessarily coincide with the public interest. The rise of what might be termed public defenders inside the agencies also is a tacit admission that the regulators appointed by the President do not contain within their supposed expert knowledge an instinctive recognition of the public interest, even though their formal decisions always and explicitly are determinations of "the public interest" or of "the public convenience and necessity."

A second and older creation of the political process of government regulation of business is the hearing examiner.[2] There are now more than six hundred hearing examiners in the federal government and they are a firmly entrenched addition to the bureaucracy. Hearing examiners are more than mere employees of the agencies. They are the creations both of Congress' desires to speed the work of the agencies and to assure that agency decisions are neither unfair nor arbitrary. Their role is provided in law. A hearing examiner always is a lawyer. He or she presides for agency members at public hearings, listening to all the testimony and then writing a so-called initial or recommended decision for the members to read. With the case thus summarized and the recommendation in hand, the regulators are spared weeks and months of sitting in on hearings and they can make up their minds after listening only to brief, summary oral arguments. Hearing examiners have more job security than ordinary federal employees and many of them are paid more than $20,000 a year.

The roles of the public counsel and the hearing examiner should not, however, be stressed unduly, because their pronouncements are not final. Moreover, the public counsel experiment has been of limited value because agency employees assigned this task have never been given much in the way of funds or manpower to seek out what the consumer's interest is. The impact of public counsels, even on examiners before whom they have argued, has in fact been very limited. The hearing examiner is a far more prestigious fellow, but with one exception his recommendations do not carry final authority.

The exception among major agencies is the National Labor Relations Board. The NLRB examiners' decisions by law may not be reviewed by the board unless a party to a case in effect asks for review. The explanation for this measure of finality which Congress conferred only upon NLRB examiners' decisions is that federal regulation of labor-management relations has remained politically more volatile than regulation in general. Pro-labor liberals and pro-management conservatives in Congress pull and tug almost endlessly at the National Labor Relations Act. In 1947 the conservatives succeeded in amending the original act with the Taft-Hartley Act, which was intended to offset in various ways the pro-labor bias of the 1935 law. The provision of Taft-Hartley concerning examiners' decisions apparently was born of the hope that examiners would be less anti-management than board members.

At other major agencies, the commission or board members have the unrestricted right to review an examiner's decision. They may, and not infrequently they do, modify an examiner's ruling to suit themselves or overturn it completely. Even at the NLRB, important cases frequently are decided by the board because the party that lost before an examiner requests review. It is then the commissioners and board members, appointed by the President, who are the kingpins of government regulation of business.

In addition to their legalistic and bureaucratic formalities, there also is a more practical side to the role of these agencies in government. It relates to the relative position of independent agencies in the federal establishment that today is very large. In 1887 when the first agency was created, government was small and a member of the Interstate Commerce Commission was a big fish. Even as late as the early 1930's, the chairmanship of the Securities and Exchange Commission was reward enough to Joseph P. Kennedy, the patriarch of the Kennedy clan, for his support of Franklin D. Roosevelt in the 1932 election. But now there are many agencies and government as a whole is much larger. The President under acts of

Congress has the responsibility of nominating for Senate confirmation persons to fill more than twelve hundred appointive positions in government. The relative prestige of membership on a regulatory agency is thus much diminished, and several consequences flow from this fact. One is that a regulator labors in relative obscurity. He cannot easily star in his own right. Washington's large press corps has neither the time nor the motivation to pay much attention to him. Another consequence is that the agencies have low priority when it comes to adornments of public office. The regulators ride around Washington in gray, government-issue Plymouth station wagons because they don't rate Buick sedans, much less long, black official Cadillac limousines in which cabinet members ride. They have great difficulty getting Congress to vote adequate official housing. Old agencies, such as the Federal Reserve Board and the Interstate Commerce Commission, eventually have moved into big, impressive buildings of their own. But the Securities and Exchange Commission for many years lived in a ramshackle temporary-type building in a Washington slum area and the Federal Communications Commission was stuck away on the top floor of the Post Office Building, under a roof that often leaked.

The agencies' lack of status is compounded by their constitutionally enforced isolation from the President, partisan politics and the mainstream of political life in Washington. They are not of course totally isolated (for that matter, neither is the federal judiciary, though federal judges have life tenure and regulators do not). If they want reappointment to a second or third term, they must look to the President, for reappointment is not automatic. They must also look to Congress. Senate confirmation for a successive term is not automatic either. They must look to the House and Senate for operating funds in addition to appropriations for buildings and for new legislation. Political pressures thus can be applied and, though the regulators are by law independent of the President, it is not unheard of for the White House or a key member of Congress clandestinely to put pressure on a regulator. Congress as a whole sometimes has overruled the regulators of an agency, not on the basis of the merit of their work but on the strength of political pressures that industry lobbyists have brought to bear on Capitol Hill.

The politics of regulation rarely is the partisan politics of Democrats versus Republicans. Rather, it is the politics of patronage and of privilege. The agencies are bipartisan and at one time or another everyone has played the game. The regulators have played because they owe their jobs to political appointment. White House aides and members of Congress have played because regulated companies are important constituents. The regulated play because they cannot afford not to. Politics has bulked increasingly large in the regulatory agencies in recent years and the only outsiders seem to be the consumers.

The evolution of the fourth branch assumes regulation of industry to be a special kind of economic discipline, a unique kind of governmental power that can be exercised outside of politics. It is not. The agencies have been accused of many things, but they have never seriously been accused of practicing technocracy.

The Regulators and the President

As does the politics of almost everything in Washington, the politics of regulation begins at the White House. The President—the sole officer of government who derives his mandate from the nation's voters at large—is both the head of his party and the Chief Executive. These two roles are intimately fused in his exercise of domestic powers.

The appointed officers of the executive branch owe the President their loyalty during his administration. When he leaves the White House after defeat or by choice, his department heads along with hundreds of appointed subcabinet officers usually depart with him, to be replaced by others who will serve at the pleasure of the new President. Although patronage motivates some appointments, particularly among subcabinet positions not subject to Senate confirmation, the spoils system does not dominate the executive branch. To the extent that it does exist, it is a necessary price to pay for our system, which requires that cabinet and subcabinet officials be loyal to the elected President and his policies.

At the other end of the power spectrum is the President's authority to nominate judges—including justices of the Supreme Court. Again, while politics does influence such appointments, once they are nominated and confirmed the judges owe no political or policy loyalty to the President. Their independence is constitutionally assured by lifetime tenure.

It is usual for Presidents to appoint men of their own political party to the lower federal courts. Generally the Senate has accepted this prerogative; in turn, presidential respect for the independence and integrity of the judiciary has yielded a generally high standard of appointments, aided by a screening device in the form of the American Bar Association's Committee on the Federal Judiciary.

A higher order of politics is involved in Supreme Court appointments. More is at stake, obviously, because the Supreme Court is the court of last resort in the interpretation of statute and constitutional law. Each President has preferred to name to the High Court men of his political party and has attempted to implant therein a measure of his political philosophy.

This exercise of presidential power does no undue violence to the constitutional independence of the court. The Senate, even when controlled by the party of the President, is capable of defeating a Supreme Court nomination to which it takes particular exception. It has not often refused confirmation, but it rejected President Johnson's nomination in 1968 of Abe Fortas to be Chief Justice. That episode was complicated by issues of presidential cronyism and senatorial propriety, but essentially President Johnson was seeking to perpetuate the liberalism of the Warren court in matters of civil and individual rights, while the Senate was exercising its power to check the President. When, as much more frequently happens, the Senate and the President are in agreement, presidential hopes of steering the court by remote control can be frustrated. This was most recently discovered by President Eisenhower, who failed to transfer his conservative philosophy to the Supreme Court when he nominated Earl Warren Chief Justice. The court from time to time does alter course, but is always its own master.

Regulators do not serve at the pleasure of the President and they owe no loyalty to his programs. However, they also are not independent of the President. Lacking the lifetime tenure of judges, they must look to the White House for reappointment at the end of their appointed terms.

In constitutional theory, the regulatory agencies are extensions of the legislative branch that speak only to and take directions only from Congress. Making law in technical areas where Congress could not or would not legislate definitively, their expertise would be their right to independence of the President. If not experts when first appointed, they presumably would gain expertise by reason of long tenure assured by reappointments.

Since Woodrow Wilson's Administration, no President has accepted that theory without reservation. Constitutional doctrine of course does not prevent the President from exercising upon the area of business regulation and consumer protection his power to recommend legislation, provided he speaks openly and to Congress. A number of Presidents have addressed Congress on the matter, but they and sometimes others also have spoken directly to the regulators, openly and secretly. The frequency, nature and purpose of these interventions by the President or members of the White House staff have varied with the aggressiveness and interests of each President. Nevertheless, the power of reappointment necessarily lies behind all interventions because that is the only real power the White House has over the regulators. No President has been willing to concede that important matters of producer regulation and consumer protection are beyond his reach. The regulators thus occupy an ill-defined and varying position in relation to the President, somewhere between the subordinate status of cabinet officers and the independence of judges. Over the more than seventy-five years of their existence, the regulators have become more subordinate. However, no President has succeeded in commanding for long their total loyalty. The politics of regulation, particularly in more recent years, has tended to go underground.

Congress has never been precise about how or where Presidents should find people with the occupational talents to be regulators. The only rule, which is unwritten but almost never violated, seems to be that the President may not nominate a regulator from the ranks of the industry to be regulated. There apparently were some doubts from the beginning that nonexperts would or could grow into experts, loyal solely to the interests of consumers. State regulation, which preceded federal regulation, certainly had not proved immune from political intervention. Judge Thomas Cooley, upon hearing rumors circulate in Washington that President Cleveland was going to name him to the new Interstate Commerce Commission, wrote to his wife: "I really begin to think that I am in danger of being named on the Railroad Commission. I don't think there is anything in it for me to feel elated."[1]

Judge Cooley, who in 1887 already had acquired a reputation as a legal scholar, for some years thereafter served as the ICC's chairman. In that early period it seemed that the regulators could make the system of expertise and independence meaningful. While the original regulators were not railroad experts when they were appointed, they had the opportunity to acquire a fair ration of expertise. A number of the men who were appointed to the ICC by Presidents Cleveland, Harrison and McKinley before the turn of the century served out their initial six-year terms and were reappointed to second and third terms. Some held office for as long as two dozen years. They acquired knowledge, and apparently their independence, of the President and of political and other pressures, remained intact. There was, from the consumers' point of view, a healthy hostility between the ICC and the railroads.

Presidential respect for the independent expertise of the regulators began to decline soon after the turn of the century. The history of the decline is difficult to reconstruct because of an absence of sure knowledge of all the facts. Presidents sometimes have intervened openly or have subsequently made known their interventions. But more frequently others have revealed the already known interventions at a later date. The knowledge that some Presidents have intervened secretly, encourages the suspicion that there have been other interventions.

A generalization which emerges from three-quarters of a century of history, is that the farther a President is removed in time from the creation of a regulatory agency, the less likely he is to respect and trust it. Most agencies have been created by Congress on the recommendation of a President, and that President has the opportunity to name the entire membership. He names people whom he trusts and who in turn believe in the agency's goals; he thus is willing and able to respect their independence. No subsequent President has the same opportunity to influence an agency, although each President following attempts to influence the quality and quantity of regulation through the appointment power and other means. Consequently, in more recent years Presidents and their aides have not had faith in the many agencies already created and have used them for patronage and other useful purposes—even while trying to turn regulation in more liberal or conservative directions.

In addition, the growth over the years in the purview of the executive branch affected White House attitudes toward the regulators. The President, insofar as he is able, often has addressed himself to matters of producer and consumer affairs through the executive branch and not through the agencies.

Theodore Roosevelt, for instance, was not so far removed in time or philosophy from the Interstate Commerce Commission as to have lost all faith in it. But President Roosevelt did complain to Congress of the ICC's independence and, in bringing the power of government to bear on the railroads, relied more on antitrust suits filed by his Attorney General than on regulation by the commission.

Woodrow Wilson also was an aggressive President who, of course, challenged the independence of postmasters and won. It is not known whether President Wilson fired any regulators, but it seems certain he believed he had the constitutional authority to do so. He once threatened, secretly, to remove all the members of the Federal Reserve Board.[2]

Presidents Harding and Coolidge, even before the Supreme Court in 1926 confirmed Wilson's right to fire postmasters and apparently also regulators, shared the Wilson view of regulators as presidential subordinates. Both of these Republican Presidents, it is said, demanded and obtained from certain regulators, prior to their appointments, signed and undated letters of resignation.[3] It is further recorded that President Harding, a vigorous advocate of shipping subsidies, dominated the United States Shipping Board, a theoretically independent agency that was a predecessor of present maritime agencies. President Harding was an old friend of the board chairman, former advertising man Albert D. Lasker. Calvin Coolidge succeeded to the interest in ship subsidies as well as to the Presidency, and Congress in 1924 set up a select committee to investigate White House relations with the Shipping Board. A Wilson appointee to the board offered the most revealing testimony given before the committee: "It was well known that the relations between the President and the chairman were intimate and constant and the board naturally felt that whatever the chairman brought to the board, he was expressing the policies of the President. In addition, the board more than once, or if not the whole board, members of the board, were called into consultation by the President and he showed his direct and personal interest."[4]

President Hoover on one occasion told the Interstate Commerce Commission that he thought railroad passenger rates should be increased and on another gave the ICC directions concerning railroad mergers. The commission, according to one historian, "somewhat reluctantly yielded to that influence."[5] President Hoover made those requests openly, having in hand the Supreme Court's decision that he had the power to fire uncooperative regulators.

The second President Roosevelt quickly seized upon the Supreme Court's 1926 decision and demanded the loyalty of a number of regulatory agencies. Commissioner Humphrey of the Federal Trade Commission balked but certain other regulators handed the President their resignations, as requested. Most regulators, it would appear, were not asked to resign; they stepped into the New Deal harness, reluctantly or not, and retained their jobs. President Roosevelt's successful and covert intervention at the Federal Communications Commission, for instance, was later described thus by a commissioner: "The commission always complied with all orders and requests made of it by the President and never raised any question about its obligation to do so."[6] It is not known what President Roosevelt specifically asked of the FCC nor whether his interventions ceased when the Supreme Court in 1935 reversed itself, saying that the agencies are not part of the executive branch and that the President has no constitutional right to fire regulators. In major respects, however, the 1935 decision made no difference to President Roosevelt because Congress created a number of new agencies during his term of office. He appointed all the original members of the Securities and Exchange Commission, the National Labor Relations Board and the Civil Aeronautics Board, for example, and had no reason to doubt their loyalty to his New Deal aims.

The Supreme Court, in any event, did not stop successive Administrations from intervening at the agencies. It was during the Truman Administration that the White House covertly asked the Securities and Exchange Commission not to proceed with the adoption of rules that would have abolished "floor trading" on stock exchanges. This episode began on August 8, 1945, when the SEC, after long deliberation, tentatively voted to abolish floor trading, a valuable privilege of stock exchange members. It ended just twenty days later, on August 28, 1945, when the commission voted for a full retreat, saying it had taken a new look at "the information available to us."[7]

While President Truman's personal role in directing the request to the SEC is obscure, it is known that the White House was informed of the extreme displeasure of the New York Stock Exchange with the SEC's action of August 8 and that the request was transmitted to the SEC, in the name of the White House, by a ranking Truman Administration official.

The importance of the intervention to the New York Stock Exchange can hardly be overstated. Floor trading is the privilege enjoyed by members of a stock exchange of entering onto the trading floor and buying or selling stocks for their own personal accounts. The privilege traditionally has been defended by the New York Stock Exchange because it adds "liquidity" to the market, meaning that the more buyers and sellers there are, the faster and better public investors' transactions can be executed. Critics traditionally have asserted that, whatever liquidity floor trading may add to the market, the privilege should be abolished because it gives exchange members too much of an advantage over public investors. Members, being on the scene (the public cannot trade on or walk on an exchange floor; it must trade through an exchange member and pay him a commission), can react to market developments more quickly and at less expense than can the public. There has been evidence too that floor trading, even though it has been regulated for many years by exchange rules, sometimes has tended to destabilize the market.

In 1945 the staff of the SEC (which had the discretionary power to "regulate or prevent" floor trading, from the 1934 Securities Exchange Act) had laboriously studied floor trading and recommended that the commission abolish the privilege. Over the well-known objections of the New York Stock Exchange, the five commissioners first decided, on August 8, that they would. Then they decided they would not. Instead, their public announcement said, they would let the New York Stock Exchange tighten its own floor-trading surveillance rules. The Big Board in 1945 did amend its rules and, a few years later, relaxed them again.

A postscript must be added to the Truman Administration's mission to the SEC. After President Kennedy came to the White House, the SEC made its massive Special Study of Securities Markets, published in 1963. One of the staff study's major recommendations to the commission was that floor trading, "a vestige of the former 'private club' character of stock exchanges," be abolished or severely restricted. And again, in the spring of 1964, the New York Stock Exchange went to the White House, by then occupied by Lyndon B. Johnson. But the Big Board's footing wasn't so good this time. Word of its scheduled visit leaked out, embarrassing the President, exchange officials and the SEC. As it turned out, the SEC in 1964 voted to restrict floor trading, this time much more severely. But the point to be made is that the commission, despite years of controversy and criticism concerning the privilege, never exercised its power to abolish it.

The Securities and Exchange Commission and other regulatory agencies were no more immune from White House intervention during the Republican Administration of Dwight D. Eisenhower than they had been during the Democratic reign of Harry S. Truman. President Eisenhower, like Mr. Truman, may not have known what was going on, but President Eisenhower's chief of staff, Sherman Adams, seemed to assume that the regulators owed their loyalty to the President.

Mr. Adams, crisp New Englander that he was, picked up his White House phone one Saturday morning in the summer of 1955 and successfully intervened in a pending SEC case that was part of what became known as the Dixon-Yates affair.[8] This case was essentially a public versus private power dispute and the Eisenhower Administration was determined to settle it in favor of the private electric utility that was headed by Messrs. Dixon and Yates.

A government facility located near Memphis, Tennessee, needed additional power. It could have been supplied either by the Tennessee Valley Authority or by the Dixon-Yates combine. Dixon-Yates was awarded the contract and then the combine applied to the SEC for approval of its financing. The Administration asked Congress for $6.5 million to build a power line to carry the electricity from the proposed generating plant to the government facility. Both these aspects of the controversial matter were pending when Sherman Adams telephoned J. Sinclair Armstrong, then chairman of the SEC. Adams asked that the commission put off a hearing scheduled for the upcoming Monday. The apparent reason was that a vote on the $6.5 million appropriation request also was upcoming and the White House feared that testimony to be given at the SEC hearing might tip the narrowly divided House of Representatives against the appropriation. The SEC agreed to postpone its hearing and, whether or not that was the reason, the House approved the appropriation.

The commission hearing then resumed and it appeared that the Dixon-Yates plant was on its way. That was not, however, the way it ended. Senator Estes Kefauver, Democrat of Tennessee, dogged the Administration and President Eisenhower finally had the Dixon-Yates contract canceled.

That call by Sherman Adams to the SEC in 1955 was not his undoing, however. His departure from President Eisenhower's staff came in 1958 after another Democratic-controlled investigative unit, the House Legislative Oversight Subcommittee, disclosed Adams' interventions on yet other matters with the SEC and the Federal Trade Commission on behalf of his friend Bernard Goldfine.[9]

Sherman Adams and Bernard Goldfine had been close personal and political friends since about 1940. Goldfine was a textile manufacturer and had other business interests in New England. Adams left the governor's chair in New Hampshire in 1953 to become the second most powerful man in the White House.

Late in 1953, Goldfine brought a problem to his friend. Northfield Mills, a Goldfine company, had been charged in a letter from the staff of the Federal Trade Commission with mislabeling some of its fabrics. Adams quickly telephoned Edward F. Howrey, the commission chairman, asking what had prompted the letter. Chairman Howrey said he would find out and shortly thereafter composed a "Memorandum for Honorable Sherman Adams" outlining the evidence which indicated mislabeling. Adams passed the memorandum along to Goldfine. Thereafter, the FTC settled the case on Northfield Mills' written agreement to label accurately the wool, nylon and vicuña content of its fabrics.

However, the FTC staff continued to snoop and in the spring of 1955 Goldfine asked Adams to make an appointment for him to see Chairman Howrey. The conference took place in April of 1955. Almost a year later, the staff drew up a detailed report alleging that the Goldfine companies had continued to mislabel fabrics, and recommending that the commission issue a formal complaint against the companies and certify the facts to the Justice Department for criminal prosecution. The commission issued a formal complaint and in 1957 settled it on the basis of another Goldfine promise to cease mislabeling.

It was in 1956 that Goldfine first took to Adams his problem with the SEC. Adams asked another White House aide to inquire and the aide was told by the SEC's general counsel that the agency was having trouble getting Goldfine to file certain reports on the financial affairs of two of his companies, East Boston Company and its subsidiary, Boston Port Development Company. Corporate annual reports are due at the SEC within 120 days of the close of a company's fiscal year but the East Boston and Boston Port Development reports had not been filed since 1948 and the SEC staff was pressing Goldfine to file them. The aide passed this information back to Adams, who later said he didn't pass it along to Goldfine because there was nothing in it the latter didn't already know.

Sherman Adams' interventions at the FTC and SEC involved matters that, in the total context of those agencies' affairs if not in the life of Bernard Goldfine, were of small import. Moreover, the intervention at the SEC did Goldfine little good in the long run. The commission brought suit in federal district court in Boston and Goldfine was compelled to file the reports. In addition, Goldfine had large income tax problems which were resolved in 1961 when he pleaded guilty to evasion of $800,000 in federal taxes and served ten months in a federal prison.

Clearly, Sherman Adams was of little help to Goldfine. Nonetheless, Adams' willingness to telephone the agencies on his friend's behalf became the major scandal of the Eisenhower Administration. In the late 1950's the Democrats controlled Congress and they revealed Sherman Adams' earlier surreptitious phone calls. The Republican embarrassment was sufficiently great that Adams was forced to resign. Perhaps he was guilty of no more than naïveté, but even he became convinced later on that "no expression of interest, no matter how innocent or slight, is ever completely disregarded" by the regulators when it comes from the White House.[10]

There is no evidence that the White House similarly intervened at the regulatory agencies during the Kennedy or Johnson Administrations. But it also is not unfair to note that, throughout the history of regulation, the evidence of surreptitious intervention usually has come to light only when the Democrats are anxious and able to embarrass the Republicans, or vice versa. During the Kennedy and Johnson Administrations, the Democrats controlled Congress as well as the White House; the Republican minority in Congress was without power to investigate the President's relationships with the regulators.

If they did not telephone the regulators, Presidents and their aides since Dwight Eisenhower's Administration certainly have not lacked interest in business regulation and consumer protection. President Kennedy shortly after his election in 1960 assigned James M. Landis, an old family friend, former Harvard Law School dean and former regulator, to the task of studying the agencies' efficiency and effectiveness.[11] The Landis report was not a secret document and it was the basis of several messages the President sent to

Congress. President Johnson, within days of the Kennedy assassination, spoke to the regulators directly and privately, although the White House press office released his statement. In it Mr. Johnson said he wanted the regulators to concern themselves with "cooperation" with business rather than "new areas of control" of business.[12] Presidents Kennedy and Johnson appointed to the agencies, as vacancies occurred, men they felt shared their philosophies. But, as Lyndon Johnson's statement indicated, their philosophies were not identical, even if both were Democrats. John Kennedy was a liberal who favored tough and expansive regulation of business and initially appointed tough and expansive regulators. Lyndon Johnson was a liberal on matters such as civil rights, but on issues of property rights he was a conservative who used his appointment power to soften and curtail regulation. Richard Nixon also was a conservative who, during the 1968 presidential election campaign, sent a form letter to three thousand securities industry leaders pledging that during the Nixon Administration the Securities and Exchange Commission would follow a soft line.

Taken together, the known evidence of interventions from Wilson to Nixon demonstrates that Presidents, Democratic or Republican, have not disassociated themselves from the substance of regulation. Contemporary regulation, in form and substance, also is influenced by a more or less constant application of patronage politics. The spoils system, roughly the equivalent of the system that remains in the executive branch, invaded the regulatory agencies in 1950. Presidents, of course, prior to that year, at times had given appointments to commissions and boards as rewards for party service. By law, no party may have a majority of more than one among the members of most agencies, but Presidents past and present usually have been able to find in the opposite party men and women to their liking. In 1950, however, a significantly larger opportunity for patronage politics came into being.

That, presumably, was not the intention. President Truman in 1950 submitted to Congress reorganization plans for the major regulatory agencies. Their main purpose was to authorize the President to designate one of the members of each agency as its chairman and to vest in the chairman the responsibility for naming key staff personnel. Previously, the members of most agencies elected one of themselves as chairman, usually rotating the position annually, and all members participated in the hiring of important staff people. President Truman told Congress that his aim was to pinpoint responsibility for efficient operation of the agencies and to speed their work, trim their backlogs and generally improve "effectiveness and economy." Mr. Truman must be taken at his word, but, as so often has happened with the regulators, the end results have been quite different from the effects intended.

Congress agreed to all the reorganization plans except one for the Interstate Commerce Commission. The railroad industry, unwilling to take its chances with a chairman of Harry Truman's choice, stirred up enough opposition so that Congress voted to bar the President from naming the ICC chairman. At almost all other agencies, the President since 1950 has designated the chairman, the chairman serves at the President's pleasure and each time the White House changes party hands the chairmanships also change party hands. The Supreme Court has never been called upon to decide whether, as a matter of constitutional law, the chairmen may serve at the pleasure of the President or are entitled to the chair for the duration of their terms as members of a commission or board. Some chairmen have been of the latter view, but not strongly enough to fight all the way to the Supreme Court. Some chairmen since 1950 also have had to be persuaded by the new President to vacate the chairmanship; most have not. Most have gone quietly, accepting the principle that the chairmanship belongs to the party in the White House.

The extension of presidential power to the chairmen has had profound effects, reaching laterally to the other agency members and seeping downward into the agency staffs. Political allegiance and alliance are more important to all than they once were. Indeed, politics has become a larger topic of concern inside some agencies than it is inside the executive branch departments. Cabinet and subcabinet officers need not declare their allegiance to the party and demonstrate their loyalty to the President endlessly; in the political limbo of the agencies, declarations and demonstrations are a useful kind of job insurance.

Some Presidents still have relied sometimes on the criteria of ability, energy and honesty in appointing and reappointing regulators to some agencies. Some few agencies still remain relatively nonpolitical. The Interstate Commerce Commission is not unconcerned with politics, but it also is not consumed with politics, because it picks its own chairman; the Federal Reserve Board is not concerned to excess, because its members have long (fourteen-year) terms. By and large, however, politics since 1950 has eroded more the expertise which supposedly is the touchstone of regulation. James Landis asserted in 1960 that the agencies had suffered "a deterioration in quality, both at the top level and throughout the staff."[13] The observation was not seriously challenged then and it remains valid.

The quality of contemporary regulators and regulation reflects another, related test which candidates for nomination must pass. The test relates in an inverse way to the qualifications for regulating a particular industry. It remains as true as ever that nominees may not come from the industry to be regulated. Pertinent experience of any sort has become so irrelevant as to produce exchanges such as this, which took place at the Senate confirmation hearing of a nominee to the Federal Communications Commission. Asked by a senator about his qualifications for regulating the communications industries, he replied, "Senator, I don't know anything about communications. I came to Washington expecting to be appointed to the Federal Power Commission."

The test of competence to which a candidate for initial appointment is subjected consists of the submission by the White House of his or her name to industry executives before sending it on to the Senate for confirmation. CAB appointees are cleared with airline executives, FPC appointees with gas and electric companies, ICC appointees with railroad officials and usually truckers too.

Every President in recent history has run some sort of check with industry before appointing or reappointing a regulator. The method of checking has not always been the same and industry reactions obtained have been given varying weights by different Presidents. But the practice is so well established that not long ago a new president of Eastern Air Lines proposed publicly that the whole thing be brought out into the open with the formation of a committee of airline presidents "to select a list of 'competent candidates' for consideration by the President in filling the next vacancy on the CAB."[14] The committee was not formed, at least not out in the open. The appointment machinery apparently works well enough, for example, to the thinking of a bank executive who said of the banking regulators: "This system works best if there's a blob in every job."[15]

Almost no President has ever sent up for Senate confirmation a name to which industry takes vigorous exception. President Truman, for instance, refused, for no reason that was apparent at the time, to reappoint James Landis. Landis, who in the 1930's had been chairman of the Securities and Exchange Commission, was chairman of the Civil Aeronautics Board in 1947. His term was drawing to an end and the White House announced he would not be reappointed. Landis subsequently said, "There is no question that the airlines were against me. I am against monopolistic practices and a number of things that they have been doing."[16] The only exception in recent history was when President Truman in 1949 tried unsuccessfully to reappoint Leland Olds to the Federal Power Commission despite gas industry opposition.

More usually the names that the White House picks pass the industry check without difficulty. President Johnson, for instance, decided in the spring of 1965 to name Charles S. Murphy to the CAB and to designate him chairman. The White House checked with American Airlines' Washington vice president and several other airline executives and found no objections. Mr. Murphy typically had no aviation experience. He was a good, sound Democratic work horse, a Washington lawyer and a long-time friend of Lyndon Johnson. Mr. Murphy had been on the White House staff during the Truman Administration; he left government and practiced law in Washington during the Eisenhower Administration and returned with the Democrats in 1961. He was named Under Secretary of Agriculture by President Kennedy, went to the CAB in 1965 and returned to President Johnson's White House staff in 1967.

All Presidents have run checks with industry before picking regulators, fundamentally because all have looked on regulation more or less as industry's preserve. They also, in the normal exercise of their duty to nominate executive, judicial and regulatory officers for Senate confirmation, want to be forewarned of opposition. If a nomination will face a stiff fight, the President must decide whether to drop it or do battle with the Senate. Another reason for the checkouts is that all Presidents, Democrats as well as Republicans, number leading industrialists among their personal friends and political contributors. Conferring with them is regarded as simply an act of courtesy.

And, perhaps most important, no President can forever ignore the business community or incur its universal and undying wrath by appointing hostile regulators. As John Kennedy learned, an excessive amount of presidential hostility toward the business community can in the long run shake business confidence in the future of the nation's economy. Badly shaken confidence means a falling stock market and perhaps curtailment of new plant construction and of new job opportunities and that is bad politics. Regulatory agency appointments are of course not the whole of business confidence or lack thereof, but they surely are part of the fabric of the White House's relations with business.

Politics and regulation being what they now are, regulators generally fall into one of two categories. The first consists of the occasional appointees who are bright, able and ambitious; they invariably stay for a few years and then resign, long before the expiration of the five-year or seven-year terms to which they were appointed. The second category takes in the majority of incumbent regulators; appointed wholly because of their political credentials and need of jobs, they usually stay indefinitely, or at least as long as their political connections and industry acceptability remain intact.

The premature resignations of men who are regarded by their peers as bright and able have been decried over and again. When the first Hoover Commission investigated the regulatory agencies during the Truman Administration in the late 1940's, it complained that the regulators were coming and going so rapidly that many "do not remain long enough to master the problems of regulation and to perform their duties well." During the Eisenhower Administration, in 1956, the chairman of the Civil Aeronautics Board in a moment of frankness told a House committee that the CAB never adhered to "a fixed philosophy for any very fixed period of time because the members come and go, and they do come and go pretty fast down there."[17]

Key staff members who are bright and able also come and go pretty fast. The politics involved is not subtle. A principal value to the President of his power to designate chairmen is the patronage potential in each chairman's authority to appoint key staff personnel. These staff officials—the head of the CAB's Bureau of Economic Regulation, of the SEC's Division of Trading and Markets, of the FCC's Broadcast Bureau—do not have the job security enjoyed by the mass of federal civil servants of lower rank in the agencies and the executive branch. They are part of the "Schedule C" layer of Washington officialdom that is below the rank of presidential appointment and above the rank of civil service protection; they can be hired and fired at will.

There was a time, before 1950, when someone who wanted one of the top agency staff jobs and who was accepted by the members of the commission or board had simply to obtain a letter of endorsement from one of the senators of his home state. Once hired, from outside the agency or by way of promotion from within, he usually stayed. A change in command at the White House didn't reach him. Now the appointments go through the same political patronage clearance procedure at Democratic or Republican National Committee headquarters that is involved in all non-civil service appointments to high federal office.

The job seeker normally goes first to his Democratic or Republican national committeeman or committeewoman, or to another party official of his home state designated to clear federal jobs for that state. If the state official looks with favor on the job claim, he submits it to National Committee headquarters and only then does the job seeker go to see the chairman of the agency for whom he wants to work. "This is normal procedure," says a Democrat who served as a top staff official of the SEC during the Kennedy and Johnson Administrations. "The chairman of any agency could argue against me or anyone else sent over by the National Committee, if he really felt strongly. But that ordinarily doesn't happen."

What does happen is that when the White House changes party hands, the chairmen of the agencies change and the top staff appointees go and come with the chairmen. When Dwight Eisenhower became President, staff heads rolled at the Federal Trade Commission, the Civil Aeronautics Board and most other agencies. When John Kennedy became President there was a wholesale turnout of Republicans. And when Richard Nixon moved into the White House the Democrats were turned out.

All this is not to say that there is no expertise left in the agencies. A few experienced staff officials at some agencies have remained through Democratic and Republican Administrations. They've usually done so by means of friendly alliances that permit the politically displaced to take lesser jobs with civil service protection in an agency, hoping to return to power when the next Administration comes along. But these are the exceptions. The rise of politics and the decline of expertise inside the agencies is described, privately, by a member of the Federal Trade Commission: "At the FTC everybody, down to Grade 13, knows who's a Republican and who's a Democrat and who contributed to what party."

5
The Regulators and Congress

The regulators in theory act for and are responsible to Congress. If in fact they were subordinates of the legislative branch, the agencies would constitute no fourth branch of government. They do because Congress is not an overriding influence in the policies or practices of contemporary regulation. After it has created an agency, and thus disposed of the point of consumer displeasure at hand, Congress as a body loses interest. But the regulators cannot similarly ignore Congress, because they continue to need appropriations, more laws and reappointments. The situation offers opportunities for political or personal gain for particular members of Congress who are in a position to take advantage of them.

Congress is not a monolithic body. The Senate, because it has the authority to confirm or reject the President's nominations, is more important than the House. Yet both houses of Congress are organized on the committee system, which means that lawmakers who are members of the committees with jurisdiction over regulatory affairs are more important than other lawmakers. It also means that legislators with seniority that makes them the chairmen and ranking members of committees such as the House and Senate Commerce Committees are the most important of all. The average member of Congress can, at the behest of an industry located in his home state or district, ask the regulators for favors and receive little or nothing; a powerful member of an important committee will receive favors without ever putting forth a direct request.

There probably is no member of Congress who has not asked something of the regulators. A senator or a congressman usually asks not for himself but for a constituent. He phones or writes to ask the ICC what's holding up a truck company's application, to ask the FCC when it will award a TV station franchise, to ask the CAB why an airline doesn't get a new route. The public records of some agencies are studded with pink slips flagging letters from members of Congress. The hearings of the House Oversight Subcommittee in the late 1950's suggested that many other congressional communications do not get into the public files. Sometimes, members of Congress have even appeared before regulatory agencies to testify in public hearings. That has not happened often, presumably because it has done the lawmaker's constituent no apparent good.

Businessmen have as much a right as any other group of citizens to petition their government, and members of Congress cannot, any more than can the White House, ignore requests from business leaders. The business community can be an important source of support and increasingly needed campaign contributions. Moreover, every senator and almost every congressman numbers among his constituents back home bankers, power companies, broadcasting stations and such. The support of a radio or TV station owner can be of exceptional value, particularly if the stations broadcast editorials come election time.

Rarely have members of Congress had to offer public explanations for their communications on behalf of constituents, but when they have they invariably have explained, as did Sherman Adams, that they merely were seeking information. In the great majority of instances, information is all they get. The regulatory agencies type out a reply to the senator's or the congressman's letter, he uses the information to reply to the constituent, and that is the end of it. On the other hand, communications from more influential members of Congress may yield more than mere information, even if by chance only information was sought. A former member of the CAB has said that "a simple status inquiry, if made often enough and by the chairman of a committee, let us say, can have some effect. It isn't hard to imagine a situation where constant, strong inquiries from a congressman can have some of the undesirable effect."[1]

It is impossible to know how much effect communications by members of Congress on behalf of constituents have had on regulatory agency decisions in individual cases because the full stories of such interventions come out so rarely. But it's no secret that members of Congress who are ranking members of key committees, intervene in behalf of regulated industries in policy matters that are pending before the agencies.

The House Commerce Committee and its communications subcommittee, for example, habitually poke their noses into FCC policy matters at the behest of the broadcasting industry. The Commerce Committee has initial legislative jurisdiction, in the House, over the

FCC; all bills concerning communications matters originate in or are referred to the committee. Sometimes the committee or the subcommittee can block an FCC action with a mere resolution. At other times, because the commission has been balky, blocking an action has required a bill or resolution approved by the committee and then by the whole House.

A mere committee resolution, for instance, was enough in the late 1950's to prevent the FCC for longer than a year from allowing any pay-television tests. When the commission in 1959 decided to defer to the committee no longer, it still permitted the tests only under extremely rigid conditions that were designed to protect the advertiser-supported commercial television industry.

In 1964 the commission dropped a proposed rule it had been considering that would have limited the amount of air time radio and television stations could use for commercials. The mild rule would not have cut back on the number of commercial announcements aired by most large stations because it simply would have adopted as a requirement for all stations the industry's own advertising code that bigger stations subscribed to anyway. However, the industry was up in arms and the FCC dropped the proposed rule when the House—by a 317 to 43 vote that was a tribute to the broadcasters' grass-roots lobbying efforts—passed a bill to bar the commission from regulating commercials.

Only a bill was involved, and not a law. Indeed, it was doubtful the Senate would have gone along with the House. Still, the FCC backed off, and broadcasters, who shortly thereafter gathered in Chicago for the annual convention of the National Association of Broadcasters, gave a standing ovation to Representative Walter E. Rogers of Texas, the chairman of the House communications subcommittee, who had sponsored the bill.

"The record shows indisputably," *Broadcasting* magazine, the bible of the business, subsequently said in an editorial, "that broadcasters have been able to accomplish more through Congress than through the regulatory commissions Congress has created."

The tobacco industry could have written a similar paean to the House Commerce Committee and to Congress in 1965 when the Federal Trade Commission was voted down on Capitol Hill. The FTC was given a stinging congressional rebuke for attempting to adopt a rule that would have required tobacco manufacturers to place a stringent health warning on cigarette packages and in all cigarette advertising.

Early in 1964, the United States Surgeon General's advisory panel on smoking and health issued its condemnation of cigarette smoking, saying, in part, "Cigarette smoking is a health hazard of sufficient importance in the United States to warrant appropriate remedial action." The FTC thereupon did what seemed its duty. It proposed rules that said cigarettes had to be labeled as a "health hazard" and that the industry was "under the legal duty to disclose the health hazards of cigarette smoking in advertising." The FTC quickly held hearings on the proposed rules and wanted to put them into effect before the end of 1964. The industry hardly bothered to argue with the FTC at its hearings, but took its case to the House and Senate Commerce Committees. The House Commerce Committee asked the commission not to put the rules into effect as planned and the commission agreed to hold off.

The result was a bill that both houses of Congress passed and President Johnson signed into law in 1965. Under the law, after January 1, 1966, all cigarette packs had to carry the message: "Caution: Cigarette smoking may be hazardous to your health." Under the circumstances of the Surgeon General's report, that was about as mild as the tobacco industry could have hoped. The industry did not have to warn cigarette smokers in its advertising and the commission was forbidden to adopt any rules requiring either a tougher warning on cigarette packs or any warning at all in cigarette advertising. The tobacco industry made no real effort to hide its elation at the outcome or, for that matter, to conceal its lobbying efforts that had taken the matter out of the hands of the Federal Trade Commission. After Congress slapped down the FTC, a grateful tobacco industry demonstrated its thanks with cash. Executives of R. J. Reynolds Tobacco Company got up a kitty of at least $10,490, to be contributed to the re-election campaigns of deserving legislators. Former Senator Earle Clements of Kentucky, head lobbyist for the Tobacco Institute, an industry association, was charged with deciding how to divide the kitty. In the end, most of it was divided among members of the House Commerce Committee.[2]

Direct congressional intervention in matters pending before the regulatory agencies, when the meddling reflects no public or consumer opposition to the regulators but rather the opposition of private industry, is on its face a substitution of politics for decision-making that is supposed to be both expert and nonpolitical. But the denial to the regulators of independence of judgment is never more blatantly portrayed than when the Senate refuses to consent to the reappointment of a regulator because of his voting record. The Senate has not refused confirmation often because the White House normally does not select for reappointment regulators who have become too controversial. Yet it has happened.

The first time was in the 1920's when the Senate refused to confirm President Coolidge's reappointment of Commissioner John J. Esch to the Interstate Commerce Commission.[3] Mr. Esch's political fences theoretically should have been in excellent condition. He had been a Republican member of the House of Representatives for longer than twenty years. His bid for re-election to the House failed in 1920 and the following year the President gave him an appointment to the ICC that the Senate promptly confirmed. Mr. Esch's undoing was a vote he had cast in a big ICC case involving railroad rates on coal. The case pitted coal producers in West Virginia against producers in Pennsylvania, Ohio and other areas. Mr. Esch, who hailed from Wisconsin and had no apparent interest in coal one way or the other, cast his vote for rates that gave the Pennsylvania and Ohio producers a competitive edge. And, in 1928, when his nomination to another term arrived on Capitol Hill from the White House, Senator Matthew M. Neely of West Virginia led the fight against confirmation. The senator, who himself was up for re-election that year, freely admitted that his coal operator constituents had told him they didn't want John Esch on the ICC.

A more recent and more celebrated case of Senate refusal to confirm a President's reappointment of a regulator was the rejection of Leland Olds.[4] Olds in theory also had a right to expect to be reconfirmed. He had not served in Congress, as Mr. Esch had, but twice before he had been confirmed to sit on the Federal Power Commission when President Truman renominated him for a third term in 1949.

Olds had come to the FPC with some experience in public utility work in New York and he had the backing of a number of people in the academic community and also of several liberal groups, including Americans for Democratic Action. Olds's undoing was the stand he had taken as a member of the FPC on the matter of federal regulation of natural gas producers, an issue that was bubbling in the forties, came to a boil in the fifties with the Supreme Court decision that producers are subject to regulation under the 1938 Natural Gas Act, and that is simmering still.

Congress' primary purpose in passing the act was to bring under federal regulation the interstate transportation of natural gas by pipelines. The law seemed to exempt from regulation the producers (frequently big oil companies whose wells also brought up gas) who sold gas to the pipelines for interstate transmission, but wasn't crystal-clear on the point.

Consistently, since 1938, a majority of commission members, in rulings on formal cases had interpreted the law to mean the FPC did not have the power to regulate gas producers. However, in the late 1940's it looked as if the commission might be wavering.

In March of 1947, after the commission had investigated the question of its authority over producers, the four commissioners then sitting took a vote. Two votes said the commission had the power to regulate producers, two votes said it did not. Leland Olds's vote was one that said the commission had the power. The vote was not a formal case ruling and, indeed, five months later, in August of 1947, the four commissioners took another vote and issued a policy statement saying that this time three votes held the FPC did not have jurisdiction over producers and one vote said it did. Leland Olds reversed himself, casting one of the three votes against asserting jurisdiction.

However, the fat was already in the fire. The 3-to-1 vote was of little comfort to gas producers who apparently were more inclined to believe Olds's first vote than his second and who distinctly saw the possibility of a fifth commissioner swinging a majority to the pro-regulation side. Nevertheless, Olds seemed, both philosophically and geographically, as if he should be a pro-regulation man. He was a liberal Democrat from the gas-consuming state of New York. Regulation of natural gas always has and still does divide the gas-consuming states of the North from the producing states of the Southwest.

As 1948 passed and the end of Olds's second term in 1949 approached, something happened that seemed to confirm his first vote in 1947, for regulation. Almost as soon as the possibility had first appeared that a commission majority might vote to regulate producers, bills were introduced by senators and congressmen from gas-producing states to amend the 1938 act so that producers once and for all would be exempt from regulation. In 1949 Olds was chairman of the FPC and the bill sponsored by Senator Robert S. Kerr, a wealthy Democratic oilman from Oklahoma, was a hot issue. Just three months before President Truman sent to the Senate his nomination for a third term, Olds as chairman testified before the Senate Commerce Committee against the Kerr bill. He took a strong stand against any legislation that would remove from the FPC for all time the prerogative to decide whether to regulate producers. His testimony was credited with having contributed substantially to the defeat in 1949 of an exemption bill that had passed the House.

Shortly thereafter, Olds's nomination for a third term arrived at the Senate and was assigned as a matter of course to the same Senate Commerce Committee before which he had appeared three months earlier. The chairman of the Commerce subcommittee that held hearings on the appointment was a rising senator from the gas-producing state of Texas named Lyndon Johnson. Witnesses against Olds, who mostly were from producing areas, vigorously attacked his views on regulation and charged that his writings back in the 1920's proved Communist leanings. Witnesses for him, mostly liberals from gas-consuming areas, defended him vigorously. But the attack was so heavy that President Truman took the unique action of instructing the Democratic National Committee to send telegrams to all of the party's state chairmen urging them to come to the defense of the embattled Mr. Olds.

The President's intervention did Leland Olds little good. The Johnson subcommittee voted unanimously to recommend that the Senate refuse to confirm him. When the nomination reached the Senate floor in October of 1949, Senator Johnson led the opposition. In an intemperate attack on Olds, Johnson charged he had "labored skilfully through ten years in public office to" create the public impression of a "knight in shining armor" protecting consumers' interests. A "myth," the senator asserted.

Senator Johnson charged that "Leland Olds' record is an uninterrupted tale of bias, prejudice and hostility, directed against the industry over which he now seeks to assume the powers of life and death." He claimed that Olds had conducted an "insidious campaign of slander" against his fellow commissioners who disagreed with him on the issue of gas producer regulation. And the senator asserted that the commissioner "in the twenties scoffed at private property; in the thirties said our democracy had been made a sham; in the forties . . . has discredited his fellow commissioners, fostered a smear on Congress and taken the law into his own hands to substitute irresponsible confiscation for responsible regulation."

During the floor debate, some senators, like Wayne Morse, William Langer and Hubert Humphrey, attempted to counter Johnson's attack. Senator Langer said the Communist charges were unfounded and that "the case against Leland Olds smells strongly of oil." The vote was a resounding defeat for Olds and for President Truman. The Senate voted 53 to 15 against confirmation.

The Senate rejection of Leland Olds was unusual because regulators are ordinarily not strong-willed, controversial figures. Indeed, the rejection of Leland Olds was atypical. It was the exception that proved the rule that sitting regulators, if they want their jobs, had better stay on the right side of industry issues.

Equally important is to stay on the right side of powerful members of Congress, and a regulator need not simply follow the negative path of avoiding words and actions. If he serves on an agency that has rich franchises and other prizes to award, he has the opportunity to think positively. He can award a few of his many prizes to particular senators or congressmen for their political or personal satisfaction.

The wise selection of recipients requires a detailed working knowledge of Congress. To the regulator, the most important members of Congress are the ranking members of the Senate and House Appropriations Committees, which pass on the agencies' requests for operating and subsidy monies, as well as of the legislative committees. But the relevant Capitol Hill hierarchy is even more specific.

The House and Senate Appropriations Committees have Independent Offices Subcommittees that are most relevant to money matters because they have initial jurisdiction over all the regulatory agencies' appropriations. Each Commerce Committee has one subcommittee for communications, another for railroad, truck and barge transportation and a third for air transportation. These subcommittees deal, respectively, with the FCC, the ICC and the CAB. The rivers and harbors program is handled on the House and

Senate sides by the Public Works Committees. The House has a separate Merchant Marine Committee. And so forth.

Splendid airline service for cities in congressmen's home districts is one of the rewards the regulators can bestow upon deserving lawmakers.[5] Another is an abundance of natural gas service. A third, useful to congressmen from coastal districts, is ship construction subsidies which keep shipyard workers busy. All members of Congress must look constantly toward the next election, and such bounties, including Air Force bases, post offices and military production contracts, are tangible evidence for the voters at home of a lawmaker's accomplishments in Washington. But these are not the biggest and best rewards for which a representative or senator can hope. It seems quite apparent that broadcasting franchises, which only the Federal Communications Commission can give, are the honorariums most fondly desired. These, of course, offer opportunities for personal investment rather than re-election. Some members of Congress acquired their investments after they came to Washington and some had them before they came; all must look to the FCC because all radio and television stations have matters pending more or less constantly before the agency. Over two dozen members of Congress are known to have personal interests in broadcasting properties, in their own names or the names of members of their immediate families.[6] No other companies in industries that are regulated by the federal government seem to have offered such attractive investment possibilities to members of Congress, and particularly to those members who sit on the House and Senate Commerce Committees or the Appropriations Committees.

When Congress wrote the Communications Act, as it has in almost all the regulatory laws, it declared that no member of the FCC could have any financial interest in any regulated company. This worry over regulatory conflicts of interest remains very much alive; each time the Senate Commerce Committee holds a confirmation hearing on a presidential appointment or reappointment to the FCC, or another agency, it questions the regulator-to-be at length concerning his personal investments. Frequently it asks little else. But Congress has enacted no such laws concerning the personal investments even of its members who deal with regulatory agency laws or appropriations.

Indeed, the predilection of so many members of Congress for

broadcasting company stocks gave rise a few years ago to a ruckus over whether the commission should issue a policy statement, applying to members of Congress in general, that would elaborate on the "public interest," or lack thereof, involved in their personal broadcast holdings. The case involved a contest over the franchise to operate a new television station on Channel 10 in the Albany, New York, area. The contestants were Veterans Broadcasting Company, which already had a radio station in Rochester, New York, and Capital Cities Television Corporation, which had a radio station in Albany and a television station in Durham, North Carolina.

In his recommended decision of 1959, Examiner J. D. Bond, detailed the facts he thought important. There wasn't much to be said about the experience, financial and sundry other qualifications of the two applicants; both were qualified in many respects, Bond said. Then he wrote at length about another qualifying standard the FCC always considered in such cases, that of "civic participation." Mr. Bond said that Dean P. Taylor, a stockholder and participant in the management of Capital Cities, had for many years been a Republican member of the House of Representatives. The examiner then said that Lee W. O'Brien, also a Capital Cities stockholder and management adviser, was a Democratic member of the House of somewhat more recent vintage. The congressional districts that Messrs. Taylor and O'Brien represented both would be within the service area of the proposed new Channel 10 TV station at Albany.

And then Examiner Bond wrote: "It cannot be ignored here that . . . these individuals have achieved civic and political prominence which denotes an ability to discern and be responsive to the interests of the people of their community; to be elected and re-elected as a member of the House of Representatives is a manifestation" of civic participation. The examiner thus found Capital Cities a "manifestly superior" applicant and recommended that it be named the winner of Channel 10.

When, in 1960, the case came before the commission, Veterans opined that it was "up against an organization" that included among its leading stockholders members of Congress as well as "several leading New York State politicians." Veterans argued before the commission that the presence of politicians on an applicant's list of stockholders "obviously" should not be given the weight that the examiner had accorded to Capital Cities' stockholders. "In fact," said an attorney for Veterans, "this case could well afford the commission an opportunity to enunciate a policy as to whether it is in the public interest for members of Congress to be stockholders in broadcast licensees."

The suggestion, made at a public session in a case that by then had drawn considerable attention, placed the FCC in a difficult position. On the one hand, the commission's own examiner in effect had recommended that the commission frankly acknowledge that members of Congress have an edge over everybody else in obtaining broadcast licenses; on the other, Veterans Broadcasting was inviting the commission to publicly repudiate its examiner and congressmen who own broadcasting stocks.

The FCC's response was that "obviously, it would be unseemly and arbitrary either to favor or penalize an applicant solely because it numbers members of Congress amongst its officers, directors or stockholders. We have had no such discriminatory policies in the past and we have none now." But the commission hastened to make plain that its statement constituted no policy statement. Anyone who wanted an official pronouncement that it was wrong for members of Congress to own broadcasting stocks should take his request to Congress, the FCC said.

Then, turning to the merits of the case at hand, the commission proceeded to uphold its examiner. First, the commission said that "participation in civic activities" traditionally had been taken into account. Second, it said that "political activities" are civic activities not at all unlike "participation in fund-raising projects for charitable purposes, music associations, Red Cross, Chambers of Commerce, Parent-Teachers Associations and professional organizations." And, third, it said that the winner of the Albany Channel 10 case was Capital Cities Television Corporation.

As it turned out, someone did take to Congress a request for an official declaration that it is wrong for members of Congress to own broadcasting stocks or at least that it is wrong for congressmen to expect or get preferred treatment from the FCC. As a result of the Albany Channel 10 case, Senator William Proxmire of Wisconsin, frequently a maverick Democrat who pursues lost causes, introduced a bill, that would have barred the FCC from considering "as a factor favoring the grant of a broadcast license the presence of members of Congress among a station's officers, directors, or stockholders."

The Senate Communications Subcommittee held a hearing, late in

1963, at which FCC Chairman E. William Henry testified, "An applicant should not obtain a grant simply because it numbers among its stockholders a member of Congress, the body which appropriates funds for commission activities and deals with the commission's legislative program. To award valuable privileges upon such a basis would, of course, be wholly improper."

The Proxmire bill never became law and, all in all, the public wound up knowing nothing more than it knew before. All the public got was a reluctant acknowledgment from the FCC that membership in Congress can and sometimes does help, and an uneasy feeling that it is impossible to know really how much of an edge politicians have with the commission.

It would seem, from the number of lawmakers who have personal interests in broadcasting properties, that they are not remiss in expecting a considerable edge. The two Democratic lawmakers who for many years were chairmen of the House and Senate Commerce Committees, Representative Oren Harris of Arkansas and Senator Warren Magnuson of Washington, both held personal interests in broadcasting properties.

Oren Harris, who came to Congress in 1941 and left in 1966 to accept the federal judgeship to which President Johnson appointed him, became an investor in the broadcasting industry in January, 1957, when he bought some stock in and became a vice president of a television station back home in El Dorado, Arkansas. Three local citizens, each of whom owned one-third of the stock of South Arkansas Television Company, Incorporated, had received in 1954 a permit from the Federal Communications Commission to build a television station. The station began operating on Channel 10 in December, 1955, first as KRBB, and later changed its call letters to KTVE. Like some other TV stations, it lost money initially, and in 1957 applied to the FCC for an increase in power and antenna height, both of which were granted early in 1958.

On January 29, 1957, the three original owners of South Arkansas Television Company sold 50 shares of treasury stock to Harris, making him a coequal 25 percent owner, and elected him vice president. The price for the 50 shares was $5,000, which Harris covered with $500 in cash and a personal note for $4500.

But Harris' investment did not turn out well. Entirely by coincidence, at least so far as recorded history tells, in February of 1957 House Speaker Sam Rayburn asked for the investigation of the regulatory agencies that led to Sherman Adams' resignation and to other embarrassments. As a matter of course, the request went to the Commerce Committee, of which Mr. Harris was by then chairman, and led to the establishment of the special Legislative Oversight Subcommittee. The subcommittee, chaired by Representative Morgan Moulder of Missouri until Mr. Harris took over, hired as its chief counsel Bernard Schwartz, a New York University professor. Professor Schwartz made headlines of his own by assuming a larger role in investigating the regulators than the committee intended him to have. Before Representative Harris fired him, the professor stumbled across the congressman's 50 shares of stock and told every newspaper reporter he could find of his discovery. The embarrassed Oren Harris thereupon announced he was selling his stock because of "harassment" by reporters.[7]

In January, 1958, just a year after he had bought the stock, Harris resold the shares to South Arkansas Television Company for $500 in cash and cancellation of his $4500 note, according to FCC records. A few years later, the three remaining stockholders sold out for $1.1 million. In 1964, after other changes in ownership, KTVE became the property of a Georgia company owned by the chairman of that state's Democratic Executive Committee.

The story of Warren Magnuson, broadcaster, is a great success story, little known in Washington.[8] It spans twenty-three years, from 1945 to 1968. Over these years, Magnuson rose to power in the Senate and invested in the KIRO broadcast stations back home in Seattle. He began with 11 shares, apparently worth about $220. He ended with 10,389 shares, which he sold for a total of $334,089. His broadcasting career closed in 1968, when the last of the shares were sold, although his Senate career of course continued.

The KIRO radio and television stations are the Columbia Broadcasting System outlets in Seattle and thus are significant properties. In 1945, KIRO was only a radio station, licensed by the FCC to the Queen City Broadcasting Company. The now-faded FCC records do not show how much Magnuson paid for the 11 shares that year, but they do show that the following year, when he bought 200 additional shares, the stock was worth $20 a share.

The FCC records also disclose that Queen City's shareholders from time to time included other Washington figures. In 1945, for instance, the stockholder list included the late Mon C. Wallgren, who was then governor of Washington. Prior to 1945 Wallgren had been a congressman and a senator. In 1949, subsequent to his term as governor, President Truman appointed him to the Federal Power Commission. In 1952, Abe Fortas—then a lawyer representing a number of broadcast stations—was elected a vice president of Queen City. His Washington, D.C., law firm, Arnold, Fortas and Porter, held stock in Queen City. Sometime later, Queen City reported to the FCC that Fortas' election had been "rescinded."

Queen City prospered in the postwar years and so did its stockholders. FCC records do not disclose what, if any, cash dividends Queen City paid to its stockholders. (Rapidly growing companies frequently pay in stock rather than cash.) But in 1946 the radio station's expanding business permitted the company to split its stock 2½-for-1, giving shareholders additional shares at no cost. In 1952 and again in 1954 it declared 5 percent stock dividends. In 1955 and again in 1956 it split its stock. In 1957, the FCC awarded Queen City a permit to operate a new commercial television station on Channel 7 in Seattle. The expense of getting the TV station on the air apparently took a tuck in the company's profits for a few years, but in 1960 Queen City declared a 2 percent stock dividend, after which Senator Magnuson had a grand total of 10,389 shares.

Magnuson did not increase his holdings from 220 to 10,389 shares at no cost. Over the years from 1945 to 1960, he bought about 2800 shares, apparently paying between $11 and $20 per share, according to the FCC records. But his holdings grew principally because of stock splits and stock dividends which cost him nothing.

The growth of the KIRO radio and television stations in the 1960's attracted the interest of other investors, who offered prices for the stock that Queen City's old shareholders found too enticing to refuse. The investor they sold out to was the Church of Jesus Christ of Latter Day Saints—a church well known for its investment acumen, which in recent years has invested its ample cash in a number of broadcast properties.

Through a subsidiary known as Bonneville International Corporation, the church early in 1963 began to purchase Queen City stock from the shareholders, paying $30.50 a share. Magnuson, who then still had 10,389 shares, sold 8839 of them for the sum of $269,589. By late 1963, the church had acquired sufficient stock so that, with the FCC's approval, it assumed control of Queen City. It then transferred the KIRO radio and television properties to a new corporation, KIRO, Incorporated, and offered the remaining Queen City shareholders the choice of accepting $39.50 per share in cash or of converting each of their shares into 35 shares of the new corporation.

Magnuson elected to sell 1500 of his remaining shares for cash, receiving $59,250. That left him with 50 shares, which he converted at the 35-for-1 rate into 1750 shares of KIRO, Incorporated. By early 1964 the church had acquired more than 99 percent of the nine million KIRO, Incorporated, shares then outstanding and the senator and the few other remaining stockholders were distinctly junior partners. The senator's broadcasting career came to an end on March 19, 1968, when he sold his 1750 shares to the church for $5250. Waiting was worthwhile. Had he sold the 50 Queen City shares for $39.50 a share in 1964 instead of accepting the 35-for-1 split of these shares, he would have received only $1975.

Senator Magnuson was never more than a minority stockholder in the KIRO stations. There is no evidence that he played any role in their management and there is none that he ever asked the FCC for any favors for the stations or for himself. He didn't have to. Without being asked by the senator, the FCC awarded Queen City a television station license and approved many other applications involving matters great and small. "Magnuson's word is almost law to the commissioners," a highly placed FCC staff member has said privately. "They bow and scrape for him. He doesn't have to ask for anything. The commission does what it thinks he wants it to do. The same was true of Oren Harris. He cracked the whip lots of times down here."

Respect for proper political connections permeates the upper echelons of the FCC staff. Said the FCC aide: "We now have before us a matter concerning a television station here in the East. I've been informed that one of the senators in whose state the station is located is interested in the matter. He's a member of the Commerce Committee and that's all I need to know."

Even former influential members of Congress who still have friends on Capitol Hill and at the FCC rate high. "Take former Senator McFarland," the aide continued. "He's a major stockholder in television station KTVK in Phoenix, Arizona, and he's interested in buying another station. We sent him a letter asking for more information but we didn't get a reply. Almost anybody else would be thrown out on his ear. But, oh no, not Senator McFarland. Him we call up, long distance, and say won't you please reply to our letter. And he hasn't been in Congress for years." Ernest W. Mc-Farland, a Democrat from Arizona, served in the United States Senate from 1941 until 1953 and during his latter years as a senator was chairman of the Senate Communications Subcommittee.

The list of present and former senators and representatives who have personal financial interests in FCC-licensed broadcast stations includes Republicans as well as Democrats. The interests of some are negligible. The interests of others are substantial and a few serve the stations as corporate officers at the same time they serve in Congress. Some have small personal holdings or no stock at all but their wives or other members of their immediate families own major interests. Almost invariably, the stations are located in the senator's home state or in the representative's congressional district. As we shall see in a later chapter, the LBJ Company of Austin, Texas, combined several of these characteristics.

Certainly it would be wrong to bar broadcasters from election to Congress on the grounds that they have a personal financial interest in an industry regulated by the federal government. The government regulates or otherwise influences so many special-interest groups in American society that to bar broadcasters on those grounds would also be to eliminate bankers, farmers, brokers, union leaders, retailers and almost everyone else from election to Congress. On the other hand, Congress has recognized the conflict-of-interest problem as it relates to all the branches of government except Congress. Aside from passing laws under which no person working for the FCC or any other regulatory agency can own stock in a regulated industry, Congress often has insisted that appointees to positions of authority sell their stocks or at least place them in trust, no matter how distant the government position may be from authority over a particular corporation.

So far as is known, no member of Congress ever has divested or even put in trust his radio or television industry stocks. (Lyndon Johnson's wife, for example, placed her large stock interests in trust only after he became President.) A few lawmakers whose personal interests in the broadcasting industry have been matters of wide public knowledge have recognized the potential conflict-of-interest problem by stating in public that they would not accept seats on the Commerce Committees. But few have done even that.

The Regulators and the Regulated

The men and women who regulate industry in the public interest deal occasionally with the White House, frequently with select members of Congress and constantly with executives of regulated industries. All manner of procedural formalities have been borrowed from the courts to ensure fairness when the regulators and the regulated meet in open public hearings. But no equally meaningful procedures or incontrovertible guidelines have been developed for the far more frequent meetings of the regulators and the regulated that do not take place in public hearing rooms. Clearly, regulators are not judges and it would be wholly inappropriate to ban all informal contact and communication between them, who are supposed to be technical experts in industry affairs, and the industries they regulate. Equally absurd would be the isolation of agencies, such as the Civil Aeronautics Board, that by law are charged with promoting as well as regulating, from their industries. The as yet unanswered question is how and where regulators may meet with private industry without compromising, or appearing to compromise, the public interest.

According to the mores of regulation, there are two types of dealings between the regulators and the regulated that take place outside of formal public hearings. The first consists of nonpublic meetings concerning specific cases or policy issues pending before an agency. These usually are small meetings, called for the purpose of disposing of small cases, and they take place constantly in almost all the agencies. The process is known as "informal adjudication." From a public point of view, it leaves something to be desired, yet the agencies could not possibly dispose of their more than 100,000 items of business annually if each case had to be decided in a formal hearing. Sometimes, closed and informal meetings involve more people and large public policy issues; when the regulators are thinking of adopting a new policy with industry-wide application, they habitually discuss the matter with corporate and trade-association executives prior to public announcement. The Securities and Exchange Commission, for example, has called in stock exchange officials before proceeding with the public adoption of new exchange rules. The Federal Trade Commission has met with automobile manufacturers before acting publicly to correct misleading new car warranty practices. All of these nonpublic dealings, on matters small or large, are not wholly consistent with the spirit of consumer protection, but all take place within the context of defined cases or issues, and the agencies' ultimate dispositions of course are publicly announced.

The second and distinctly different type of dealing among the regulators and the regulated consists of the infinite variety of informal contacts that are, or are supposed to be, outside the setting of specific cases. In this large gray area of nonpublic communications, at business and social gatherings, the boundaries of propriety are poorly marked and consumers cannot know the ultimate consequences.

Regulators uniformly and consistently attend the national and regional conventions of the industries they regulate, addressing the business sessions and mingling during the social hours. The chairman of the SEC traditionally addresses the annual December get-together in Florida of the Investment Bankers Association. The chairman of the Federal Communications Commission speaks before the National Association of Broadcasters and sometimes all seven FCC commissioners attend the NAB convention. A few regulators have attempted to limit their outside, informal contacts with industry people to the open sessions of conventions, where the press if not the public is invited. William Cary, the straight-backed professor President Kennedy named as chairman of the SEC, refused, for instance, to attend some of the cocktail parties thrown by securities industry people in Washington. The great majority of regulators, however, are unable or unwilling to follow Chairman Cary's example. Most would be unrealistic to try. Their opportunities for contact with industry are too frequent and their responsibilities to industry are too large for the regulators to limit their contacts to public forums. Therefore, they also see and hear industry representatives in private. A regulator's office door normally is open to industry folks for private chats. Some of the regulators frequently take trips out of Washington to visit a factory or home office of a regulated company. Frequent business contacts lead to occasional social contacts. It is as common for a member of the Securities and Exchange Commission to show up at the cocktail parties as it is for members of the Civil Aeronautics Board to be guests on the gala inaugural flights with which airlines begin service on a new route they've been awarded by the board. And it is not unusual for members of the Interstate Commerce Commission to go fishing with railroaders.

The accepted decorum for all these informal, off-the-record contacts, whether they occur in the regulators' offices in Washington, in an airline president's home or on a fishing lake, is the same. Propriety, as developed by the agencies, means that talk is fine but not talk of a pending case. But in the regulators' world, it's a difficult rule to make stick. An airline lobbyist says on the subject: "Of course, we never bring up a pending case. Let's say we have pending a case concerning a route application. Of course I wouldn't mention the route matter. I talk about equipment, about new airplanes, new hangars. I know and the board member knows that the only reason we're talking about equipment is the use we hope to make of it on the new route."

Even if an airline, a railroad, or a gas pipeline lobbyist doesn't have a case pending, the ground rules are less than meaningful. It pays to keep a regulator well informed and thinking well of a company because sooner or later the company will have a case pending. Indeed, regulation is so pervasive that it's rare when major regulated companies like a big airline or a big railroad don't have at least several cases pending simultaneously.

A regulated company can hardly be blamed for using every opportunity for attempting to influence a regulator. It legitimately fears that if it doesn't a competitor will. Indeed, considering what's at stake a company would be remiss in its duty to its stockholders if it didn't try to exert influence. A piece of paper from the CAB awarding a major route can be worth more than $50 million in annual revenue to the winning airline. A license won from the FCC to operate a television station in a medium-size city can be worth $20 million, in terms of what the station will bring on the open market, and a big station in a very large city like New York may be worth close to $100 million. Approval of a railroad merger by the

ICC is worth more than $100 million in terms of annual cost reductions the applying railroads eventually can achieve. Many, many millions of dollars hang on FPC regulation of gas rates, on SEC regulation (or lack thereof) of stockbrokers' commissions and on FCC regulation of long-distance telephone rates.

Corporate executives who wine and dine the regulators are only doing what's expected of them. Consider the sarcasm publicly flung at the executives of American Telephone & Telegraph Company at its annual stockholders meeting, held in Detroit's Cobo Hall, in 1966. It was a time when AT&T was embroiled in an FCC investigation of its long-distance rates. Grabbing a microphone and addressing the chairman of the board, a stockholder declared, "Apparently our present directors have zero influence in Washington."[1] At that time, AT&T had nearly three million stockholders, far more than any other corporation in the nation, but for many years it had not maintained a large Washington office. More recently the company has augmented its Capital staff.

Big government as a whole has attracted to Washington armies of corporate, industry association and union emissaries, but regulated industries long have been the best represented. Consider the airline industry. The Air Transport Association, long headed by former CAB staff lawyer Stuart Tipton, has a large Washington staff of lawyers, public relations men and lobbyists, though the ATA is not as influential a behind-the-scenes force as are the officers of individual airlines who reside in Washington. Almost every major airline is represented by a corporate vice president. Some smaller lines have resident vice presidents as well, and others are represented by lesser corporate officials or by hired hands who usually are Washington lawyers representing several clients in regulated industries. Each vice president is backed up by a staff that usually includes public relations men and lawyers, and each invariably outranks CAB members, so far as salary is concerned.

Other industries are almost as well represented. All three of the radio and television broadcasting networks, ABC, CBS and NBC, have vice presidents in Washington, and the National Association of Broadcasters is a Federal City resident. American Telephone & Telegraph and Western Union, both of which are regulated by the FCC, have vice presidents too. The railroads, truckers and barge lines each have their trade-association headquarters and some companies have officers in Washington. The Pharmaceutical Manufacturers Association is there to represent the drug makers who are regulated by the Food and Drug Administration. Gas companies regulated by the Federal Power Commission are represented by corporate officers or by law firms. Tommy Corcoran, a prominent Washington lawyer who was a government official in New Deal days, testified before a House subcommittee in 1960 that the law firm of which he was a member was on a retainer of $60,000 a year from Tennessee Gas Transmission Corporation.

Industry has sent many ambassadors to Washington, they invariably have large expense accounts and they engage the regulators in frequent nonpublic communication. But the net result is not as sinister as the people—the consumers—may imagine. Bribery of a public official is not often proved nowadays and in fact probably is rare. The growth of the industry establishment in Washington poses a number of more subtle problems, like jobs and salaries.

Many of those bright young men who resign as regulators long before their terms expire leave to take higher-paying jobs in industry or to join Washington law firms that represent industry before the regulatory agencies. Assuming that the job seeks the man, rather than the man in government using his position to seek a job, the departures would seem to raise no ethical problems. But the distinction normally is difficult to draw. The ethical problem is potentially always present, as a high-ranking staff official of the Securities and Exchange Commission acknowledged when he said, privately, that the interest in industry job opportunities "does get bad when it's blatant and open."

The ethical question aside, the agency-to-industry movement unquestionably aggravates the government's loss of genuine talent and therefore undercuts the theory that the regulators would become experts by reason of many years of service. Certainly the cumulative loss of talent has been great and many of the industry ambassadors are able men who certainly did not have to beg for jobs but who were sought after by industry. One such was Everett Hutchinson, a Texan who was appointed to the Interstate Commerce Commission by President Eisenhower and who handed his resignation to President Johnson in order to become president of the National Association of Motor Bus Operators. Frederick W. Ford, who had been on the Federal Communications Commission since 1957, in 1964 resigned the FCC job, which at that time paid about $20,000 a year, to become president of the National Community Antenna Television Association, reportedly at $50,000 a year.

Big-name law firms in New York and in Washington are filled with men who once were with the SEC, as commissioners or staff members. Some SEC folks have departed for brokerage concerns and mutual funds like the giant Investors Diversified Services. Some moved to seats in corporate executive suites. Donald C. Cook, once on the staff of the SEC's Public Utilities Division and then a commissioner, became president of American Electric Power Company. Ralph T. McElvenny, once on the staff of the same division, became president of American Natural Gas Company. The other agencies' talent losses perhaps haven't been as great, but they have lost too. Washington law offices that specialize in broadcast matters are as full of former FCC commissioners and staff members as law firms specializing in securities law are crowded with SEC alumni.

The conclusion suggested is that, in general, industry has sought out the more capable people in the regulatory agencies and paid them for their talents. There is almost no evidence that industry has offered high-paying jobs as pay-off's for favorable decisions. Boorish regulators who seek private employment, on the other hand, often don't find it. The problem, then, is not one of ethics so much as how government can retain talented men—at least for the duration of a President's and agency chairmen's terms of office, until the opposition party installs its own talent in key agency positions.

Similarly, the presence in Washington of many corporate vice presidents and trade-association executives seems to pose no overriding problem of ethics in the sense of regulators giving their votes in exchange for a particular company's hospitality. A regulator who accepts the hospitality of a company might be suspected of favoring that company over other regulated companies, such as one airline over another. But, upon examination, it would appear that the regulators attempt to avoid such favoritism by an equitable acceptance of all the hospitality offered. The conclusion is supported by bits of evidence that have come to light, including a pertinent incident which forced its way into the public annals of the Civil Aeronautics Board.

A board member named Chan Gurney, a veteran regulator, was

first appointed to the CAB by President Truman in 1951 and twice was reappointed. He and other board members apparently often had gone out of Washington to visit airlines at their home offices and to inspect their facilities. On the afternoon of September 19, 1960, he made a routine call on Central Airlines in Fort Worth, lunching with its president, Keith Kahle, and other officials, inspecting its hangars and shops and winding up the day by visiting the home of Kirk Johnson, Central's board chairman. When Mr. Gurney got back to Washington, he dropped Mr. Kahle a letter that began "Dear Keith" and thanked the airline president for "the super de luxe reception you gave me." Regulator Gurney complimented him on running Central "in apple pie manner" and concluded, "It was a pleasure to meet Mr. Johnson in his home and I hope that I can see him again sometime."

Chan Gurney's call on Central turned out to be not so routine because his "Dear Keith" letter somehow fell into the hands of Ozark Air Lines and into public print. Ozark happened to be vying with Central for some new routes that the board was going to hand out and less than a month after Mr. Gurney's return to Washington the board voted, with Mr. Gurney concurring, to make substantial route awards to Central. Ozark thereupon claimed that Central had been trying improperly to influence Mr. Gurney's vote and that Mr. Gurney had compromised his independence.

The charge wasn't much in the scale of Washington events, but it was enough to convene the five members of the CAB in an extraordinary session that began at 10 P.M. on a cold November night in 1960 when the "Dear Keith" letter was getting to be a hot issue. After the meeting, the board issued an equally extraordinary press release which publicly disclosed, for the first time, the details of Chan Gurney's trip and his letter. In the press release the other four CAB members absolved Gurney of any wrongdoing and dismissed the charge against him. The four declared that his actions had been "entirely proper" and in accord with CAB ethics and practices.[2] Apparently they were. In 1964 he retired from the CAB to go home to Yankton, in South Dakota, the state he had served as a United States senator until he was defeated for renomination in 1950. On the occasion of his retirement, the entire airline industry joined to give him a big farewell dinner at the Statler Hilton Hotel in Washington.

Large, expensive, black-tie dinners that bring together government officials and industry executives are of course commonplace in Washington. The social intercourse among Defense Department officials and defense contractors no doubt was an element of President Eisenhower's expressed concern about the "military-industrial complex." The permanent presence in Washington of registered lobbyists for all sorts of industry, labor and other special-interest groups makes possible the frequent fund-raising dinners held there in honor of individual senators or representatives who need cash to wage re-election campaigns back home. Dinner at the White House was one reward for corporate executives who gained membership to the President's Clubs of John Kennedy and Lyndon Johnson by contributing at least $1000 yearly to the Democratic party's war chest.

Businessmen don't give their hard-earned dollars expecting no return. What they normally expect, in buying twenty-dollar tickets to dinners for lawmakers or in contributing through the President's Club, is political recognition and friendship. They don't buy commitments of members of Congress or Presidents any more than they buy votes of regulators. They buy, or hope to buy, a government official's willingness to lend a sympathetic ear, at luncheon someday or in the official's private office, on pertinent matters of legislation, administrative action or procurement.

Regulated businessmen do more and expect more because they have more at stake in Washington. They are among the most prominent members of the President's Club. They are the dependable mainstays of fund-raising dinners for members of Congress, and particularly those members who sit on the Commerce Committees. In addition, they entertain the regulators with whom normal businessmen are not concerned. The Washington vice presidents of regulated companies normally are registered with Congress as lobbyists. Their work is almost entirely in the area of informal, off-the-record contacts. They scout Capitol Hill, dropping in to see members of Congress in their offices; they frequent the agencies, visiting with regulators in their private offices, and sometimes they go to the White House. They also entertain legislators, regulators and White House personalities at lunch and in their Washington homes. The best of them receive selected regulators, legislators and White House aides in their homes for an evening of convivial mixing. These Washington vice presidents usually are lawyers. But formal, on-the-record appearances at public hearings before congressional committees and regulatory agencies normally are left to a separate staff of corporate lawyers located in Washington or at the company's home office. On the other hand, corporate presidents and board chairmen frequently come to Washington to mix in the informal gatherings and often they also hold membership in the President's Club.

What regulated businesses expect in return for their considerable hospitality and contributions is an appropriately large opportunity to be heard. Specific expectations must be considered in terms of the interrelations of the regulatory agencies, Congress and the White House. From the regulators, a lobbyist can hope to purchase, if not a vote for his company, then sympathy for the interests of the industry of which his company is a part. From members of Congress he hopes for committee and floor votes that someday may be necessary to pass or block a regulator's confirmation, a piece of regulatory legislation or some part of an agency's appropriation. From the White House, he hopes to be included among industrialists who are consulted before regulators' nominations are sent to Congress.

The interrelationships of the regulated, the regulator, Congress and the White House are known to all concerned and the lobbyists' hospitality and contributions are part of the mortar of the politics of regulation. Indeed, regulated industry has no real power over the regulators, except for the power to offer jobs, and industry's influence thus comes in large part from the power that can be brought to bear indirectly, through Congress and the White House.

No one, including the Washington vice presidents, knows precisely how much influence the hospitality and contributions purchase. Pressures from various sources are brought to bear on larger issues of regulation and some cancel out others. A President or member of Congress may side with an industry most of the time but not always and lobbyists can't know all the reasons for an official's action on every issue. They do know that Presidents usually consult regulated industry before they nominate regulators, that White House aides have intervened at the agencies, that the Senate has refused to confirm some nominees and that regulated industries generally have been quite successful in taking their cases to members of Congress.

So knowing, regulated industry in recent years has invested ever more heavily in Washington hospitality and campaign contributions. Some companies are more politically-minded than others. But their total investments certainly amount to some millions of dollars, at least in a presidential campaign year.

An illustration was provided in 1965, which wasn't a campaign year. The Democratic party, through an adjunct known as the Democratic State Committee on Voter Education, decided to raise money by publishing a tribute to Lyndon Johnson's Great Society. The tribute took the form of a slick-paper book, in magazine format, titled *Toward an Age of Greatness*. In addition to text and pictures of the President's achievements in education, health and other fields, it contained many pages of advertising which the Democrats sold at $15,000 per page. Some of the purchasers were defense contractors and many others were companies regulated by the government. Each of the nation's major airlines bought a page. So did several subsidized ship lines and some railroads, including Southern Railway, the Milwaukee Road and Union Pacific.

The $15,000 check each company wrote was an investment in Democratic good will. Most corporate political contributions are more specific, as to recipients and issues. For example, more corporate cash flowed into both Democratic and Republican campaign treasuries during the 1968 elections than in any previous national election year and probably more of it than ever before was specifically earmarked.[3] Member firms of the New York Stock Exchange, banded together under the name Exchange Firms Campaign Committee, collected more than $125,000 to give to selected candidates for House and Senate seats. The Securities and Exchange Commission earlier in 1968 had sought quite actively to force the New York Stock Exchange to make some changes in its commission rate schedule that, while relatively minor, were not to the liking of all exchange members. "We are absolutely not trying to buy votes," declared the counsel to the firms. "This is simply an attempt to support candidates who have shown . . . a willingness to listen to the industry's problems. It's an example of political awareness in an industry that has tended to stay away from politics."[4]

The nation's largest securities firm, Merrill Lynch, Pierce, Fenner & Smith, in 1968 established its own campaign chest, named the Effective Government Association. Through it, Merrill Lynch officers and employees, as well as some outsiders, made political contributions as individuals. Merrill Lynch at the time was faced with formal SEC charges of having prematurely disclosed information to certain large customers about the earnings of Douglas Aircraft Company.[5]

Many other firms or their officers contributed to 1968 national and state political campaigns through organizations with equally nebulous names. Savings and loan associations organized the Savings Association Political Education Committee. Textile manufacturers had the Committee on American Principles. Truckers had the Truck Operators Non-Partisan Committee. In each instance, contributions were not channeled to the candidates of a single party but were given to individual candidates of both parties who were on or might be on committees of Congress influential in the affairs of particular industries.

Election-year contributions such as those are matters of public record because they must be reported to Congress, and newspaper reporters have dug through the records. Yet they are no more than the surface layer of political activity, at least as practiced by the most energetic and, presumably, effective industrialists.

An outstanding example was a trucking industry leader, Neil J. Curry, who was very well known inside government and industry circles, yet almost unknown to the public. He headed California Cartage Company and rose to industry leadership positions, serving as president of the California Trucking Association and then as president of the Washington-based American Trucking Associations. He was a gregarious man, standing more than six feet tall, an effective public speaker and an able proponent of his industry's point of view, in public or private speech. He was well known to all the members and staff officials of the Interstate Commerce Commission. He was equally well acquainted with members of the House and Senate Commerce Committees, which have jurisdiction over ICC matters, and the Public Works Committees, which oversee federal highway construction spending.

In the area of political fund raising, Curry was not a party partisan but he became a fund raiser mainly for Democratic candidates, perhaps because the Democrats controlled Congress and the White House during most of his career. He coordinated truckers' political contributions, first in California and then nationally. His role broadened, as he raised money for John Kennedy in 1960 and

Lyndon Johnson in 1964. He became an officer of the President's Club and was the chairman of a $100-a-plate dinner held in the cavernous District of Columbia Armory on the evening of June 3, 1965. The dinner was a Democratic fund-raising event honoring several key members of Congress. The speaker was Lyndon Johnson and Curry had the honor of introducing the President of the United States to the large gathering of government officials, industry executives and Democratic stalwarts.

The privilege was one measure of Curry's political standing; it is rare indeed that the President is introduced to large gatherings by private persons virtually unknown to the public. Further evidence of his standing was offered on his death, later in 1965. An unusual number of lawmakers offered tributes to Neil Curry in speeches on the House or Senate floor. These official utterances of course became part of the *Congressional Record.* In one, a congressman from California said Curry was a model of the modern corporate executive who must know and master "the intricate interplay between government and industry."

Later, an American Trucking Associations official confirmed in private conversation that Curry was "our main contact with political life." A Democratic National Committee aide said, also in private, that Curry was "a very active fund raiser and extremely good friend of the party."

Neil Curry could not have been absolutely certain of the benefits to the trucking industry of his political activities. Yet, the trucking industry over the years that Curry was active in Washington was highly successful in urging its points of view. He certainly is not to be denied a substantial part of the credit for the industry's accomplishments. Truckers after World War II wanted more highways and their lobbying was part of the reason that Congress in 1956 began the $50 billion interstate highway system. Another very major accomplishment came in the early 1960's. President Kennedy proposed that Congress give the railroads more rate freedom to compete with truckers. The truckers were very much opposed, as was the Interstate Commerce Commission. Congress, after a time of intense lobbying by truckers and railroaders, rejected the Kennedy proposal.

Neil Curry and every other industry representative in Washington has a constitutional right to petition his government and none is lacking in funds to petition effectively. It takes skill as well as cash and, if Curry was most skilled in his day, perhaps the railroads' day will come. No one need lose all the time, except the public. The politics of regulation is a merry-go-round on which there is a place for all, except consumers. The merry-go-round is propelled by the self-interests of industry that must ride for the preservation of revenues and profits; of the regulators who want to keep their jobs; of members of Congress who need campaign cash and of White House figures who want business' confidence and use the regulatory agencies for political ends. The interrelationships of self-interests leave no room for consideration of the public interest. The agencies tend to become umpires not of consumer versus industry interests but of industry versus industry. Taken together, regulation tends to perpetuate the protection of industry and the disregard of consumer interests, including the consumer interest in industrial competition.

One illuminating example of these effects was offered by Louis Hector who in 1959 resigned as a member of the CAB and also left with the White House a devastating critique of the regulatory system. In the document was a description of what had transpired behind closed CAB doors when the board earlier in 1959 had been forced to announce an investigation of the Air Transport Association, the scheduled airline industry trade organization.[6]

A House Antitrust Subcommittee headed by New York Democrat Emanuel Celler, who frequently takes a dim view of the regulatory agencies, had accused the CAB of being too friendly toward the Air Transport Association. When Mr. Hector and his four colleagues sat down to figure out how best to reply to the Celler charges, Mr. Hector related, there was "long discussion." The ATA conducts certain activities that would violate the antitrust laws, were they not exempted from antitrust prosecution by board action. But the board, though empowered to keep an eye on such activities, had never investigated the association since it was set up in 1936, according to Mr. Hector.

Some members who sat around the table felt there still was no need to investigate, Mr. Hector related, "and that in any event there should be no public order because it might reflect adversely on the [ATA]. Others felt that the board's duty was clear and that no discredit would be caused by a public order."

A majority of the five men around the table voted finally to issue a public order. But before it was issued, Mr. Hector said, "phrases were changed, sentences omitted, footnotes altered and, as a final concession to the members who did not see any necessity for an order, the word 'Investigation' was changed to 'Inspection and Review.'" The order finally was issued but the ensuing inspection didn't amount to much. Mr. Hector departed the CAB with this conclusion: A regulator faces a "serious conflict . . . between the responsibility for investigation and prosecution of law violations and the responsibility for formulating plans and policies to promote the well-being of an industry. It is this conflict which explains the failure of the FCC, CAB, ICC, FPC to crack down vigorously on law violators within the industry except in those cases where actions of one member of the industry threaten the economic stability of the industry as a whole."

Mr. Hector was an unusual regulator. So was Newton Minow, who resigned from the FCC in 1963. In the memorandum he dropped on President Kennedy's desk on his way out, Mr. Minow wrote: "Those who make policy and regulate must necessarily have frequent contact with the industry in order to be well informed. Under the present system, the possibility of improper influence or at the least of charges of such influence is always present."[7]

And there was a third. When Howard Morgan, an Oregon Democrat, in 1963 told President Kennedy he didn't want to be reappointed to the Federal Power Commission, he inserted in his letter this rather purple prose:

> Ordinary men cannot administer [the regulatory] laws today in the face of pressures generated by huge industries. . . . The big problem in the regulatory field is not influence peddling and corruption as that word is commonly understood. In my experience as a regulatory official I have been approached only once with a veiled intimation that money or stock was available in return for a favorable decision, and that was at the state level, not here in Washington.
>
> But abandonment of the public interest can be caused by many things, of which timidity and a desire for personal security are the most insidious. This commission, for example, must make hundreds and even thousands of decisions each year, a good many of which involve literally scores and hundreds of millions of dollars in a single case. A commissioner can find it very easy to consider whether his vote might arouse an industry campaign against his reconfirmation by the Senate.[8]

The Question of Competition

The impact of government regulation of business on consumers is not to be found in the occasional political scandals that have involved the independent regulatory agencies. Politicians are the master mechanics of regulation and politics keeps the machine greased and running. Big money and big politics occasionally make big headlines. But the day-in, day-out product of the machine is the tens of thousands of decisions and rules and orders concerning consumer prices and services, routinely ground out in the course of regulating competition, that do not ordinarily make headlines.

What is industrial competition, as traditionally defined by antitrust law and normally accepted by the consumer? Competition is the rise of a retail discount house, which undersells an older department store, which in turn took business away from a mom and pop dry goods store, all because each offered lower prices than the next. Competition is the demise of Ford Motor Company's Edsel and the success of the Volkswagen and other small foreign cars, because the Edsel wasn't the right car at the right price and the Volkswagen was. Competition is buying two bars of soap for the price of one because a soapmaker wants to introduce you to his new, fragrant brand. Or competition is two gasoline stations on opposite corners of the street undercutting one another's prices simply to meet competition. And competition is the government collecting $1,926,000 in fines from twenty-nine electrical goods manufacturers that conspired to fix prices in violation of the Sherman Act. Competition is, in summary, a maximum amount of rivalry among producers that yields for consumers the lowest prices and the best and most up-to-date goods and services—enforced, as necessary, by the antitrust laws.

What then is regulation? Regulation is many things, depending upon its origin in transportation, communications, energy supplies, banking, trade, the labor market, and pricing. But all regulation is government direction of private economic endeavor and all regulation tends to produce similar economic consequences which are in conflict with the basic definitions of competition and with antitrust law.

Federal regulation of business, whether directed to particular industries or to certain practices common to all industries, could never have remained confined to its modest/original purpose of keeping consumer prices low. It tried to do that and complications arose because industrial pricing is a highly complex matter. If prices are kept too low, then the quality and quantity of goods and services available to consumers tend to deteriorate. When that happens, government has three choices available to it: allow prices to increase, subsidize ailing producers with tax monies, or allow deterioration to run its course. Government has tried all three. It has armed the regulatory agencies with the power to increase prices and to restrict the number of competitors in industry. It has, in the area where regulation is the oldest, directly and indirectly awarded billions of dollars of subsidies. It has curtailed the public availability of some services, though deterioration is more likely to be stemmed with subsidies instead of being allowed to run its course.

Federal and state regulation of business' selling and pricing practices owes its birthright to government's desire to protect the small businessman from the big businessman—to protect the corner grocer and the neighborhood drugstore from the chain supermarket and the chain department store. The laws, with the inspired names of "fair-trade" laws, laws to ban "discrimination" by a manufacturer among its retail customers, were made by the political pressures that small business lobbies have brought to bear on state and national legislatures. They were made for the specific benefit of a particular class of businessmen, not with the consumer interest in mind. In practice, these laws also have contradicted competition and in fact have been sustained by explicit and implicit repeals of federal antitrust laws.

Fair trade is the name inspired by propagandists of retail-level protectionism for a practice under which a manufacturer of bicycles, breakfast cereal or some other consumer goods fixes the retail price at which its products are to be sold. The result, if the scheme is successful, is to ensure that all retailers in a particular area sell at a uniform price and that none indulge in price-cutting. All manner of devices have been used to enforce fair trade but the basic technique is the manufacturer's refusal to sell to retailers who cut prices. States that have fair-trade laws generally do not have regulatory agencies created specifically to enforce such laws. Agency enforcement is unnecessary because manufacturers are authorized to enforce the laws through private lawsuits against offenders.

The legality of fair-trade price-fixing has been a topic of recurring dispute for longer than half a century. Absent state or federal law sanctioning such price-fixing, the practice clearly would violate the Sherman Antitrust Act. Indeed, the Justice Department as far back as 1911 won from the Supreme Court a decision that manufacturers violate the Sherman Act when they attempt without appropriate state sanction to enforce fair-trade prices through contracts with their retail dealers.[1] Almost immediately, many states began to enact fair-trade laws that allowed manufacturers to fix uniform retail prices throughout the state and to refuse their products to retailers who refused to abide by the fixed prices. As many as forty-five states enacted such laws, although some in recent years have been repealed and others have been held by state courts to be in violation of state constitutions.

Bills have been pending in Congress as far back as 1914 to legalize retail price-fixing on a national scale. The pressure has ebbed and flowed in the intervening years, but never has disappeared completely. Congress has not succumbed but it has attempted to resolve the legal conflict between state fair-trade laws and federal antitrust law. In 1937 Congress passed the Miller-Tydings Fair Trade Act, which declared that fair-trade contracts executed under state laws are exempt from federal antitrust prosecution. But the 1937 law turned out to be an incomplete resolution of the conflict. Some years later, an enterprising New Orleans retailer who wanted to cut liquor prices brought suit under federal antitrust law, claiming he could not be forced to enter with distillers into price-fixing contracts despite the Miller-Tydings Act and Louisiana fair-trade law. The United States Supreme Court agreed with the retailer, deciding in 1951 that to require rebellious retailers to sign price-fixing contracts would "have a vast and devastating effect on Sherman Act policies."[2] But the Supreme Court decision didn't stand for long. Congress overrode the decision in 1952 by passing the McGuire Act which further amended federal antitrust law. The McGuire Act said federal law could not be used to void state law under which all retailers, whether or not they executed fair-trade contracts, may be forced to adhere to prices fixed by manufacturers.

Although Congress has not seen fit to devastate the Sherman Act, it has been persuaded not only to permit fair trading under state law but also to administer a direct blow, by means of the Robinson-Patman Act, to federal antitrust law. A fitting companion piece to state fair-trade laws, the act does not permit manufacturers to fix uniform prices that their retail dealers charge consumers. Rather, it attempts to accomplish much the same objective by saying that manufacturers and other producers of goods and services may not "discriminate in price" among wholesale or retail purchasers. The act, like many other exemptions from antitrust law which Congress has enacted, was grafted directly onto antitrust law; the Robinson-Patman Act is an amendment to the Clayton Antitrust Act. Congress said that the Robinson-Patman Act was to be enforced by either the Federal Trade Commission or the Justice Department, or through lawsuits brought by private parties. Not surprisingly, the Justice Department has never brought an action resting wholly on the Robinson-Patman Act. The Federal Trade Commission has become the government enforcement agency, although many private actions also have been brought.

The Robinson-Patman Act illustrates, better than any other single piece of federal regulatory legislation, the national confusion between competition and protectionism that gradually is resolved by political means. The legal concept of just prices, equally available to all, has medieval roots. The Sherman Act of 1890 did not specifically speak of the evils of discriminatory pricing, but it implicitly condemned price-cutting whereby a manufacturer and its favored dealers conspired to cut prices for the purpose of driving a competitor out of business. The original Clayton Act of 1914 went further by explicitly making it unlawful to "discriminate in price between different purchasers . . . where the effect may be to substantially lessen competition or tend to create a monopoly."

Price-cutting for the purpose of driving a competitor out of business obviously does not in the end serve the best interests of consumers. Price-cutting that is not so motivated clearly does serve the public interest. The distinction is often difficult to make, particularly because price-cutting, however motivated, usually reduces sellers' profits even if not to the point of driving anyone out of business. In 1914 Congress attempted to meet this difficulty by saying in the original Clayton Act that price-cutting was not to be viewed as illegally discriminatory if it was based on lower costs, on quantities of goods purchased or on a seller's "good faith" attempt to meet competition. In the twenty years that followed enactment of the 1914 act, the Federal Trade Commission issued only about forty price discrimination complaints and most of these the commission itself dismissed after hearings. It accepted the evidence offered that the price reductions challenged were based on manufacturers' differences in the costs of serving different retailers, on the varying quantities retailers bought or on simple good-faith efforts to meet another company's price cuts.

It was precisely this rational administration of the 1914 law that generated political pressures on Congress to do more to protect small retailers from big retailers. Small retailers normally do not buy in large quantities and a manufacturer's costs in serving many small dealers normally are higher than the cost of selling to big super-markets and chain department stores. These economic facts of life took on added meaning in the 1920's with the rapid growth of chain stores, such as the Great Atlantic & Pacific Tea Company, and of mail-order retail houses, such as Sears, Roebuck and Company. These larger retailers often bought directly from manufacturers, and by eliminating middlemen in the distribution system they tended to erode the business of wholesalers through whom smaller retailers often did their buying. The Depression of the 1930's hit wholesalers and smaller retailers particularly hard and together they turned to political channels for relief.

In response to their plight, the Federal Trade Commission made a study and in 1934 sent to Congress a report tracing the rise of chain stores. The report found no present threat of monopoly in their growth but said that "to the extent that chain stores consistently undersell independents," the chains would continue to thrive at the expense of smaller wholesalers and retailers. With the report in hand, a special committee in the House of Representatives began its own chain-store investigation and it investigated principally A&P. The bill that came out of the investigation was drafted by one of A&P's chief antagonists, a lawyer-lobbyist employed by the United States Wholesale Grocers' Association.[3]

The controversial bill was debated at length when it arrived on the floor for House action. Representative Emanuel Celler, the New York Democrat who even then was an influential member of the House Judiciary Committee, which has charge of antitrust legislation, tried to block it. The bill, he said, was "intended, under cover of devious but innocent appearing wording, to assure profitable business to a trade class regardless of the efficiency of service rendered the consumer." The consumer was "made the goat. . . . The legislation strikes directly at the primary interest of the public by denying consumers the assurance of obtaining the benefits of the lowest prices [which] the most efficient methods and equipment can bring about under free but fair competition. The consumers owe no business a living."

Advocates of the bill replied in the idiom that later made Senator Joseph McCarthy famous. The bill, they declared, had "the opposition of all cheaters, chiselers, bribe takers, bribe givers and the greedy who seek monopolistic powers." Representative Wright Patman, the Texas Democrat who shepherded the bill on the House side, said the measure would "compel the Golden Rule in business."

Given its purpose of protecting a special class of businessmen from the rigors of price competition, the Robinson-Patman Act that became law in 1936 could not have been a model of clarity. It was not and still is not. The act began with the original Clayton Act's proscription of price discrimination "where the effect may be to substantially lessen competition or tend to create a monopoly." Then it expanded on the old law by extending the proscription to price discriminations that "tend to injure . . . any person"; the legal effect of this provision was to allow the FTC to rule out a price reduction on a finding of injury not to competition but to a particular company or individual. Robinson-Patman also authorized the FTC to proceed against retailers who "knowingly receive a discrimination" as well as against sellers.

The new act retained the old law's defenses of price reductions based on costs, quantities purchased and meeting competition in good faith. Or so it seemed. "Nothing herein," the new law said, shall prevent price cuts based on "cost . . . or quantities" and "nothing herein shall prevent a seller from showing that his lower price was made in good faith to meet an equally low price of a competitor." But the new law made a drastic change by in effect shifting from the FTC to the accused company or person the burden of proving the legality of a price reduction. The shift meant that the FTC could rest its case after making what was termed a "prima facie" showing that the accused had cut prices and that the cut might injure a competitor. Moreover, the act's peculiar affirmation of the legality of price cuts made to meet competition seemed to mean that a company could meet a competitor's lower price but no "good faith" could be ascribed to undercutting competition.

Finally, Congress threw into Robinson-Patman three catchall provisions making it a crime to sell at "unreasonably low prices," to be "a party to or assist" in a discrimination and to sell goods in one part of the country "at prices lower" than those charged elsewhere.

Justice Robert Jackson said of the Robinson-Patman Act that "the commercial discriminations which it forbids are those only which meet three statutory conditions and survive the test of five statutory provisos."[4] A member of the FTC has asserted in private conversation that "the people who wrote it didn't understand English."

The Act is still the butt of sophisticated jokes among jurists and lawyers who must deal with it. One story is that a distinguished judge on a United States Circuit Court of Appeals one day listened in court to an FTC lawyer defending a commission decision. Then, turning to the judge sitting next to him on the bench, he said in a loud whisper intended for hearing throughout the courtroom that the Robinson-Patman Act "doesn't parse." At another time, the late Mr. Justice Jackson, writing of another lower court's decision, said of the act, "The Court of Appeals seems to have thought it almost beyond understanding."[5] James M. Landis, telling President-elect Kennedy in 1960 about the "muddled" FTC, said of the act: "Congress must make up its mind what this legislation really intended to accomplish."[6] Jokes are made sometimes even by FTC people. A commission aide, in a 1966 address to a group of lawyers who specialized in antitrust practice, gave witness to the endless litigation and legal fees the act has spawned by making this comment: "Today there are second generation experts in this field who were born, weaned, raised and educated on the fees that flowed from its bounty."[7]

More serious criticisms also have been made. Justice Felix Frankfurter once cautioned that the FTC's enforcement activities "might give rise to a price uniformity and rigidity in open conflict with the purposes of other antitrust legislation."[8] Frederick M. Rowe, a

Washington lawyer and respected student of the Robinson-Patman Act, once declared that the commission's actions "foment . . . industry-wide restraints of trade," as well as "screwball litigation and forensic giggles."[9]

Nevertheless, the Federal Trade Commission has plowed ahead and by and large the Supreme Court has acceded to the commission's supposed expertise. By law, the FTC's enforcement jurisdiction covers virtually the entire nation. In practice, the commission has never had financial or manpower resources commensurate with the vastness of its legal jurisdiction. If the commission had the resources to "regulate the conduct of the majority of business in a $675 billion dollar economy," as a recent FTC chairman remarked with unusual candor, everyone from the corner druggist to General Motors Corporation would live in "a police state."[10]

The meanings of Robinson-Patman thus have evolved since 1936 case by case, mostly on the basis of cases brought by the FTC but involving some filed in courts by private litigants.[11] Enforcement began cautiously, as it does with most new federal programs; administrators tested their new powers first on the specific issues that most bothered Congress and then moved on to explore unknown avenues.

In the 1930's, the FTC concentrated on eliminating discounts or "brokerage" given by food processors to A&P and other large grocery retailers. It also cracked down on a few companies that unquestionably had cut prices to drive competitors out of business and that probably could have been disciplined under the old Clayton Act or the Sherman Act. Becoming more confident, the FTC in the 1940's brought cases where the predatory intent of the price-cutters was more debatable. It ruled, for example, that the Morton Salt Company could not give quantity discounts to certain large customers because these customers passed the savings on to consumers while smaller stores had no similar savings to pass on. The Supreme Court upheld the FTC in this and other cases.[12] In the 1950's the FTC grew more aggressive and the Supreme Court began to blow the whistle. The agency successfully blocked producers' price reductions on products ranging from bakers' yeast to auto parts. When it attempted to prevent Standard Oil Company of Indiana from reducing gasoline prices to jobbers, the High Court decided Standard was meeting competition and the FTC was going too far.[13] And when the commission tried to force up the price a vending machine company paid for candy, nuts and chewing gum, the Supreme Court intervened with Justice Frankfurter's warning of "open conflict with . . . other antitrust legislation."[14]

In retrospect the 1950's were years not of reform but of indecision.[15] The Supreme Court's warnings had no permanent effect on the FTC and in the 1960's the court ceased even its warnings. The commission, for example, outlawed United Biscuit Company's discounts on cookies and crackers and the court abstained. The agency said Borden Company could not package low-priced brands of evaporated milk for sale to big supermarket chains and the court agreed, without bothering to discuss the consumer's interest in low-priced milk.[16] And in 1967 the court significantly expanded small business protectionism by ruling, in a case brought not by the FTC but by a local Utah pie company, that price-cutters can be sued even when their local competitor remains dominant in its market and is by no means forced to the brink of bankruptcy.[17] In reaching this conclusion, the Supreme Court issued no warning and made no mention of the sharply reduced prices Salt Lake City housewives were paying for frozen dessert pies.

Protectionism thus has grown and now it is only occasionally that a voice on the FTC or the Supreme Court is raised against the Robinson-Patman Act. Justice Stewart objected when the court upheld the FTC's ban on Borden's low-priced milk. Commissioner Philip Elman took exception when the FTC rescued local jelly manufacturers on the East Coast from price reductions on national brands. The government should not "protect businessmen against the inevitable risks and losses resulting from competition," he declared. "All successful competition necessarily diverts business from rivals and no competitive tactic is more effective than a reduction in price." But these are minority voices, heard only in dissent to majority decisions.

As a practical matter, the Supreme Court can warn but, lacking a constitutional basis upon which to issue orders to other branches of government, it is poorly equipped to resolve conflicts in laws enacted by Congress. The FTC, given its vulnerability to pressures brought on members of Congress by special-interest groups, seems incapable of rationalizing protectionism with competition. It is illuminating that the great majority of price discrimination cases brought by the FTC have not originated with agency investigators combing the country for commercial misdeeds. Rather, they have originated in letters, sent directly to the commission or forwarded by members of Congress, in which small and not-so-small businessmen complain of their competitors' price reductions. The letters are not ordinarily in the commission's public files. But the pattern of enforcement is not denied. The commission's charge against Standard Oil of Indiana in the 1950's originated with the Retail Gasoline Dealers Association of Michigan, which complained of a gasoline price war in Detroit, according to one authority.[18] According to another—a former FTC staff official who deserted to the Justice Department—"The FTC has become the mouthpiece of small business lobbies."

It is axiomatic that consumers have paid dearly for the hundreds of price discrimination orders issued by the FTC since 1936 and the additional court actions brought by companies. Yet, the total effect on consumer prices is difficult to measure. Obviously, the commission has not halted all price competition; neither the law nor the commission's resources would permit any such result. The law has been applied in no logical pattern, but on a hit-or-miss basis to companies scattered throughout the nation. And even where the FTC has hit, protection of small companies and increases in consumer prices have not always been the inevitable results; for example, there is no law to prevent a supermarket chain, denied a manufacturer's lower prices on jelly or any other item, from building its own jelly factory to reduce its costs and its retail prices.

Still, there is no doubt that the nation's consumers have indeed become the "goat" of Representative Celler's prediction. Although national enforcement of the Robinson-Patman Act is far from complete, the law is a competition-stifling smog that hangs threateningly over all producers of consumer goods. "It has become dangerous to compete by selective or localized price reductions," a former FTC chief economist has concluded.[19] Realism requires noting also that large companies usually are no more enthusiastic than are small businesses about price reductions as a method of competition. Indeed, large manufacturers frequently are arm-in-arm with small retailers in advocating and enforcing fair-trade laws. Price-cutters, large or small, usually are renegades; they are newer companies seeking to take business from established rivals, or they are older companies seeking to regain business lost.

Unlike the FTC's thinly spread and less than totally successful effort to regulate consumer goods pricing practices throughout the nation, other agencies concentrate on single industries and achieve more complete results. Total control of an industry's pricing, however, also leads to rather awesome economic complexities.

Government regulation of an industry can be reasonably successful when the industry involved has a true monopoly or something close to a monopoly. In that event, the complications presented to regulation are not so great. Traditional monopoly industries in the United States are local utility companies, franchised under state law, which offer electric, gas, water or telephone service. If the state regulators fix rates that are too low to yield the company sufficient revenues to maintain good service, regulation does not run the risk that service will deteriorate to the point of disappearance; consumers have no practical alternatives to paying the prices. On the other hand, the state regulators can guard against excessively high prices by knowing the utility's costs and allowing it no more than a fair profit.

The federal regulators' task is infinitely more complicated because, with one exception, there is no national monopoly in any federally regulated industry. The exception is the telephone industry and the government has been reasonably successful in regulating interstate telephone rates. In all the other industries which the federal government today regulates, there is competition among numbers of producers. This difference between state and federal regulation of business is frequently ignored but it is fundamental to both politics and economics. If the federal regulators were politically independent and economically expert, as they are constitutionally assumed to be, perhaps they could have regulated competition more effectively by fixing prices low enough to satisfy the consumer interest and high enough to ensure an adequate quantity and quality of goods and services. Instead, they uniformly have resolved their dilemma by minimizing the number of competitors in regulated industries, by condemning price competition among a few competitors and by restraining industrial change in the form of technological innovation.

Thus, despite variations in the powers and attitudes of agencies, certain universal truths emerge today. The agencies have institutionalized industrial protectionism. They are umpires not of the consumer interest versus business interest but of competing business interests. They are supported and favored by business, even though the old animosities of business and government still sometimes show through. And they are the nemesis of competition, as defined by the antitrust laws and the Department of Justice.

The institution of protectionism is not easily penetrated. The paraphernalia of government and the 100,000 decisions a year are too imposing. Professional economists only rarely have tried to take the measure of the agencies. Sometimes, however, one who is not intellectually burdened with knowledge of the complexities can better go to the heart of a matter. One such, an unimpressed young man in Omaha, did so. His name was Tom Hilt.

One day in March of 1965, Hilt, who had studied transportation in and graduated from college, was home in Nebraska, working with his dad, who owned Hilt Truck Line. He had spent most of the day in the office, performing the onerous chore of typing a new rate schedule on frozen potatoes, meat and grain products. The document had to be mailed off to the Interstate Commerce Commission in Washington.

Any ICC tariff is a bore, except possibly for the few "tariff experts" who study the ICC's minutely detailed tariff regulations as a lifetime occupation. Once, when Hilt had to type a tariff covering rates for almost everything carried by Hilt Truck Line—a company of respectable size operating in nineteen midwestern states—the job covered ninety pages and took nearly a month. On this day, he had particular reason to be annoyed. Some weeks earlier Hilt Truck Line had sought to cut some rates on frozen potatoes, meat and grain products, but after that tariff had been typed and sent to Washington, a number of big railroads had protested to the ICC that Hilt's rates were too low. As a result, the ICC's Board of Suspension had suspended the rate cuts, telling Hilt Truck Line it could not put them into effect unless it proved they were legal.

Tom Hilt was angry. The railroads had claimed Hilt Truck Line's new, low rates were lower than the company's costs, and therefore illegal. Hilt felt he was in a better position than the railroads or the ICC to know what his costs were and he knew the company could make money hauling frozen potatoes or almost anything else at a rate of about 33 cents a hundred pounds. Hilt Truck Line had wanted to cut the frozen potato rate only to about 42 cents, from 50 cents. "The ICC is a railroad lover," he grumbled.

Rather than going through all the cost and trouble of fighting the railroads, Hilt Truck Line had decided to abandon the rate cut. So Tom was typing out the new tariff, putting the rates on frozen potatoes, meat and grain products back up where they had been. After he had typed the last line, raising the frozen potato rate back up to 50 cents, he added something new:

YAK FAT, Omaha to Chicago. Rate: 45 cents per hundred pounds, to become effective April 11, 1965. The yak fat, he continued, had to be shipped in minimum quantities of eighty thousand pounds (two truckloads). But Hilt Truck Line would accept yak fat in glass or metal containers, in barrels, boxes, pails or tubs.

Then he mailed the new tariff off to Washington, seven pages all legal and official-looking. Tom Hilt's yak fat rate was duly clocked in at the ICC as "Hilt Truck Line, Inc., Tariff MF-ICC 7, third revised page 62, Item 1810," and sent on its way from the mail room through the hushed, government-green corridors to the sixth-floor Public Tariff File Room where the "tariff watchers" spy to make sure that nobody undersells anybody. A sharp-eyed railroad man quickly spotted "yak fat" and dispatched a communiqué to the Western Trunk Line Committee, a large rate-fixing office maintained by railroads, including railroads with tracks between Omaha and Chicago that compete with Hilt's trucks.

Before March was out, the Western Trunk Line Committee's formal, fully documented complaint was in, requesting the ICC to suspend the yak fat rate because it was patently below cost and therefore illegal. The railroads cited the commission's own decision in a case titled "Paper Articles from Atlanta to Cincinnati, 314 ICC 715 (716)." Exhibit A, attached, purported to show in some detail that Hilt's yak fat hauling costs added up to 63 cents a hundred pounds and therefore the 45 cent rate would mean an 18 cent loss. Exhibit B compared a railroad rate of 63 cents, not on yak fat, but on comparable traffic.

On April 7, the Board of Suspension—five experienced employees to whom the Commission had delegated the power to block rate cuts and increases—voted to suspend yak fat. In the board's defense, it is only fair to note that it was a particularly busy day, with thirty suspension applications to be acted upon.

"It appearing," the board's order said in what now became a federal case, Docket M-19432, the yak fat rate may be "unjust and unreasonable in violation of the Interstate Commerce Act . . . it is ordered that an investigation be, and it is hereby, instituted. . . ." Two days later Commissioner Howard Freas issued a full-fledged order in M-19432, getting the investigation under way and giving Hilt thirty days to make an opening defense of yak fat. By mid-April the growing file on M-19432 included a letter with which the railroads informed the ICC they'd formed a yak fat arguing committee, on which were represented some of the biggest names in western railroading: the Burlington, the Rock Island, Chicago Great Western, the North Western, Milwaukee Road and the Illinois Central.

They never had the chance to swing into action. The thirty days Commissioner Freas had given Hilt to begin its defense passed and of course the opening statement never arrived. The ICC and the railroads by now suspected they were being hoaxed. Apparently not sure, but anxious to be done with yak fat, the commission issued an order stating that Hilt had been "afforded ample opportunity" but had failed to sustain the burden of proving its rate legal. M-19432 was closed.

Hilt Truck Line never had hauled any yak fat, and never intended to. Tom Hilt never heard of a truck line or a railroad that had. But he had heard of a yak. There was one in the Pioneer Park Zoo in Lincoln, Nebraska, a rather skinny specimen of the wild ox native to Tibet, although he (or she, the zoo keeper was not sure) was not for rendering.

Tim Hilt wanted only to prove that "the railroads will protest anything and the ICC will go along." He did, at perhaps greater personal risk than he realized. The victimized ICC dusted off Title 18 of the U.S. Code which states quite clearly that the filing of false or fraudulent representations with any department or agency of the government shall be punishable by a $10,000 fine or five years in jail, or both. But young Tom was saved by the ICC's acute embarrassment, which prosecution could only have made worse.

The sooner forgotten, the better. Yak fat was but a ripple upon the bureaucratic sea. The railroads were as anxious to forget it as the commission. The trucking industry wasn't laughing very hard because it plays the rate game too, even if its tariff spies aren't quite as well organized as the railroads' watchers. And, except for a few barge lines that also play, a few trade-paper reporters and an occasional associate professor of economics from some midwestern university, nobody else pays much attention to what the ICC says and does. Forgotten it was!

Tom Hilt exposed, if but briefly, a price-fixing institution so hoary it almost is no longer questioned within government and so removed it is almost unknown to the public. The Western Trunk Line Committee is one of many rate-fixing conferences which are maintained by railroads, trucking lines, barge lines, steamship lines and international airlines. The rate conference is the medium by which American companies in each transportation industry confer among themselves to fix the passenger fares or freight rates all of the supposedly competing members of an industry uniformly will charge the public. The agreed-on fares and rates must be submitted to the pertinent regulatory agency—the Interstate Commerce Commission, Federal Maritime Commission or Civil Aeronautics Board —which approves or rejects them, as the public interest supposedly requires. Approval or rejection does not disturb the industry's price uniformity; it means that all members of an industry, except the renegades, if any, raise or lower their fares and rates together. In deciding whether the public interest requires an industry's fares and rates to go up or down, the agency does not consult consumers. If it consults anyone, the consultation takes the form of testimony and exhibits against the fare or rate change filed by a competing industry.

Rate conferences are a cartel-like institutionalization of price-fixing. They represent the most advanced form of price uniformity developed by the federal agencies that regulate particular industries and they represent the largest area of conflict between regulation and competition. The conflict has been resolved in favor of regulation through the political processes of Congress. But the resolution was neither automatic nor simple. Indeed, transportation companies fixed prices, apparently for the better part of fifty years, in violation of the Sherman Act and without exemption from that law. The Supreme Court in 1897 held the railroad conferences illegal and it was not until 1948 that Congress enacted the law exempting railroads and other transportation industries from the Sherman Act. It is apparent from ICC records that some railroads, during the years prior to World War I, had returned to rate-fixing conferences.[20] Precisely what the railroads talked about is not clear, but it would appear that the ICC knew and that it tacitly approved. As far back as 1898, the commission said publicly that "to one familiar with actual conditions" it was plain the railroads should be allowed to confer on rates.[21] It's not clear either why the Justice Department did not renew its attack on the rate conferences. These years prior to World War I were of course the years when the ICC was rapidly acquiring from Congress additional powers over the railroads. It would appear possible that the department shied from a direct confrontation with the commission, preferring to leave the 1897 Supreme Court decision stand undisturbed rather than risk its overturn either by Congress or the Supreme Court.

After the war the conferences were revived and continued unchallenged until the late 1930's, when the trust busters began sniffing around once more. By then, there were trucking industry rate conferences, too. Congress had extended ICC regulation to trucks in 1935 and if the railroads could assume that regulation allowed them to confer on rates, so could truck lines.

The Justice Department's antitrust division investigated both railroad and trucking industry rate conferences and in 1942 it began to present evidence to a federal grand jury in Chicago with the intention of obtaining Sherman Act indictments. But the secrecy of the grand jury's deliberations developed leaks and soon the Army and the Navy were pleading with Justice Department officials in Washington to call the whole thing off. Their plea was that the transportation of war goods was, at the moment, far more important than the legality of rate conferences. History does not record all the events that transpired, but the generals and the admirals did obtain from the War Production Board a certificate that said the rate conferences were legal and the grand jury in Chicago apparently did not issue an indictment.

But that was by no means the end of it. The trust busters persisted and early in 1943 they did obtain an indictment in Denver against a group of truck lines and their rate conferences. The case went to trial and a jury acquitted the truckers.

Still the trust busters kept at it. In 1944 they brought an injunction suit in United States District Court in Nebraska naming as defendants all the western railroads and the Association of American Railroads. Quickly, the state of Georgia filed a parallel action in the United States Supreme Court seeking to enjoin twenty railroads operating in the East and South from participating in rate conferences. The entire railroad industry was under attack. On March 26, 1945, the Supreme Court decided the case brought by Georgia, ruling that rate conferences violated antitrust law.[22]

Now the action shifted from the Supreme Court across the street to the Capitol. Bills to immunize the rate conferences from the antitrust laws had begun flowing into congressional hoppers in 1943. In 1946, the House, by a lopsided vote of 277 to 45, passed a bill to exempt rate conferences from the jurisdiction of the antitrust laws. But the Senate didn't go along with the House and the fight continued. Many shipper organizations supported the railroad and truck arguments for exemption and the ICC testified that rate-fixing "conformed to necessity and realities."

Finally, in 1948, the House and Senate passed the Reed-Bulwinkle bill that exempted railroad, truck and barge line rate-fixing conferences from the antitrust laws, provided only that the conference agreements were filed with the ICC and that such agreements specifically give each party to an agreement the right to take independent rate action. President Truman vetoed the bill but Congress passed it over his veto and over the objections of a few like the late Senator Charles W. Tobey, a maverick Republican from New Hampshire, who railed without effect against "cartelization of the transportation industry . . . a dangerous precedent, encouraging other powerful groups to seek legislation immunizing them from established laws."

Since 1949 the ICC has approved agreements covering more than sixty conferences at which hundreds of railroads, truck lines and barge common carriers, day in and day out, fix thousands of rates. Industry's preference for rate-fixing was vividly displayed as recently as 1962, when President Kennedy sent his Transportation Message to Congress. The railroad industry for longer than a decade before John Kennedy became President had been pamphleteering against government policies and programs that they felt discriminated against the railroads. The campaign, spearheaded by the Association of American Railroads, eventually mounted into one of the biggest long-term lobbying efforts ever conducted in Washington. The railroads had a lengthy, but selective, list of recommendations. They wanted the Treasury to collect user charges from trucks, barges and airlines that operated on federally built or maintained rights of way; they wanted their own tax bills reduced; they wanted the right to own airlines. But what they probably wanted most was the elimination of the double standard of freight rate regulation. All railroad rates of course were subject in full to the ICC's authority over rate increases and decreases. But when Congress in 1935 had extended regulation to trucks it said the ICC would have no control of truck rates for agricultural products and fish; when Congress extended regulation to barges in 1940, it gave the ICC no control of barge rates on bulk commodity traffic.

The railroads campaigned for the repeal of those truck and barge rate exemptions or, as a second choice, they wanted rail rates on agricultural products, fish and bulk commodities also freed of ICC regulation. The former had a nice "free enterprise" ring, of which the railroads made the most.

The inequities in federal transportation policies and programs of course had been recognized for many years, although not necessarily in the order listed by the railroads. The industry got a sympathetic hearing during the Truman Administration and President Eisenhower gave the railroads his moral support. The industry didn't get much more than that. And then, on April 4, 1962, President Kennedy sent to Congress his Transportation Message, which for the first time put the prestige of the White House squarely behind an overhaul of federal transport law.

It was unexpected for a Democratic President to identify himself so closely with a major and traditionally Republican industry, but John Kennedy's list of reforms read pretty much like the railroads' own proposals. Mr. Kennedy paid no special homage to the railroads; he addressed himself to the "patchwork" of the Interstate Commerce Act and his most significant proposal was that the inconsistencies of ICC freight rate regulation be eliminated.

However, the message was not a source of unrelieved joy for the railroads. It also said, "Congress should make certain that such practices by [railroads] freed from minimum rate regulations would be covered by laws against monopoly." The Administration wanted to free the railroads of some ICC rate controls, and thereby permit them to meet truck and barge competition. But President Kennedy at the same time wanted to take away the antitrust immunity of their rate-fixing conferences and thus force railroads into rate competition among themselves.

A crucial point was reached on the morning of June 5, 1963. The Kennedy Administration's program, on which congressional committees had been taking testimony for longer than a year, had become extremely controversial. The proposal to free the railroads of much ICC rate regulation was under extremely heavy attack by the truckers, the barge lines and the Interstate Commerce Commission. Oren Harris, who was the powerful chairman of the House Commerce Committee, was giving the railroads another hearing. Daniel Loomis, the president of the Association of American Railroads (whose $7 million annual budget powered most of the long drive for rate freedom), had brought along some of the industry's most progressive executives—men like Ben W. Heineman, the chairman of the Chicago & North Western Railway.

As Loomis finished his testimony and Heineman began, the committee's interest focused more and more on the railroad rate conferences, on the use shippers make of them to request new rates and on the antitrust immunity conferred on them by the Reed-Bulwinkle Act.[23]

Finally, Chairman Harris leaned forward: "Let me ask you this sixty-four-dollar question."

Mr. Heineman: "Yes sir."

The Chairman: "Suppose the recommendation of the Administration to repeal [the Reed-Bulwinkle Act] were to be approved. How would you feel about the entire bill?"

Mr. Heineman: "Are you asking me my view of the industry's position?"

The Chairman: "I am. . . ."

Mr. Heineman: "I would say, sir, that . . . the industry would prefer to see the bill die than pass with such a provision."

And die it did. Maybe it would have died anyway. Perhaps the trucking industry, whose influence was great in the Senate Commerce Committee, could have blocked enactment even if the House had passed the bills. But it seems more likely that Congress would have enacted some version of the Kennedy proposal, if Mr. Heineman had been able to respond differently to Oren Harris' question.

There was and is a minority of railroad presidents and chairmen that would have supported the Kennedy proposal. Some unknown number of railroad executives would have given up their privilege of fixing rates with other railroads, in exchange for the freedom to engage in unrestrained price competition with trucks and barge lines. One such was the Southern Railway's D. W. Brosnan, who said this to the Harris committee: "I don't think that competition should be restrained at the expense of the public in order to take care of any railroad or any truckline."[24]

Mr. Heineman also was an enlightened railroader and, had he been asked his own opinion, his answer to Representative Harris might have been different. But he was asked for the opinion of the majority of railroad executives in America and without question he accurately gave the industry's opinion. An equally progressive railroader, chatting in the privacy of his own executive suite and pleading anonymity "because I still have to live with the ICC," delivers this indictment of the railroads: "In this industry we have many managers—presidents, chairmen of the board and vice presidents—who are frightened to death of real competition. The ICC encourages these fears. It's forever talking about the horrors of price competition that would result from deregulation."

Indeed, the commission has paraded the alleged horrors before Congress. It told the Harris committee that President Kennedy's proposal would mean "destructive and damaging rate wars" and in the end transportation companies would be "prostrated financially."[25]

Price-fixing, as sanctioned by the ICC, today bears no relevance whatsoever to the consumer. A commissioner who was appointed by President Kennedy said as much in 1963 when he urged upon his fellow regulators a "positive search for the public interest."[26] It has not been found. The Interstate Commerce Commission's authority over transportation rates is an exercise in settling disputes among the railroad, the trucking and the water carrier industries. It is a process in which no consumer voice is heard.

No fewer than 203,721 new rail, truck and barge rates and rate changes were filed with the Interstate Commerce Commission in 1964, a typical-enough year. (In the wonderful world of freight rates, there are separate rates for horses for slaughter and draft horses, on sand for glass manufacture and sand for cement, on lime for industrial use and lime for agriculture.) The commission received protests on 4959 of the filings. No less than 90 percent of those protests involved proposed rate cuts and only 10 percent involved proposed rate increases. And the great bulk of the protests (3654 of them) were pleas filed by the railroad, truck and barge line agents stationed inside the ICC's cavernous rate-filing room. "Such a distribution of protests," said the President's Council of Economic Advisers, "reflects an attempt to orient regulation to the settlement of disputes between competitors" rather than disputes between transport companies and the shipping and traveling public.[27]

The conflict between transportation price-fixing and antitrust law and its resolution by enactment of the Reed-Bulwinkle Act is an example of what has happened time and again. For roughly forty years, Congress has been resolving conflicts between regulation—federal and sometimes state—and competition and it again and again has repealed antitrust law. The bits and pieces today add up to a vast cartelization of a large number of industries.

Congress in the early 1920's legislated a bit of immunity from antitrust prosecution for farmer cooperatives that market certain agricultural products and in the years since it has broadened the immunity to cover the pricing practices of dairy farmers and vegetable growers. Many years ago Congress also passed laws to immunize labor unions and manufacturers' export trade associations from antitrust law. Sometimes the exemptions were enacted on the ground that the business involved regulated itself. More often, exemptions were passed on the ground of state regulation. Congress, for instance, passed the McCarran-Ferguson Insurance Regulation Act in 1945 to exempt insurance companies from federal antitrust prosecution because they were regulated by the states. The occasion for the passage was a Supreme Court decision the previous year which held that insurance companies were subject to the Sherman Act. But the Supreme Court has not always found industry to be within the reach of antitrust law when Congress has failed to enact a specific exemption. On occasion, the High Court has ruled that federal regulation implies exemption, and once upon a time it gave the professional baseball business an exemption even though Congress has never regulated baseball.

No areas of private economic endeavor enjoy such complete immunity, explicit and implicit, from antitrust law as industries that are regulated by the federal regulatory agencies. There are exemptions of one sort or another for railroads, truck lines, water transportation companies, airlines, banks, stock exchanges, telephone and telegraph companies, natural gas pipeline companies, oil producers and coal operators, among others. These are, by and large, big businesses. But Congress also has enacted some impressive exemptions for small business.

It has been estimated that the exemptions, carved out of antitrust law in bits and pieces over many years, now apply to one-quarter of the nation's commerce. In other words, more than $150 billion of annual business, in terms of a gross national product that has been running over $600 billion annually, today is excused from the antitrust law and from the legal necessity to compete.[28]

Services and Prices

Economic democracy requires and consumer protection demands vigorous competition in pricing, products and services among the greatest possible number of producers and sellers. Antitrust laws were made not only to assure consumers of the greatest possible amount of price competition and product innovation but also to ensure freedom of entry into businesses and foster maximum numbers of competitors in all industries. Even the Robinson-Patman Act rested ostensibly on a premise of maximizing the number of competitors; its error was the preservation of competitors who dislike price competition. Antitrust law recognized but one type of exception: natural monopolies, such as privately-owned electric and other utilities. Granted an exclusive franchise by state or local government, its rates and services regulated, a utility cannot freely quit business and no one can enter to compete with it.

The federal agencies that regulate industries which are not natural monopolies, but which Congress has decided are clothed with a large public interest, must attempt to rationalize competition with control. In regulating rates and prices, they have tried to treat all the component companies of an industry as a single entity, utilizing rate-fixing conferences that are legalized only by legislative exemption from antitrust law enforcement. Economic democracy still recognizes the rights of dissenting minorities—the Tom Hilts and other nonconformists—to a point. But efficient regulation of rates among multiple competitors obviously requires a large measure of conformity, which has been achieved by controlling entry into an industry and minimizing the number of competitors. And here too Congress has rolled back antitrust law for the benefit of the regulators and their industries and the Department of Justice has fought a losing battle all the way.

The federal regulators today control entry into and exit from the railroad, trucking, airline and steamship businesses; the telephone, telegraph and the television and radio broadcasting industries; the business of operating natural gas pipelines, hydroelectric dams and nuclear electric generating stations; and the commercial and investment banking businesses. Some of these businesses, such as banking, still can be entered on a limited, intrastate basis on the authority of state regulators. Telephone regulation is a joint state-federal undertaking. But by and large, the power to control entry and exit rests in Washington. No private enterprise of significant size can be started without a finding by the federal regulators that the venture is required by the "public convenience and necessity."

The need for and effectiveness of limitations on entry vary among the agencies and their industries. There are relatively few airlines and entry by a newcomer is virtually impossible. There are many truck lines and entry should be relatively easy. How difficult it can be to enter even the trucking business was discovered by one Joe Jones and the Small Business Administration, a unit of the executive branch of the federal government. His case reflects what many other aspiring small businessmen have encountered. Jones was an Atlanta Negro with ten children and an ambition to own a truck line. He had experience in the trucking business and he lined up customers—a candy company and a chemical concern—for the business he proposed to establish. Then he went to the Small Business Administration and obtained a $25,000 loan; SBA was satisfied with his qualifications and it happened that SBA at the time was anxious to promote the Johnson Administration's war on poverty by helping blacks to establish their own businesses. Jones next went to the Interstate Commerce Commission and applied for a certificate of public convenience and necessity to haul candy to northern cities and return southbound with chemicals.

The ICC turned him down, not once but several times, because, it said, there already were enough trucking companies hauling candy north and chemicals south on the highways where Mr. Jones wanted to run his trucks. Or, in the ICC's more formal way of putting it, Mr. Jones had failed to show that "the public convenience and necessity" required additional trucking service.

Ever since 1935 the ICC has minimized truck competition. When the Depression-minded Congress in 1935 placed the truckers under the ICC's wing with enactment of the Motor Carrier Act, the lawmakers were openly fearful of an "oversupply" of trucking services. The commission has a rigid formula for trying to keep the quantity of trucking competition within bounds: Certificates, of "operating rights," it hands out specify in great detail the type of freight a trucker can haul and the route over which he can haul it. Typically, a trucker can haul nuts and bolts between Bridgeport, Connecticut, and Providence, Rhode Island, but he can't haul nuts or bolts on to New York City and he can't haul nails anywhere.

Such detailed regulation, of course, has generated thousands of applications for certificates to enter the trucking business, to extend routes and to haul additional kinds of freight. The paper work is enormous. The ICC regulators decide each with a large amount of protectionism in their hearts for the companies already in business. Joe Jones finally was given a certificate because he was black, but many more applications are rejected on findings that the public interest does not require additional competition.

While the ICC has carried out Congress' intent by limiting the number of competitors, the commission has issued more than seventeen thousand trucking certificates. The largest trucking company has nothing approaching a monopoly. Entry into other regulated businesses is progressively more difficult—especially because more capital is usually needed—and the number of competitors is relatively smaller. A charter to open a new national bank is probably a little more difficult to obtain. A license to operate a commercially viable television station is more difficult still. Entering the railroad, telephone, stock exchange or natural gas pipeline businesses is almost impossible because the regulators won't permit new competitors to enter, or because companies already in the business are large enterprises with monopolistic or near monopolistic power, or for both reasons.

The rationalization of competition with regulation varies with capital requirements, industry prosperity or recession at any given time and other factors. Everything considered, however, the airline industry is the most tightly closed and least competitive of all. About twenty domestic airlines were in business in 1938 when the Civil Aeronautics Board was created. They received "grandfather" franchises from the board. Since 1938 no new company has been licensed to engage in scheduled, domestic trunk-line service.[1] The number of trunk lines has since declined, principally because of mergers, to fewer than a dozen. The CAB has authorized direct-route competition among no more than three airlines and it has sanctioned this limited amount of competition only on the nation's most heavily traveled routes. Following World War II, the board did begin to license and subsidize thirteen local service airlines to serve smaller cities. But it carefully avoided any substantial amount of route competition among local service lines or between the local lines and the trunk lines.

When Congress created the first regulatory agency in 1887, it clearly did not intend to limit competition or confer monopolistic powers. Subsequently, in creating new agencies or amending the jurisdictions of older agencies, Congress sometimes has told the regulators explicitly to curtail competition and at other times clearly did not intend that competition should be further curtailed; Congress' intentions varied with the times, politics and state of concentration already existing in an industry. Nonetheless, all of the agencies that were given authority to control entry have used it to restrict competition, even when the authority was given only to protect the public against entry by unethical businessmen or unsafe business practices. The curtailment of entry has become so commonplace that it almost is no longer questioned in Congress or in the Justice Department's antitrust division.

On the other hand, the agencies' second means of reducing competition remains highly controversial. Congress has passed laws saying that companies in regulated industries may not merge without the prior approval of their regulators. The agencies are to weigh the public interest in competition between two companies against the cost-saving and other financial benefits that would accrue from the merger.[2] Far more frequently than not, the regulators vote against competition and for mergers, and many of the mergers they approve would violate antitrust law. The courts frequently have banned these mergers on such grounds. Time and again Congress has resolved this dilemma with laws that explicitly immunize agency-approved mergers from antitrust attack. When mergers are immunized, the Justice Department frequently appears before the agencies to argue for competition and against proposed mergers, but, almost invariably, the regulators approve the mergers. The department then is powerless to bring suit charging illegality under the Sherman and Clayton Antitrust Acts. It may go to court and charge that the agency improperly weighed the desirability of competition against the benefits of merger. The courts usually are sympathetic but in the end they submit to the agencies' presumed expertise.

A prime example was the application, filed in 1960 by the Seaboard Air Line Railroad and the Atlantic Coast Line, that posed a most direct confrontation between the philosophy of regulation and the philosophy of competition. The two railroads for years had been direct competitors in a vast stretch of the southeastern United States and both were prosperous. The Justice Department told the ICC it was opposed, contending that approval of the merger would eliminate two vigorous competitors, that their consolidation of facilities would leave some shippers and smaller communities without any rail service and would jeopardize the continued existence of some smaller railroads in the Southeast that would have to compete with this new behemoth.

On December 2, 1963, a majority of the eleven ICC commissioners approved the Coast Line–Seaboard merger. "We cannot agree," the majority said, "that the merger will create a potential monopoly in the region served." It did agree that "some lessening of competition will inevitably result" in a six-state area. But after weighing the curtailment of competition "with the advantages of the merger, including improved services, safer operations and lower costs, we are convinced the advantages far outweigh the potential disadvantages." There was dissent within the commission. Charles A. Webb, a Republican regulator from Virginia, said, "In no prior case, has the commission destroyed so much competition with so little justification." The majority had "disparaged competition and exalted regulation." The ICC decision went finally to the Supreme Court, which bowed to the ICC's expertise, and the merger took place in 1967.[3]

This approval by the ICC and the Supreme Court was a giant step along the way to other consolidations of huge railroads that took place in the mid-1960's. In 1966, the commission, over the initial objections of the Justice Department, unanimously approved the merger of the Pennsylvania and New York Central Railroads.[4] The ICC decision was appealed by a group of other eastern railroads and the Supreme Court in 1967 sent the case back to the commission for further proceedings; Justice Fortas dissented, saying the courts "are not the chief administrators" of the economic destiny of the people.[5] Justice William O. Douglas wrote a separate opinion in which he agreed with the majority that the case should go back to the ICC but asserted that the commission on remand should review the entire eastern railroad merger situation. "The commission's piecemeal, hands-off approach to the merger problem is not commanded by the Transportation Act," he asserted.[6]

The commission conducted only limited proceedings on remand and when the case again came before the Supreme Court, railroad merger case law as well as the Penn Central took another leap forward. The court approved the merger and Justice Fortas wrote the majority opinion. In it he said positively that it is the policy of Congress to encourage "consolidation of the nation's railroads."[7] The Pennsylvania and New York Central thus were merged in 1968 into the Penn Central, a $4.5 billion corporation, the largest merger in American railroading history, to date.

The growth of regulation and decline of competition, over the years from 1887 when the ICC had no power over rail mergers until 1968 when Justice Fortas spoke the final words, is portrayed in the storied efforts of three western railroads to merge. The Great Northern Railway, the Northern Pacific Railway and the Chicago, Burlington & Quincy Railroad first attempted to combine more than sixty years ago. They were joined in a holding company, which the Justice Department challenged as a violation of the Sherman Act. The Supreme Court in 1904 ruled that the holding company was illegal and ordered it dissolved.[8]

In the 1920's, after the ICC had acquired its authority to approve rail mergers but before it was fully disposed to use the authority, the three railroads tried again. The commission ruled in 1928 that the Great Northern and Northern Pacific could merge, but only on the condition that they divest the joint ownership of the Burlington. The three called off the matter rather than agree to the ICC's condition.

In 1961 the three returned to the commission with a merger application. The Justice Department was as much opposed to the transaction as ever. Its hostility was such that department lawyers became involved in a personal feud with the ICC examiner who heard argument on the merger proposal, accusing him of "shocking personal bias in favor of the merger," which he approved in a 456-page opinion. In 1966 the commission itself by a 6-to-5 vote decided the merger was not in the public interest—and in passing commented unanimously that the Justice Department lawyers' charges against the examiner were "baseless and reckless." Then, in 1967, the commission reconsidered and reversed itself. Its approval of the merger was upheld by the U.S. District Court for the District of Columbia, which relied in large part on Justice Fortas' words in the Penn Central case.

The right of regulators to curtail competition and the futility of Justice Department objections apparently are settled, insofar as the railroad industry is concerned. But for many other regulated industries, the law remains less clear and the battles between the regulators and the trust busters continue. A noteworthy conflict involves the banking industry, surely a worthy symbol of the free enterprise system, and its preference for regulatory law as opposed to antitrust law.

The recent history of this battle began with the wave of bank mergers that followed World War II. The mergers were approved by the Comptroller of the Currency, the principal regulator of national banks, and after a time the Justice Department concluded that all the mergers might not necessarily be in the public interest. Congress addressed itself to this conflict with the Bank Merger Act of 1960, which applied to bank mergers a scheme rather like the one that gives the Justice Department an advisory role in ICC consideration of railroad merger applications. The 1960 law required the department's antitrust division to render to the bank regulator opinions concerning the effects on competition of proposed mergers. Further, the law told the Comptroller to weigh the financial desirability of a merger, in terms of the banks' capital structure, profits and so forth, against "the effect of the transaction on competition." The Comptroller thus was to arrive at a decision on whether a proposed merger would be in "the public interest."

The 1960 law did not explicitly exempt approved mergers from the antitrust laws. But the fact that Congress had bothered to pass a law, and the very decision process created by that law, led many lawyers, bankers and regulators to the conclusion that bank mergers implicitly were exempt from antitrust prosecution. The opinion was so widespread that even the Justice Department apparently shared it for a time.[9]

But early in 1961 the department decided to put the assumption to a court test. The case that initially prompted the department to take on the banking industry was the merger of the second and third largest banks in Philadelphia, the Philadelphia National Bank and Girard Trust Corn Exchange Bank. More precisely, what prompted the trust busters to attack was that the regulators themselves had disagreed on the Philadelphia case. The Federal Reserve Board and the Federal Deposit Insurance Corporation were against the proposed merger, feeling it would have anti-competitive effects outweighing its advantages, but the Comptroller took a contrary view and approved it. The approval came on a day in February, 1961, and the Justice Department the next day filed an antitrust suit charging the merger violated both the Clayton and the Sherman Antitrust Acts.

In the months that followed, the trust busters sued to stop eight more bank mergers. They didn't try to steamroller all bank mergers; between 1961 and 1965 the regulators approved some seven hundred bank mergers. The Justice Department chose carefully, trying to single out significant mergers where the regulators were in disagreement.

The Philadelphia case was the first to reach the Supreme Court, which decided in June of 1963 that bank mergers enjoy no blanket immunity from antitrust prosecution.[10] The High Court ruled the Philadelphia merger was in violation of the Clayton Act and, having reached this conclusion, the court did not pass on the Justice Department's second argument that the merger also violated the Sherman Act. But the High Court corrected that omission the following year. It ruled in 1964 that the 1961 merger of two Lexington, Kentucky, banks, the First National Bank & Trust Company and the Security Trust Company, violated the Sherman Act.[11]

Then, in March of 1965, a federal district court ruled on the suit the Justice Department had brought against one of the largest postwar mergers, the 1961 merger of Manufacturers Trust Company and Hanover Bank in New York. The lower court judge, citing the Supreme Court's ruling in the Philadelphia case, ruled the New York merger illegal.

That prompted Senator Willis Robertson, the aging Democrat from Virginia who was chairman of the Senate Banking Committee, to act. He introduced a bill which led, in 1966, to the enactment of a law novel even in the annals of regulatory statutes. Mr. Robertson's original draft in 1965 would have excused from antitrust prosecution the Manufacturers-Hanover combination plus five other mergers that then were still under Justice Department challenge in the courts. Moreover, the bill would have forbidden the future challenge of any bank mergers solely on antitrust grounds, leaving the whole matter in the hands of the three regulatory agencies. The senator claimed the Justice Department and the Supreme Court had ignored Congress' intent in passing the 1960 Bank Merger Act. "My bill will reinstate the original purpose and intent of Congress," declared the crusty Virginian.

The original Robertson bill was actively supported by the American Bankers Association, but the senator had to make some concessions, concerning the application of antitrust law to future mergers, in order to get fast Senate action on the other part of the bill excusing Manufacturers-Hanover and the other five mergers. The concessions made, the Senate in June of 1965 passed the bill almost casually. On the House side, the measure ran into some difficulties but these were largely personality problems and the two houses of Congress voted approval of a compromise that President Johnson signed into law early in 1966.

The law excused from antitrust prosecution several of the challenged mergers which the courts already had held to be violations of antitrust law—one was the Manufacturers-Hanover merger—and even halted the court-supervised proceedings then pending to unmerge Manufacturers Trust and Hanover Bank. Other mergers—of banks in Nashville, St. Louis and San Francisco—that the Justice Department had challenged were not excused, but the new law said the pending court proceedings on these mergers should be resolved under a new standard set forth. That standard, applying to those pending cases plus all future bank mergers to come before the regulators or the courts, was that the financial benefits of a merger must "clearly outweigh" any reduction in competition. Beyond that, the law said that, in the future, the Justice Department would have thirty days after a merger was approved by the regulators to bring an antitrust suit and if no suit was brought within the thirty days a merger would forever be exempt from antitrust prosecution.

What Congress clearly did was to repeal the antitrust decisions against a powerful New York bank, Manufacturers-Hanover, and several other banks. Also clearly, the 1966 law circumscribed the time limit within which the Justice Department in the future could act to challenge bank mergers approved by the regulators. But beyond that the meaning of the new standard was unclear. A half-dozen lower courts that ruled, after enactment of the 1966 law, on Justice Department challenges decided unanimously that Congress had intended to exempt all bank mergers from antitrust prosecutions even though Congress had not precisely said so. In March, 1967, the Supreme Court had its first opportunity to interpret congressional intent and it reversed a lower court, ruling that Congress had created for banks an antitrust "exception" where a merger's "adverse effects are outweighed by considerations of community convenience." But the burden of proving that anti-competitive effects were outweighed rested on the banks, and the two Houston banks involved had not met the burden, the court said.[12]

The Justice Department cheered and the American Bankers Association groaned that it was "very disappointed." But the meaning of the 1966 law remained sufficiently unclear to ensure for future years more antitrust suits, more Supreme Court decisions and eventually more bills in Congress. Senator Robertson, however, will not be submitting the bills, for a few months after the Bank Merger Act of 1966 was enacted, he was defeated in a Virginia primary election by an opponent who made an issue of the cash that bankers were contributing to the senator's campaign for re-election.

The consumer finds himself equally at the mercy of the regulatory agencies in the matter of free and open price competition. Some containment of price competition is easily seen by the consumer: A passenger who wants to fly nonstop between New York and San Francisco can buy a ticket on any one of three airlines—American Airlines, Trans World Airlines or United Air Lines—but the price he pays is exactly the same for each. An investor can buy ten shares of stock of General Motors Corporation, or any other stock listed on the New York Stock Exchange, from any one of dozens of members of the Big Board, and the price he pays for the stock and the commission rate he pays the broker is the same for any member.

But much of the proscription, the suppression and the discouragement of price competition is hidden from the view of the average consumer—the transportation of freight, for example. There is a freight charge in the price of virtually everything consumers buy. The transportation charge may run between $50 and $100 on the purchase of a new automobile. This the consumer can see because auto manufacturers must list the charge on each new car sold. But transportation charges are not so listed on other products, even though freight may amount to 25 percent of the consumer price of bulk commodities such as coal and fuel oil and it may add 2 percent or so to the price of relatively expensive items such as television sets.

To prove that uniformity in the prices or rates charged by a limited number of competitors causes consumers to pay higher prices than they otherwise would pay is no less difficult than to prove beyond doubt that antitrust law results in lower prices. The evidence, in both, is largely circumstantial. Evidence that uniformity denies consumers lower prices cannot, of course, be obtained from those who observe uniform prices. It can come only from those relatively rare instances where uniformity has been broken temporarily.

One such outbreak of price competition occurred in the airline industry immediately following World War II. Hundreds of military pilots came home from the war full of excitement about the future of commercial aviation and anxious to break into the business. By 1948 they had set up as many as 142 new airlines, termed "large irregular air carriers" by the Civil Aeronautics Board. They operated under a section of law that, the CAB willing, exempts such flying from economic regulation. They had secondhand airplanes and they flew no fixed routes or schedules. Under the circumstances, the only way they could compete with the older and larger airlines was on the basis of price. So, they became the nonscheduled lines, as they were popularly known, and they pioneered cut-rate air coach service. The nonsked industry grew rapidly, though not always profitably. By 1957, two years before the jet age dawned, the scheduled lines also were offering coach service, and the price of a one-way ticket between New York and Los Angeles on any one of the three scheduled airlines on the route was $99 by coach or $158.85 first class. The nonskeds' price for the same transportation, but without service frills and usually in smaller, unpressurized aircraft, was $88 one-way or $160 round-trip.[13]

The nonskeds' success, however, proved to be their undoing. The scheduled airline industry fought them all the way, at the CAB and in the courts, and it still is fighting even the remnants of an industry that once numbered 142 airlines. The CAB had begun to investigate the nonskeds in the late 1940's. In 1950 it began to suppress their operations with a new series of regulations which said, for instance, that no such carrier could operate more than three flights during any period of four successive weeks between thirteen pairs of named cities that were the country's thirteen biggest markets for the scheduled airlines. But still the intruders grew and in 1955 the CAB decided it would give them a small, carefully carved-out niche in the world of aviation. The board decided it would give them official franchises and an official name, the "supplemental air carriers." They had the right to operate charter flights for group travel, plus ten flights per month, for which they could sell tickets to individuals—in other words, the supplemental would have rights like the scheduled airlines, but very sharply restricted rights.

By mid-1961, when the number of nonscheduled airlines was down to about twenty-five, the New York–to–Los Angeles fare charged by these survivors still was $88 one-way and $160 round-trip, while all of the scheduled airlines' fares were up. A one-way New York–Los Angeles ticket cost $171.45 first class or $109.15 in coach on a piston-type aircraft. In a jet-propelled airliner the price was $181.45 first-class or $138.60 in coach. It cannot be concluded, simply from these figures, that the government curtailment of the nonskeds resulted in the higher fares charged by the scheduled airlines. But the nonskeds, while they were permitted to thrive, clearly offered consumers a price alternative to the uniform fares of the scheduled airlines.

Then in July of 1964 the nonskeds by act of Congress lost their right to operate as common carriers, selling tickets to individual travelers in direct competition with the domestic scheduled airlines. The dozen or so nonskeds that were left were reduced largely to charter and tour service. "The supplemental segment of the industry," a CAB staff report in 1965 said, "25 years after its inception, finds itself with authority more highly restricted than it has ever known, and with fewer carriers than at any time during its history."[14]

Another aspect of the airline industry offers an example of the extremes to which uniform pricing can go. Perhaps the most institutionalized price-fixing in which any American corporation legally engages is the rate-setting machinery of the airlines that fly international routes. By leave of the CAB, and with full immunity from antitrust prosecution, Pan American World Airways, Trans World Airlines and lesser American lines that fly international routes meet regularly with some ninety other foreign-flag international airlines under the auspices of the International Air Transport Association.

The IATA, which is based in Montreal, is an international cartel in the classic mold. It has a permanent staff organization, and executives of its member airlines usually meet twice yearly at elegant watering places, picking, say, a resort in the Arizona sun in the wintertime and a hotel beside a cool lake in Switzerland in the summertime. The member airlines meet behind closed doors, but their purpose is no secret; IATA exists for the avowed purpose of fixing the prices all the competing lines will charge on transatlantic and other international routes. The cartel has teeth, too. Member lines that sign a price-fixing agreement can be fined if they subsequently don't charge the agreed prices or otherwise abide by the finest detail of agreements. For instance, there was the "sandwich war" of the late 1950's when the transatlantic airlines temporarily got out of step by trying to outdo one another with appetizing snacks for passengers. The IATA fined Scandinavian Airlines System $20,000 just for making disparaging remarks about another line's sandwiches.

The irony of IATA is that it is a cartel made up primarily of the airlines of the free world. And of course many of the lines that fly the flags of western European countries are owned or controlled by their governments. Each government usually has given to its airline a national monopoly of international air transportation and IATA is the medium through which national monopolies fix uniform international air fares. The world's only major airline that for years refused to join the international cartel, despite IATA's invitations, was Aeroflot, the Soviet Union's state-owned airline.

Competition is more closely controlled in the transportation industries than in others and it is not unreasonable to conclude that consumers as a result pay higher rates. This is with the approval or at least with the knowledge of Congress. But it also can be demonstrated that the regulators are unwilling or unable to foster competition even in industries where Congress in the relatively recent past has enunciated a policy of favoring competition. Stock market regulation, for example, is taken for granted by most consumers and by Congress, but shouldn't be.

The regulatory scheme Congress adopted in 1934 when it created the Securities and Exchange Commission provided in effect for licensing by the SEC of existing and new stock exchanges and for commission regulation of commission rates each exchange's members charged the public. In 1934, almost every larger American city had its local stock exchange and a Senate committee said it was the policy of Congress to "create a fair field of competition among exchanges."[15] The policy was restated as recently as 1963, when the SEC's own Special Study of the Securities Markets commended "the general public benefits of competition in securities markets, which . . . are not unlike the benefits of competition in other types of markets."[16]

But the number of local stock exchanges available to compete with one another for public investors' business declined substantially after 1934. There were a number of reasons for the disappearance of stock exchanges, frequently by merger with exchanges in other cities. But as a result, attention turned to the authority of the SEC to regulate the commission rates fixed by members of each exchange. And attention turned principally to the New York Stock Exchange, at which are traded more than 70 percent of the shares in American business that public investors buy and sell annually on all exchanges. Neither the New York nor any other stock exchange has been given an explicit antitrust exemption by Congress.

An avowed purpose of the New York Stock Exchange, ever since it was organized under the legendary buttonwood tree at the foot of Wall Street in 1792, is to fix the minimum commission rates that members charge the public.[17] It also is true that, as a recent chief of the Justice Department's antitrust division put it, the New York Stock Exchange always has been, "by its very nature, a repository of anti-competitive practices that fly in the face of the philosophy undergirding the antitrust laws."[18]

The commission's authority since 1934 to regulate the commission rates that exchange members fix has never been questioned but the SEC has never done anything of significance to regulate New York Stock Exchange commission rates. Thus the exchange was a sitting duck for an antitrust suit. A suit might or might not have been successful, depending on the Supreme Court, but apparently no antitrust suit was filed against the New York Stock Exchange until 1959. The Supreme Court, at any rate, had never in its history had an opportunity until the appeal of the 1959 suit to decide whether antitrust law applied to stock exchanges.

In 1959, a Dallas, Texas, securities concern (not a member of the New York Stock Exchange) brought an antitrust suit against the exchange, seeking the triple damages to which successful litigants are entitled under the Sherman Act. It was not a frontal assault on the Big Board's commission rates or its ancient rate-fixing practice; rather, the suit involved the less sweeping question of whether the exchange, as an association of private companies, could order the disconnection of direct lines connecting certain member firms and the Dallas securities concern established by an entrepreneur named Harold J. Silver.

Although the antitrust attack was not of a sweeping nature, the New York Stock Exchange not unexpectedly argued in court that it was implicitly exempt from any and all Sherman Act attacks because it was regulated. When the suit reached the Supreme Court, the Justice Department entered the case as a friend of the court and argued that "nothing in either the legislative history or the general plan of the 1934 Act . . . suggests that Congress intended to confer sweeping antitrust immunity on stock exchanges." The department's brief, however, also said, "There may be situations in which an exchange, in order to perform its function of regulating [under the 1934 Act] its members, may be required to take action which might otherwise violate antitrust standards."

The Supreme Court, during the years of the 1950's and 1960's when Chief Justice Earl Warren led a liberal majority, consistently went along with the Justice Department as far as regulatory statutes would permit. Thus it was no surprise that the court in 1963, ruling for the first time on whether the Sherman Act applied to stock exchanges, declared that the New York Stock Exchange was not entitled to a blanket exemption from antitrust law.[19] But because the case was a narrow one, it didn't really settle the broad issue. The Supreme Court said the action the exchange had taken against the Silver concern would obviously have been "a violation of the Sherman Act . . . had it occurred in a context free from other Federal regulation." The court went through the familiar ritual of "the difficult problem [of] the need to reconcile" antitrust law with regulatory law. And it concluded, in effect, that the exchange's action was not immune from antitrust attack because it was a particular area of exchange conduct that apparently was not subject to SEC review. But then the court went on to recognize that most areas of exchange operation are subject to regulation and to suggest that if it were asked to rule on the broader question, say in a case where the Sherman Act was pointed directly at the Big Board's commission rate system, it might have to find an implied antitrust immunity.

The Silver case did inspire a number of other private litigants to bring just such direct attacks on the New York Stock Exchange and arouse both the SEC and the Justice Department to the dimensions of the questions raised. The commission began to draft legislation that would explicitly confer antitrust immunity on stock exchanges.[20] The Justice Department countered by beginning a major closed-door investigation of the commission rate practices of the New York Stock Exchange. It was a waiting game that ended in 1967 when the Supreme Court declined to disturb a lower court's grant to the New York Stock Exchange of immunity from antitrust attack. The vehicle was a private suit brought in 1966 against the New York Stock Exchange and several of its largest member firms by a Chicago lawyer named Harold Z. Kaplan. Kaplan charged that the exchange and its members fixed "uniform minimum rates of brokerage commission in violation of the Sherman Antitrust Act." His suit declared that "the investing public is paying over $1.2 billion annually" to exchange members for the privilege of buying and selling securities listed on the exchange but added that the SEC had never attempted to regulate NYSE commission rates. A federal district court and the Court of Appeals for the Seventh Circuit dismissed the suit, ruling that although the Securities Exchange Act of 1934 "contains no express grant of immunity from the antitrust laws . . . the exchange's power to fix minimum rates exist[s] by implication."

Mr. Kaplan took his case to the Supreme Court, which, on November 13, 1967, upheld the lower courts by refusing to accept the case for review.[21] Chief Justice Earl Warren, dissenting to the High Court's denial of certiorari, wrote: "This is no ordinary case. It is of utmost importance to millions of investors. The claims advanced by [the suit] raise important questions not only as to the compatibility of the exchange's rate-fixing practice with this nation's commitment, embodied in the antitrust laws, to competitive pricing, but also as to the fulfillment of the goal of investor protection embodied in the securities laws."

Chief Justice Warren was the lone dissenter and his words were lost on the court, the SEC and Congress. And in the end, the curtailment of competition, the uniformity of pricing and the stifling of technological innovation are interwoven in hundreds of industrial patterns that defy the consumers' interest. The patterns suggest an industrial stagnation to which a member of the Interstate Commerce Commission recently made reference: "On purely abstract grounds, a strong case can be made against the popular concept of economic progress, but the idea of suppressing technological advance is so alien to the American spirit that, for this generation at least, it must be dismissed as visionary."[22]

As throughout regulation, the innovative standards by which the majority of regulated companies must be judged necessarily are drawn by the occasional maverick with the courage and cash to innovate. A case in point is the Big John case. It began in 1958, a year when the railroads needed more business and the industry, for the seventh time since World War II, had put into effect an across-the-board freight rate increase. Southern Railway was the innovator that broke ranks with the rest of the railroad industry by refusing to raise its rates on a long list of commodities. Southern's idea, which would seem quite reasonable outside the railroad industry, was that the rate increase would only cause the loss of more freight business. Southern determined that the proper course was to go in search of business rather than drive it to trucking or barge lines. From its headquarters in Washington, Southern, the only railroad based in the nation's capital, which may account for its unique ability to size up the regulators, dispatched a research team to study the southeastern transportation market and the costs and rates of railroads, trucks and barges serving that market. The researchers' market study showed that the growing South was eating more meat and poultry, that more grain was being used in the Southeast to fatten cattle and hogs and chickens for slaughter and that most of the new demand for grain was being met by shipping it in from the Midwest. The new grain traffic was not moving by railroad, however. The great bulk of it was moving by trucks and barges whose low rates were not subject to ICC control, because the law exempts from regulation all agricultural commodities that move by truck and most that move by barge.

Thus the research team located a potential source of new business for the Southern Railway and identified the nature of the competition Southern would have to meet to get the business. Then the researchers went the logical next step and figured out what Southern would have to do. They began by taking a look at the standard, fifty-ton-capacity steel boxcar that railroads traditionally had used to haul grain. It was inefficiently small and awkward. Loading and unloading was costly and time-consuming. Grain had to be carted in and out through the center door and each car door had to be fitted with a temporary paper "grain door," costing $11.27 apiece. The grain had to be carried manually to fill the ends and corners of the cars.

What Southern needed, the research team said, was a far more efficient car that would allow the railroad to undercut competitive grain rates but still yield at least as much net income per ton of grain carried as the old boxcars. Specifically, the researchers prescribed a car twice as big as an old boxcar but still light enough to stay safely within load limits on Southern tracks; a car that could be loaded quickly at the top through watertight hatch covers and be unloaded quickly at the bottom, like a bathtub. The car had to keep grain clean and free of insect infestation, yet it must reduce the time and cost involved in repeated cleanings of the old boxcars.

Southern went to a car builder practiced in the use of steel, the traditional building material of the railroads. Its designers could combine Southern's economic needs in a car holding no more than eighty-five tons—not big enough to do the competitive pricing job Southern had in mind. It happened that Reynolds Metals Company for several years had been trying with little success to interest railroads in the merits of aluminum for bigger, lighter freight cars. Word got to Reynolds of Southern's problem and Reynolds, a big aluminum producer, was only too happy to assist. Lockheed Aircraft Corporation, practiced in the uses of aluminum in aircraft construction, was called in as a design consultant. And the Big John grain car was born.

The Big John was mammoth, capable of hauling one hundred tons of grain, compared with the fifty-ton capacity of an old boxcar. It was light, cheaper to maintain and much easier and faster to load and unload. By doubling the capacity and reducing idle time spent in loading or unloading or in a railroad repair shop, Southern would obtain a car more than four times as useful as an old boxcar.

After the Big John was designed, Reynolds had to help train a railroad car building company's welders to work with aluminum. The use of aluminum by railroads had been so slight that when Southern in the spring of 1959 ordered 455 Big John grain hopper cars, plus 750 aluminum gondola cars for good measure, the order represented by far the largest use of aluminum in railroad history.

That took Southern to the ICC's doorstep, on a hot morning in July, 1961. There followed one of the biggest, most bitter and most incredible rate battles ever fought before the Interstate Commerce Commission. The case was four years at the ICC, it was nine times in lower federal courts and twice before the United States Supreme Court.

Southern told the ICC it wanted to slash its rates, effective August 10, 1961, by 60 percent on five-car lots and up to 66 percent on ten-car and twenty-car lots of grain transported in Big John cars. Protests rapidly started coming in and the ICC reacted, just as it did to the yak fat challenge, by issuing an order that prevented Southern from putting the new rates into effect August 10. The commission suspended the rates for the maximum seven months the law allows.

Dozens of companies and organizations began lining up to have their say. The opposition included a number of barge lines and truck interests, as well as others whose interests were in keeping grain traffic patterns and privileges as they were. They included the Chicago Board of Trade, the Oklahoma Corporation Commission, the Southeastern Association of Local Grain Producers and southern grain merchandisers like Cargill and Central Soya. Many midwestern milling and grain elevator companies opposed the rate slash out of fear that grain they had for years been storing and milling into flour for shipment to the southeastern market now would be shipped directly from producers to mills and elevators in the South. Uncle Sam's Tennessee Valley Authority lined up against Southern's Big John rates. The TVA was afraid that barge traffic would dry up on rivers in the TVA domain, where $200,000,000 of federal funds had been poured into locks and dams for the benefit of commercial barge traffic.

The Department of Agriculture supported the Big John rates. So did the American Farm Bureau Federation and a number of the southeastern states and regional organizations such as the Southern Governors' Conference, the Alabama Cattlemen's Association, the

Georgia Poultry Federation and the North Carolina and Virginia Departments of Agriculture.

Railroads that directly compete with the Southern, including the Louisville & Nashville, Atlantic Coast Line and the Illinois Central, were defensively neutral: if the ICC allowed Southern Railway to slash its rates on grain carried in Big John cars, they wanted to slash theirs on grain they carried in little, old boxcars.

The initial hearing on the case was only getting a good start when, in the spring of 1962, the commission's seven-months order that had prevented Southern from putting the new rates into effect ran out. That was on March 9. Southern that day could legally have put the rates into effect, but, for strategic reasons of its own, agreed voluntarily to postpone the fateful day until August 7.

As that date approached, the hearing still wasn't finished. Almost in panic the opposition asked a federal district court in Alabama to enjoin Southern from putting the rates into effect pending an ICC decision. That failing, the group obtained a temporary restraining order from the Court of Appeals, and the Big John case was on its way to the Supreme Court. Supreme Court Justice Hugo L. Black extended the temporary restraining order and finally, in April of 1963, the High Court decided that the federal courts do not have the power to enjoin proposed rates, once the seven-month suspension period prescribed by Congress runs out.[23] So Southern Railway's Big John cars finally began moving grain at cut rates on May 11, 1963.

Meanwhile, the ICC hearing finally did end, and there was issued a preliminary decision that settled nothing. A panel consisting of three commissioners decided that Southern's progress should be encouraged, not condemned. The panel held that the reams of statistics amassed by the opposition did not prove that Southern's rates were below cost and therefore illegal, that barge lines would not be swept off the rivers and there was nothing sacred about transit privileges or the location of flour mills in the Midwest. In approving Southern's rates, the three commissioners moreover held that the fruits of Southern's Big John innovation should not be nullified by allowing other railroads to charge the same rates with their old boxcars.

But the panel's decision represented only a recommendation to the full eleven-member commission. The commission on July 15,

1963, reversed the panel, rendering a decision that was a flawless example of a regulatory agency conceiving of itself not as a representative of the public interest but as the umpire of competitive fights among private interests. The commission's 8-to-3 decision, with the three panel members dissenting, ordered Southern to cancel its Big John rates. The majority ruled that Southern's reductions of 60 percent and more were not "adequately compensatory" and therefore were illegal. But the majority decided that Southern could, if it wanted, cut its grain rates by 53.5 percent and, "in the interest of equal treatment," Southern's railroad competitors could cut their old boxcar grain rates by 53.5 percent, too. The commissioners did not disclose their methodology in picking 53.5 percent, but they made no secret of their objective: The 53.5 percent railroad cut would "preserve for the barge lines the cost advantages they enjoy" on grain shipments.

The ICC's attempt at consensus finding was an utter failure from the Big John point of view. For Southern, a 53.5 percent cut would have been almost as useless as no cut at all. Not only barge lines, but also unregulated truckers "would have been able to continue to haul the bulk of the grain at a price just below the resulting rail rates," Southern asserted. Back to the Supreme Court.

First, Southern obtained from a district court a temporary restraining order against the commission's decision; the court order allowed Southern to keep the 60 percent and up reductions in effect. As the autumn of 1963 became winter and winter turned to spring, 1964, a three-judge U.S. district court reversed the commission's decision, ruling it wasn't supported by adequate findings. The Supreme Court, early in 1965, said, too, that it was not convinced by the ICC's opinion and sent the whole mess back to the commission for further consideration.[24]

The end finally came on September 10, 1965, when the commission decided that the Big John rates Southern Railway had filed in 1961 were, after all, legal. The opinion was brief and its author was anonymous; the three-man panel's and the commission's earlier opinions had been thick and were signed by the commissioners who authored them. Having "undertaken a complete view of the extensive record," the commission now decided not only that the Big John rates were legal, but also that Southern's railroad competitors could not make the same reductions on their boxcar grain traffic.

The opinion recited the pertinent figures all over again and this time concluded that Southern's Big John rates were compensatory and would "not result in destructive competition against barge lines."

"In sum, we see no probable cause to believe Southern's rates are unlawful."

Those words were a tribute to tenacity: They were four years in coming and required a bigger outlay for lawyers' fees than Southern Railway cares to talk about. But the rewards for Southern appeared handsome, indeed. Its grain revenues in 1964, the first full year the Big John rates were in effect, were 43 percent greater than in 1962. Southern's victory prompted some other railroads to buy Big John cars, and it probably hastened the construction by many railroads of special-type cars and the wider use of aluminum in the railroad industry.

Beyond all that, the Big Johns had significant effects in the grain-growing Midwest and the grain-consuming Southeast. There was evidence that significant tonnages of grain that had been stored or milled into flour in the Midwest now were moving directly into the Southeast. Typically, the William Kelly Milling in Hutchinson, Kansas, was finding that a flour mill in the Southeast was under-bidding it by more than thirty cents per hundred pounds in quoting flour prices to a large southeastern bakery that once bought as much as 125 million pounds of flour a year from Kelly. Indeed, the mid-western flour milling industry was so aroused that it hired a former Texas congressman as its Washington lobbyist. In the Southeast, new grain elevators were rising and it appeared that the cattle- and poultry-feeding business was growing more rapidly.

This shifting of grain distribution into more efficient patterns, which Southern Railway did not initiate but certainly encouraged, was satisfying to Southern and to academic economists, but what did the Big Johns do for consumers in the Southeast? The evidence again suggests strongly that consumers benefited, perhaps by many millions of dollars yearly. In the first place, there is evidence that the lower transportation charges generally were passed on to receivers in the Southeast who as a result paid less for their grain. A study by the University of Georgia's College of Agriculture, for instance, showed that grain middlemen were passing the savings in corn rates on to Georgia cattle and poultry feeders. Other agricultural colleges in the South came up with estimates that the Big John rates would reduce the production cost, in the Southeast, of a dozen eggs by one and one-quarter cents, of chickens by one cent a pound and of beef by eighty cents per hundred pounds. Another bit of evidence was presented when the Georgia Milk Commission, early in 1965, reduced the price of a home-delivered quart of milk in Atlanta to twenty-eight cents from twenty-nine cents, attributing the reduction to lower milk production costs stemming mainly from lower feed grain prices.

The evidence that penny-a-quart and penny-a-pound savings by housewives may mount into millions a year for southeastern consumers is contained in some detailed figures Southern Railway compiled on its Big Johns. Between May 11, 1963, the date the reduced rates went into effect, and September of 1963, Southern moved some six thousand Big John loads of grain and collected revenues of $2,616,269. The same volume of grain shipped under the old boxcar rates would have brought in revenues of $5,832,108. The saving in transportation charges was $3,215,839. The calculation illustrates the depth of Southern's rate cut very well, but it does not mean grain receivers or consumers in the Southeast saved as much as $3,215,839 during those four months of 1963. The reason, of course, is that most of the grain was not moving by boxcar; it was moving at a cheaper rate by truck and by barge. How much cheaper will never be known, because truck and barge lines do not file their grain rates with the ICC. But it can be assumed, from Southern's dramatic success in winning grain business from the trucks and barge lines, that the Big John rates have reduced very substantially the shipping and consuming public's cost of transporting grain. It seems reasonable to estimate that, on the basis of Southern's revenue calculations, the real savings in transportation charges on grain moving into the Southeast between May and September of 1963 were at least $1 million.

The Big John case inspired various estimates of how much Interstate Commerce Commission regulation of railroad freights may, in total, be costing American consumers in the form of higher prices than they otherwise would pay. One such inspiration came to W. D. Brosnan, then president of Southern Railway, at a time when it appeared that the ICC would succeed in preventing the Big John rate reductions. Mr. Brosnan asserted that the ICC's "witchcraft" is costing the public "at least $1 billion a year through unnecessarily high freight rates."[25]

After the case was settled, a number of more cautious academic economists undertook studies of ICC regulation of freight rates and arrived at similar, if more modest, conclusions. The President's Council of Economic Advisers, for instance, in 1966 estimated that if the ICC allowed "rates to be appropriately geared to costs . . . on railroad transportation alone savings from possible rate reductions would come to more than $400 million a year."[26] Merton J. Peck, an economist, estimated the "public benefits [in] lower transportation rates at $460 million yearly."[27]

If these estimates are correct, then government regulation of industry as a whole clearly is costing America's consumers some billions of dollars, year in and year out.

PART THREE

Planners vs. Consumers

Introduction to a Labyrinth

Comprehending the public significance and consumer costs of government's efforts in behalf of private industry demands taking more into account than the independent regulatory agencies alone. The agencies are America's original state planners, but government planning nowadays seldom involves one agency and one industry as though they were a unit. Planning would indeed be less complicated and more efficient, as was suggested by the ICC commissioner who spoke of "suppressing technological advance," if industry were more concentrated and government more centralized. However, our "Puritan ethic," as an aide to President Kennedy once disapprovingly described it, does not yet permit a solution so absolute.

Most planning is, in fact, still done by larger corporations, rather than by government. Ideally, each company independently engages in its own product research, cost estimates, market projections and sales pitches. Yet in one degree or another, planning by government today reaches all large corporations and many smaller companies. Most government planning is accomplished by indirection and through the offices of what John F. Kennedy once described as a "chaotic patchwork" of laws and bureaucracies.

It is appropriate to begin with the transportation agencies and industries, for federal transportation planning probably affects the daily existence of the average consumer more directly and intimately than any of Washington's other programs of planning for private endeavor. Transportation accounts for twenty cents out of every dollar that consumers and corporations spend annually. Transportation and shipping expenditures by individuals and business total well over $100 billion annually.[1]

It is in transportation that government has involved itself most completely in all three aspects of planning—pricing, technological innovation and allocation of resources. And it is here that government has fashioned the most complete set of planning tools. The transportation planners all are equipped with controls over pricing and the number of competitors in an industry, and most, in addition, have a third tool—the subsidy.

Some subsidies come from the independent agencies that regulate transportation industries, and others are given to transportation companies by bureaucracies within the executive branch of government. Regulation and subsidization generally go together, whether or not they are administered by the same agency. Even transportation industries generally not thought of as being regulated, such as automobile manufacturers, are discovering that as the beneficiaries of subsidy-like programs, they are increasingly subject to regulation.

A subsidy is rarely so called in Washington. Government expenditures that directly or indirectly accrue to the economic benefit of identifiable private groups are generally referred to by other terms. The Merchant Marine Act of 1936 is the only major federal law, among the many that prescribe special monetary benefits, that even uses the word "subsidy."[2] All the other laws use words such as "mail pay," "operating differential" or "construction grant." Semantics notwithstanding, Washington's expenditures on transportation programs have been running about $7 billion annually in recent years, more than the federal government has spent in those years to improve the nation's health, to educate its young or even to subsidize its farmers.

A second and more fundamental semantic problem is posed in the transportation laws, which are the mandates of the various offices of government concerned with transport economics. The Interstate Commerce Act, for instance, speaks as if the people had placed in the Interstate Commerce Commission their sole trust for coordinated national transportation planning. The act has a preamble, titled "National Transportation Policy," which says:

> It is hereby declared to be the national transportation policy of the Congress to provide for fair and impartial regulation of all modes of transportation subject to this act, so administered as to recognize and preserve the inherent advantages of each; to promote safe, adequate, economical and efficient service and foster sound economic conditions in transportation; to encourage reasonable charges without unjust discriminations, undue preferences or advantages, or unfair or destructive competitive practices; to cooperate with the States; and

to encourage fair wages and equitable working conditions; all to the end of developing, coordinating and preserving a national transportation system by water, highway and rail, as well as other means. . . .

However, the Interstate Commerce Act applies to only the Interstate Commerce Commission, which is but one of the more than thirty bureaus of transportation. The ICC regulates all rail and some domestic water and highway transportation, but it has no control over "other means" like aviation and ocean shipping. Also, the ICC doesn't develop much of anything. The Army Corps of Engineers is the development agency for waterways, and the Bureau of Public Roads develops highways.

Congress passed a separate law, wrote a separate policy and created separate bureaus for air transportation. The Federal Aviation Act contains one "Declaration of Policy" that cradles in the arms of the Civil Aeronautics Board "the encouragement and development of an air transportation system" and a second "Declaration of Policy" that charges the Federal Aviation Administration with "the promotion, encouragement and development of civil aeronautics."

There is a separate law, policy and bureaucracy for ocean shipping. The Merchant Marine Act charges the Maritime Administration with "promoting, encouraging and developing" shipping and it directs the Federal Maritime Commission to regulate as well as promote the merchant marine.

The ICC, the CAB and the FMC are independent agencies. The Army Corps of Engineers is in the Department of Defense. The Bureau of Public Roads is in the new Department of Transportation and the Maritime Administration is in the Department of Commerce. But both the Bureau of Public Roads and the Maritime Administration maintain a high degree of independence from executive authority because they are principally spending agencies and Congress controls the level of spending. The Federal Aviation Administration is in the Transportation Department; it also is largely independent of executive branch control because it also is a spending agency.

The rest of the transportation bureaucracy is scattered all over town, although not so scattered as before the Transportation Department came into being. The Coast Guard, provider of navigation aids for water transportation, is in the Transportation Department. The federal program, begun in 1961, to rescue commuter trains and other forms of mass transit was in the Department of Housing and Urban Affairs until 1968 when it was transferred to the Transportation Department. The National Aeronautics and Space Administration, which does air transportation research work as well as space tasks, is in the executive branch and under the control of the President; but it is not within any one of the great departments of the executive branch. The NASA administrator reports directly to the President and thus is more or less on a par with the cabinet secretaries who head the great departments. Tucked away in one place or another are agencies such as the Coast and Geodetic Survey, the St. Lawrence Seaway Development Corporation, the Great Lakes Pilotage Administration, the Railroad Retirement Board, the United States Travel Service, the Alaska Railroad and the Panama Canal Company.

To begin to comprehend this patchwork, one must go back to the beginning and separate its pieces. A good point of departure is the year 1817, when John C. Calhoun proposed to Congress, "Let us bind the Republic together with a perfect system of roads and canals." The lawmakers responded with funds to build a "national pike" that began in the East and later was pushed westward into Ohio and Indiana. Congress in 1824 formalized its promotional ambitions by directing the President to make "surveys, plans and estimates of the routes of such roads and canals as he may deem of national importance" and authorizing him to turn the Corps of Engineers to the task. A month later Congress appropriated $75,000 "for removing sand bars from the Ohio and planters, sawyers and snags from the Mississippi" and the Army Engineers have been in the rivers and harbors business ever since.

Thus began the bureaucratization of transportation. America's system of highways, waterways, railways and airways today is pretty much taken for granted as the result of natural forces, but it actually is the product of almost 150 years of patchwork political decision-making. The fragmentation of transport policy is indeed a particularly sharp reflection of the pressures and compromises that always have been the hallmarks of the legislative process in Washington. Fragmentation feeds on itself. Each new bureaucracy becomes its own best lobbyist. Each, with the backing of an omnipresent corps of industry lobbyists lending moral and other appropriate support, promotes its own brand of transportation, while the public cost, both economic and social, goes up and up and up.

Engineering Waterways

The Army Engineers are certainly the best, as well as the oldest, of the transportation promoters. By the grace of congressional appropriations, they have spent more than $18 billion since 1824 to build and maintain the nineteen thousand miles of waterways that are in commercial use in the United States today.[1] Without begging for it, they have received more and more money. Their annual appropriation reached $650 million in 1950, rose to the billion-dollar mark for the first time in 1963 and headed for $2 billion in 1966. The Engineers don't have to be pushy even about their future needs; Congress comes to them, as it did in 1960 when the Engineers coolly said that another $28 billion would carry them through 1980.

The Engineers like to say in proper military fashion that they are neither policy-makers nor promoters, they simply make engineering and economic feasibility studies and present the facts to Congress. As the major general in command of public works explained: "Congress is responsive to the desires of the people and the Corps is responsive to the will of Congress."[2]

That's one way of describing what the Engineers among themselves call "the eighteen steps to glory." These are the steps that a waterways or harbor improvement project must take, set out in a 1913 law which gave Congress a control of waterways spending that the White House has never been able to break. Step number one is for local interests to get together with their congressmen. The project must show promise of stimulating local or regional commerce. The congressman takes the proposal to the House Public Works Committee with a request that the Engineers be authorized to investigate and report their findings. By resolution or bill, the Engineers are told to make surveys and preliminary "economic justification" studies. The rest of the steps to glory are more surveys, engineering and cost studies, approvals by the Corps' district engineer, the Board of Engineers, the Chief of Engineers and finally the Secretary of the Army, who presents the grand design to the Public Works Committee. Congress authorizes the project and only then is the White House informed. The Army Secretary asks the President's Budget Bureau for an appropriation to start work on the authorized project. The Budget Bureau sifts through the Engineers' money requests for "new starts" and continuing projects for the coming fiscal year and decides on a total rivers and harbors figure that's fitted into the President's over-all annual budget. But Congress perennially votes more money for more projects than the President recommends.

It is cumbersome, but this system has served congressmen and the Army Engineers well. On Capitol Hill, it is an effective means of rationing the rivers and harbors appropriation, the annual "pork barrel" bill, which is never big enough to satisfy everybody no matter how large it grows. The Army Engineers don't have to lobby because members of Congress do it for them. But the Engineers' money machine is not fully automatic. The Corps keeps it oiled with an image that would be the envy of any corporate public relations man. So well has the Corps avoided controversy that the "pork barrel" ("an increasingly obsolete cliché," says the major general in command) taint never rubs off on it. Too, the Engineers have avoided having to fix "fair" tolls or user charges on their ways, a messy business that distracts the federal highway and airway planners; barges simply pay no tolls.

The Corps' image is splendid mainly because it sincerely believes in waterways. Waterways are the beginning and the end of the Corps' public transportation spectrum, and the Engineers are quite naturally the best promoters of water transportation. The Corps' general officers, resplendent in uniform, say, for example, in after-dinner speeches, "The importance of comprehensive development of water resources throughout the nation can hardly be overstated. Water is a basic resource—along with air, of course."[3] They cultivate a nationwide network of grass-roots contacts with "the people" who initiate the desires to which Congress responds. Each district office, which is headed by a general or a colonel, is in constant contact with large and vocal waterways betterment associations like the Mississippi Valley Association or the Arkansas Basin Association. Commercial barge line interests are almost always well represented in such associations.

Grass-roots support for the Engineers' work has expanded considerably in more recent years as the Corps has broadened its own perspectives. For a century after 1824, the Corps' waterworks were limited to improvements for navigation. Most river improvements by their nature serve dual purposes. A dam or a bank revetment built primarily to ensure a year-round water depth sufficient for commercial navigation, for instance, usually helps to control seasonal floodwaters. Though navigation remains the major concern, the Engineers in recent years have spread out to projects for flood control, power, irrigation and even recreation.

The "economic feasibility" studies are critical to the promotion and health of the Corps. The 1913 law said that if the Corps of Engineers is unable to establish an economic justification for a project, showing it will cost less than the benefits it will return to "the people," the proposal is dead. The law, in a broad sense, purported to coordinate rivers and harbors spending with the national good and the transportation whole. In practice, the studies often are masterpieces of uncoordination.

The Arkansas River project is a typical and important example.[4] This project, authorized in 1946, will by 1970 open the Arkansas River to commercial navigation from its mouth at the Mississippi River below Little Rock all the way up to the Tulsa area. Its navigation and other benefits will, the Engineers have promised, open up a vast area in Arkansas, Oklahoma and adjoining states "to a long-range future of tremendous economic development." The initial cost to the general taxpayers will be $1.2 billion and the annual maintenance bill will run to some $10 million. The annual construction outlays make the Arkansas project one of the biggest the Engineers have going. President Johnson, whose home grounds were nearby, dedicated one of its showpieces, the Eufaula Dam.

The nation's taxpayers are shelling out $1.2 billion on the basis of "facts" with which the Corps of Engineers ostensibly demonstrated that the Arkansas River project was economically justified. It would, said the Engineers, return to the people $1.40 of "benefits" for each $1 spent. To arrive at this wonderful figure, the Engineers began with a plan for the comprehensive development of the Arkansas Basin that included a series of dams, locks and reservoirs for navigation, bank stabilization, flood control, power generation and other purposes. The navigation aspect was pivotal to a finding of economic feasibility because the navigation features would cost $850 million to build and close to $10 million a year to maintain. The

Engineers held public hearings and made studies and ultimately told Congress that the project would return to the public a "benefit" of $65.7 million annually over a projected fifty-year life. Of the $65.7 million, the Engineers proclaimed, $40.5 million would derive from navigation "benefits," $11 million from power "benefits" (the estimated annual revenues from power sold), and $7 million from flood control "benefits" (an estimate of flood damage that would be avoided). The remaining $7 million of "benefits" were credited to boating, fishing and the like.

There is no evidence in the documents the Engineers presented to Congress that the Arkansas Basin had lacked, currently lacked or in the future would lack adequate transportation services.[5] Quite to the contrary, the Engineers' pivotal finding on navigation "benefits" couldn't have been made but for the availability of existing transport facilities in the basin.

The incredible calculation of $40.5 million went this way. First the Engineers estimated the Arkansas River, once it was opened to commercial navigation all the way to Tulsa, would carry 13.2 million tons of freight annually. They looked at railroad freight rates in the area and calculated how much the charges might be on 13.2 million tons. And then they looked at going barge line freight rates and calculated again. They subtracted the cheaper barge bill for carrying 13.2 million tons on the toll-free waterways from the rail bill and came up with an estimated annual saving of $40.5 million.

The Corps of Engineers' definition of "navigation benefits," which has been used to build $18 billion worth of waterways projects in the nation, is simply "savings in transportation charges." Local development associations all over the country and their representatives in Congress egg the Engineers on. At hearings on the Arkansas project, local interests justified the spending because, they said, their freight rates were too high and barge line competition would force the rail and even truck rates down. The same argument is used by local interests all over. Barge rates are cheaper than railroad rates and barge competition has been used to beat down railroad rates. The primary reason is that barge freight rates are subsidized by the government and railroad freight rates are not; the taxpayers build and maintain the rights of way barges ply, railroads build and maintain their own rights of way. The Army Corps of Engineers has been cashing fraudulent checks made out to navigation "benefits" that are in fact subsidies. They've been getting by with it because Congress endorses the checks.

Is it any wonder that every President since Harry Truman has failed to talk Congress into setting up toll booths on the nineteen thousand miles of commercially navigable waterways? Tolls would raise barge freight rates; higher barge rates would destroy the Army Engineers' ability to calculate the economic justification of waterways projects; and congressmen would lose the billion-dollar plums they ship to their voter constituents back home.

Another burden for the taxpaying consumer, and obsolete in its present-day functions, is the merchant marine. Intended, by the definition of congressional laws, to be adequate to the needs of the nation's foreign commerce and its national defense, America's merchant marine remains less than sufficient for these needs, even though subsidies paid out under the 1936 Merchant Marine Act alone total some $3 billion. Moreover, experience suggests that the government subsidies have discouraged the incentive American shipowners once had to meet foreign competition with superior technology and greater efficiency, as other American producers must do to compete on the world market.

The only time that the American merchant marine came anywhere close to ruling the waves was in the first half of the nineteenth century when Yankee ingenuity produced this country's magnificent clipper ships, the fastest and most efficient vessels afloat. Clipper ships were even exported. Then came steamships, which the British were faster to build than the Yanks. Congress responded in 1847 with a subsidy, disguised in ocean mail contracts, and the American merchant marine has never been the same.

In the eleven years following 1847 that the first mail subsidy program was in effect, the government paid out about $14 million. Congress finally concluded that the experiment wasn't producing results and had the good sense to abandon it. But in 1891 a new generation of lawmakers decided to try again. The size of the American fleet continued to decline but Congress still didn't abandon mail subsidies. On the contrary, it enlarged the mail subsidy program in 1916, and at the same time the Wilson Administration created the United States Shipping Board. The board was directed to regulate the rates and practices of steamship companies that transported passengers and freight across the oceans. It was unique in that Congress for the first time entrusted to a single agency both the authority to regulate and the duty to promote an industry. Congress off and on for many years had given various kinds of subsidies to steamship lines and time and again the results were political scandals. It embellished its mail subsidy program in 1928 with ship construction loans, and once again enlarged it in 1936, this time dropping the "mail" disguise after government and industry skulduggery in the mail contract negotiations was revealed in hearings conducted by the then Senator Hugo Black. The 1936 act tried to do with subsidies what technology does for other American industries competing in the world market. It prescribed government subsidies to cover the amount by which American ship construction costs and operating outlays exceeded costs of building a vessel in a foreign shipyard and operating a vessel under a foreign flag. The construction outlays under the 1936 act have proved to be controllable, by the simple expedient of building fewer ships; in recent years the construction subsidy has been running about $100 million yearly to pay about 55 percent of the total cost of about fifteen ships launched annually.

The operating subsidy bill has proved much less controllable, because Congress made a moral commitment to pick up the difference in the cost of running American and foreign ships, and that gap has been steadily widening as U.S. wage rates have gone up and foreign shipowners have slashed crews with the introduction of automated vessels; the operating subsidy bill has skyrocketed to a current figure of about $200 million yearly from $6 million in 1950.

Those Treasury checks by no means exhaust the list of Washington handouts for shipping industry and labor. For shipyards, ship lines and ship unions there is a law that says no construction or operating subsidies will be paid except for vessels built in American yards and operated under the U.S. flag with American crews. There's another thinly disguised $80 million annual subsidy in another law that says at least 50 percent of all U.S. foreign aid shipments and other government-sponsored cargoes must be shipped in American bottoms. There are bargain prices for surplus government ships and federal mortgage insurance for privately built ships. Then there are a raft of trading and rate protections for the ship lines: membership in international rate-fixing conferences, effective bars on competition between companies that are subsidized under the

1936 act and the ancient watery wall that keeps all but American ships out of the domestic trade between ports.

The railroaders never had it so good, and fervently wish they had.

For its $3 billion plus, Congress has bought an industry with the biggest crying towel in Washington, a steadily declining merchant marine and a built-in barrier to change. The United States is the world's largest importer and exporter, but while American flag ships in the clipper ship era carried 90 percent of the nation's total ocean-borne foreign trade, they now carry less than 10 percent. The fifteen shipping companies that operate under the 1936 act have built about three hundred reasonably modern ships, but the $3 billion hasn't gone nearly far enough to help dozens of other companies whose ships are old and rusting. The total merchant fleet, including government-owned ships in reserve fleets, of about 2500 vessels has shrunk by 25 percent since 1949; it will shrink much more unless the government pours more billions into the subsidy program. American shipyards are, by European standards, the least competitive of all American industries; one study of forty-four major industries, using productivity in the United Kingdom as a standard, ranked ship-building forty-fourth among American industries in productivity relative to European competitors. With only about fifteen merchant ships being built in this country each year, the twenty-one shipyards have little incentive or cash to invest in capital improvements.

In most businesses, profits can be raised by increasing revenues or cutting costs. In the business of a subsidized shipowner, seeking new revenues by going after business on a new route requires the ordeal of a painfully long and frequently frustrating hearing in Washington. There's little incentive to cut costs because the government will simply pay less subsidy. There's little incentive to resist union demands for higher crew wages because the government pays 72 percent of the cost of wages of every deck hand, engine-room wiper, mess boy and officer on a subsidized ship. And there's not much incentive to research a faster power plant or a more efficient cargo boom or a less complicated bill of lading system when some bureaucrat in Washington may well substitute his judgment for that of management. When a civil servant has before him a rule on cargo boom specifications that the agency has been following for years he's much more likely to reject the innovation than suggest a rule change. When he has to weigh safety and efficiency considerations, his career in government is much safer if he overdoes safety.

Not only does the subsidy system fail to encourage innovation, but in some ways is downright discouraging. Because of the way the system works, a shipowner might well decide, for instance, that he wants to build a 20-knot ship instead of one capable of doing 25 knots. A 25-knot vessel is 25 percent more productive than a 20-knot ship with no increase in crew costs. Four 25-knot ships will do the work of five 20-knot ships. But a ship moving through the water at 25 knots normally burns 50 percent more fuel than one cruising at 20 knots and the government does not pay any part of fuel costs because a subsidized ship can refuel at any place in the world and pay the same fuel price as foreign ships pay. So, the shipowner may well want to build five slow ships instead of four faster ones because his total fuel bill may be less and the government will pay 72 percent of the crew wage cost on all five ships. Clearly it's in the interest of ship unions that the decision be five ships.

The National Academy of Sciences in 1960 studied the merchant marine and concluded that "the subsidy system, as it now stands, is actually hindering maritime progress." The Academy said the long-range effect of the 1936 act, the merchant marine's Magna Charta, "has been to hide the symptoms while allowing further deterioration of the basic difficulty." The Academy further believed that research and development could lead to "an efficient fleet, able to face world competition, with substantially less subsidy assistance." It called for quick and wholesale automation of ship operations.[6]

The Commerce Department, which began doing the maritime industry's research several years before it took on the railroads' R&D work, reached the same conclusions. The government researchers even believe they're on the track of a surface-effect ship "capable of carrying general cargo in ocean trade at the speed of airplanes and the price of ships."

Both John F. Kennedy and Lyndon B. Johnson pressed for more maritime research in the hope eventually of lowering maritime subsidies; both the New Frontier and the Great Society had spending priorities that ranked considerably higher than spiraling merchant marine subsidies. President Kennedy made no progress in getting maritime labor to accept the government researchers' crew-cutting automation devices. President Johnson invited the shipowners and unions to come reason together at the White House, but with little more success. Also, LBJ appointed in 1964 a bright, twenty-nine-year-old professor named Nicholas Johnson (no kin, but the personal choice of the President) as Maritime Administrator. Nick Johnson was an able, articulate spokesman for reform who traveled the country widely, advocating automation, more competition and the construction of U.S. merchantmen in foreign shipyards. And maritime management and labor both hooted for his scalp. His reward for his faithful services to the Administration came in 1966: President Johnson gave him a new job, as a member of the Federal Communications Commission.

President Johnson abandoned reform of the merchant marine program, at least for then, for good political reasons. He knew very well that to try to force automation on the merchant marine under existing law would inevitably mean more maritime strikes in which the government again would become directly involved as a party to the dispute. And LBJ knew that to attempt to force through Congress an overhaul of the 1936 Merchant Marine Act, which would have been necessary to allow construction of ships abroad, would have required an investment of more of his prestige and persuasion than he cared to risk. The ship unions had good friends on Capitol Hill and the fifteen subsidized ship lines were banded together in a powerful, well-heeled lobby called the Committee of American Steamship Lines—CASL, pronounced "castle" by its friends and foes alike on Capitol Hill.

11
Railways

Over the years, the federal government has been a fickle promoter of transportation services. In the very beginning, men such as Calhoun pressed for a national pike and the Conestoga wagons rolled westward on what later became part of U.S. Route 40. Government also promoted the construction of canals and other waterways. But Washington's fascination with roads and canals as catalysts of national economic growth was dimmed by the obviously superior technology of the oncoming railroads. The federal government from about 1850 until roughly 1870 promoted railroad construction with grants of approximately 130 million acres of public lands. The railroads in the East did not share extensively in these land grants because railroad building already was well advanced east of the Mississippi River.

About twenty-five major railroads, principally those pushing westward but also some in the South, did, however, benefit handsomely from the grants. For them, Washington provided rights of way plus alternate sections of land on both sides of their tracks. These alternate "checkerboard" sections of land usually were sold by the railroads to attract the settlers who would generate the railroad traffic. In exchange for the grants, the government collected an early kind of user charge. The land-grant railroads had to agree to haul government traffic at substantial reductions, normally half their usual rates. Estimates of how much the 130 million acres were worth at the time range from $31 million to some $400 million. A congressional committee has estimated that the rate reductions given in return were worth $900 million to the government.[1]

Whatever the value of the land grants and the sufficiency of the rate reductions, government by 1887 was done with helping railroads to expand and was ready to control the rates they were charging the public at large. If government helped to make the railroads into big businesses, government also could control what it had created. The Interstate Commerce Commission for the first thirty years of its life was a modest planner. It was created to keep railroads' freight rates and passenger fares low and that, by and large, is what it did. There were, to be sure, a few inconsistencies. One was between the low rate philosophy and the ICC's apparent willingness to allow railroads to get together among themselves to fix rates and fares. A second inconsistency was its unwillingness to allow some railroads to publish freight rate reductions based on volume shipments. The agency's repeated rejection of volume rates, on the grounds that they discriminated against small shippers, may have had an effect on railroad technology, as has been suggested.

There is reason to suspect that the ICC's relatively modest powers in those early decades may have had another negative effect on railroad technology. As Congress year-by-year enlarged the ICC's authority to deal with rate and fare increases proposed by the railroads, it also expanded the commission's powers over railroad safety matters. The commission was empowered not only to require safe ashpans under coal-burning locomotives but also to prescribe safety standards for train braking systems and speed limits for passenger trains. Accidents were a problem and Congress decided that trains were being wrecked because rival railroads, particularly in the East, were racing one another in carrying passengers between major cities such as New York and Chicago. If railroads back then were not any longer competing on the basis of fares, they still were competing for the business of hauling passengers in the red velvet luxury of George Pullman's hotel cars. So, the ICC wrote speed limits and slowed the trains down. Perhaps it was necessary at the time for the government to regulate train speeds, but as a result the passenger train speed record that stood in the United States for 64 years was set June 12, 1905, when the Pennsylvania Railroad's Broadway Limited streaked across the Ohio countryside at 127.06 miles per hour.[2] The record was not approached until 1969, and then by the Penn-Central's Metroliners, developed with government aid.

Although the Interstate Commerce Commission's powers over railroad safety and rate practices grew steadily in those early decades, the commission did not emerge as a true economic planner until 1920. It is to be doubted that the Transportation Act of 1920 was necessarily a reward to the ICC for a job well done. The commission doubtless had kept rates and fares down, as Congress had originally intended. But along the way, a number of railroads went into bankruptcy because they were caught in a squeeze between controlled rates and uncontrolled costs. When World War I approached, the situation was sufficiently bad that the government deemed it necessary to seize the industry and run the trains itself.

The degree to which the commission was responsible is debatable. But the railroads were in trouble and, when the war ended and the government returned the carriers to private ownership, Congress decided that the solution was not less but more government control. Indeed, there is no evidence that Congress gave any serious consideration in 1920 to the alternative of less regulation. Railroads were bigger than ever and Congress believed more firmly than before that railroads had a transportation monopoly. Absurd as it may seem today, that firm belief resulted in the enactment of a law that assumed the railroads were public utilities and could be regulated as such.

The Transportation Act of 1920 remade the ICC and it frankly attempted to remake the railroad industry. Fares and rates no longer were to be regulated on the rather hit-or-miss basis of railroad applications to raise or lower rates and the commission was not to be guided simply by a philosophy of keeping railroad pricing low. The new law directed the commission to take a far more comprehensive approach to regulation. The statute said railroad fares and rates, like those of any other public utility, should and could be fixed by the government to produce a fair return of approximately 6 percent on railroad companies' investment. Congress supplemented the ICC's old authority to bar fare and rate increases with a new power to bar fare and rate reductions. Appropriately, Congress also provided in the 1920 act for the "recapture" by the government of railroad earnings that in any future year exceeded the fair rate of return to be fixed by the commission. The ICC in addition was given large new powers over subsidiary matters such as railroad securities, directorates, construction of tracks and abandonment of tracks.

Finally, the 1920 act directed the ICC to draw up a national master plan of railroad consolidations. Congress, coming full-turn from its 1887 chastisement of railroads as the biggest of big businesses, concluded in 1920 that a solution of their problems lay in fewer and still bigger railroad companies. So it determined to encourage mergers and its method was to direct the ICC to draw up a plan for merging the nation's railroads into a limited number of regional systems. The commission was given no shotgun to force an unwilling railroad into a merger. But the law said that those mergers conforming to the ICC plan would be blessed with immunity from any antitrust challenge the Department of Justice might otherwise bring.

State economic planning has never before or since been attempted in the United States on so grand a scale or in such infinite detail. The failure of government planning in this nation consequently has never been larger. But failure was not admitted until twenty years later.

The ICC tried to make the Transportation Act of 1920 work. First off, if railroad fares and rates were to be fixed to yield a 6 percent return in investment, the commission had to find out how much the railroads' capital investment was worth.[3] It spent tens of millions of dollars and years of work on the so-called Valuation Project, and at one time employed more than fifteen hundred for the effort. This was a waste of money and manpower. Briefly and simply put, the railroads did not enjoy a transportation monopoly and the government consequently could not assure them sufficient patronage and revenues to guarantee a 6 percent return on investment. A public utility, such as a local gas or electric company, does not require an absolute monopoly to be regulated on a rate-of-return basis but effective utility regulation assumes a sufficient degree of monopolization so that consumers have little alternative to patronizing the utility and paying the rates charged. The railroad industry has never grown so large as to deny the traveling and shipping public all transportation alternatives and no single railroad company in the United States until recently has enjoyed a substantial regional monopoly of rail service.

What railroads did have was transportation dominance. They were big and they were growing—until 1920. Prior to that year, railroads expanded more rapidly than the American economy as a whole. After 1920, railroads no longer grew as rapidly as did industry in general nor did they keep pace with population growth. Congress could not have known that railroads were going over the hump in 1920. On the other hand, it is not unfair to conclude that, had Congress looked around, it would have known that transportation alternatives were increasing and a public utility-type of regulation for the railroads was impractical. By 1920, United States automobile manufacturers already were turning out yearly almost two million passenger cars and more than 300,000 trucks and buses. In the 1920 Transportation Act itself, Congress rather incongruously authorized the Army Engineers to set up a commercial barge line (the Inland Waterways Corporation, which President Eisenhower sold off to private interests in 1953) to demonstrate anew the merits of water transportation.

Without disturbing the 1920 act, Congress itself recognized the growth in highway transportation in 1935 when it placed the highway trucking industry under ICC rate and route controls. In 1940 Congress extended the commission's rate and route powers to domestic water transportation.

Through these years, as highway, waterway and then airway transportation alternatives grew, the ICC came to the realization that it could neither regulate the railroads on a rate-of-return basis nor execute its grand plan for railroad mergers. In the 1930's, the idea of a 6 percent return on investment became a fiasco as railroad profits disappeared almost completely and many railroad companies went into bankruptcy. Congress passed special bankruptcy statutes, which the ICC helped to administer, so that bankrupt railroads would not be taken over by creditors and dismantled. So far as the merger plan was concerned, the ICC eventually produced a national consolidation plan, but bankrupt railroads ordinarily cannot engage in mergers. Eventually, the ICC told Congress the plan was no good and, in 1940, Congress repealed its directions to the commission to plan mergers and to fix railroad rates on a rate-of-return formula.

That's all Congress repealed. It did not repeal the authority of the ICC to bar rate cuts or to fix specific rates, nor did it take back the antitrust immunity of mergers proposed by industry and approved by the commission. Congress in 1940 left all of these and many more powers in the law and capped it with the declaration of National Transportation Policy that directed the ICC to "foster sound economic conditions" in transportation by water, highway and railroad, "as well as other means."

The fiction that was engrained in the 1920 act was thus maintained with refinements in the 1940 law.[4] The ICC is expected to foster sound economic conditions in at least the barge line, the trucking and bus and the railroad industries. But today the transportation alternatives available to the traveling and shipping public go far beyond those industries that are regulated by the ICC. The commission has no authority over airlines. It cannot prevent people from buying automobiles as an alternative to patronizing the regulated railroads and bus lines. And it cannot prevent shippers from buying their own private truck fleets instead of patronizing regulated railroads, truck lines and barge lines.

Life for the ICC is further complicated by the nature of the 1935 law with which Congress extended regulation to the trucking industry and the 1940 statute by which regulation reached water carriers. Congress in those laws said the ICC's powers to regulate rates and to license routes would not apply to trucks hauling agricultural products nor to barges transporting bulk commodities such as coal and grain. These exemptions from regulations resulted from the lobbying efforts in the 1930's of farmer groups, which knew that ICC regulation would mean higher truck and barge freight rates.[5] Because of the exemptions, unregulated truck and barge lines have undercut the rates charged by regulated haulers of agricultural and bulk products and there is nothing the ICC can do about it.

President Kennedy proposed to do something about it. He proposed to de-regulate railroad rates on these same products. But that solution didn't suit the ICC or Congress. It also did not satisfy the railroads when they found that President Kennedy wanted to take away the legal right of the railroads to confer among themselves to fix all freight rates and passenger fares.

The ICC since 1940 has thus planned as best it can, attempting to "foster sound economic conditions" with basically two techniques. One is to encourage mergers, on the theory that bigger railroads will be healthier railroads. A result of this pursuit, ironic certainly when one looks back to the years that preceded 1920, is that today individual railroad companies are indeed acquiring regional monopolies of railroad transportation. The ICC's second technique is to limit as best it can both price competition and the number of new competitors in the industries it regulates. It attempts to keep rates and revenues reasonably high and to allocate the available business among the railroads, truck, barge and bus companies it regulates.

But if the effort is a fraud on consumers, it also is no great success from industry's point of view. The long-term decline in the railroads' freight tonnage, relative to national economic and population trends, resumed after World War II and there is no positive evidence the decline has been halted permanently. In the general prosperity of the mid-1960's, most railroads have done well. Yet, a few railroads in the East, including the New York, New Haven & Hartford, again plunged into bankruptcy. Railroads in general have not been so well off as to forego the financial benefits, principally in the form of reduced costs, that the ICC has found to be the principal reason for finding mergers in the "public interest." Truck traffic has grown much more than rail traffic, but truck freighting subject to ICC regulation has not grown nearly as much as truck freighting not subject to regulation. Moreover, truck lines subject to regulation perennially run on paper-thin profit margins. The barge industry presents much the same story. Barge lines subject to regulation have not grown as rapidly as barge operations that run free of the ICC.[6]

The commission on occasion has come close to admitting its failings. One commissioner, Rupert L. Murphy, wrote in a law journal that rate-fixing, "especially where different modes of transportation are concerned, is something like a tightrope walker crossing the chasm of the Niagara—there is plenty of room for a spill."[7]

The ICC once had an idea for solving its problems, or anyway solving some of them. In fairness to all regulated companies, but particularly the railroads, the commission said, the freight rates charged by regulated barge companies should be raised to include the amounts spent by the Army Engineers in improving rivers for navigation. Secondly, the commission said, truck rates should be increased to reflect truckers' benefits from the sums spent by the federal government on highway construction. The thought apparently was that regulated barge line and truck line rates should be so increased, even though (or perhaps because) Congress has refused to collect so-called user charges in full amount from these companies, in fairness to the railroads. But the commission quickly rejected the idea because it would be "diametrically opposed to the long established policy of Congress" to provide free or partially free barge and truck rights of way. The commission shuddered at "the size of the Pandora's box" it might open.[8]

12
Highways

From the point of view of an automobile-happy America, highways are an unmitigated private blessing. From Washington's point of view, highways always have come under the heading of public works, with all the political meanings that attach to those words. Federal highway construction projects, like river and harbor improvement projects, mean local benefits and construction contracts that can be distributed with political patronage in mind. Throughout history federal highway funds have had larger political meanings. Early in the nineteenth century, before the government began to promote railroad construction with land grants, Congress helped to finance the building of a national pike and other roads as a means of hastening economic development and westward expansion. That spurt of federal road building lasted only briefly, and when Congress again appropriated funds for highways it was not motivated so much by desires to improve the nation's transportation facilities as by the need, or desire, to assist agriculture by improving mobility, and, during the depression of the 1930's, to make work for jobless thousands. Road building required for transportation was left largely to the states. It was not until the end of World War II that Washington once more began building highways for the sake of highways.

The Army Corps of Engineers has so much waterways money nowadays that it no longer misses its loss of highway jurisdiction. Under the 1824 law that established its water domain, the Corps of Engineers also was the federal highway builder. But that small measure of transportation coordination began to disappear in 1894, when the Secretary of Agriculture set up an Office of Road Inquiry that blossomed into what today is the Bureau of Public Roads.

The feeding and growth of the Bureau of Public Roads demonstrates very well why the federal transportation bureaucracy today is uncoordinated and chaotic. The Federal-Aid Road Act of 1916, which marked the humble beginning of modern federal highway planning, was primarily aimed at "getting the farmer out of the mud." Consequently, the 1916 law and the $5 million Congress appropriated were administered by the Office of Road Inquiry that had been set up in the Agriculture Department in 1894. In the 1930's when federal road building became principally a public works measure to get the country out of the Depression, the highway planners, by then called the Bureau of Public Roads, were shifted to the New Deal's Public Works Administration.

The Depression over, PWA was abolished and the bureau was moved to the General Services Administration, the government's humdrum housekeeper. And after World War II, when highways once more became important to the federal government, Harry Truman reorganized the Bureau of Public Roads and put it into the Commerce Department. Lyndon Johnson reorganized some more, and in 1967 the Bureau was placed in the new Department of Transportation.

Federal highway spending never stopped growing after 1916, but still Washington didn't become the nation's chief road planner until after World War II. Before the war, federal money could be spent only on rural highways, and Washington limited its contribution to 50 percent of the cost of these roads. In 1944 Congress said the federal planners could enter the nation's urban areas. Gradually Washington lifted its share to 60 percent, and then, in 1956, came the 90 percent federal, 10 percent state ratio on which the 41,000-mile National System of Interstate and Defense Highways is being built.

The road show that Congress began with a $5 million authorization in 1916 has grown since 1956 into the largest single federal transportation spending program, with annual outlays running about $4 billion.[1]

The grand total of federal funds authorized in all the years between 1916 and 1956 was about $8 billion (not including make-work highway funds spent directly by PWA in the 1930's). Bureau of Public Roads annual spending didn't cross the billion-dollar-a-year mark until 1957. Since then, the grand total has topped $30 billion, of which about $20 billion was earmarked for the Interstate System and $10 billion for other primary and secondary roads and their urban extensions. The 41,000-mile Interstate System will require a total federal outlay of $50.6 billion by the time it is finished in 1972. Total cost of the Interstate System is expected to be greater than $55 billion including the states' 10 percent share.

Washington is now paying for almost half the grand total of $8.5 billion that all levels of government in the United States spend annually on new construction of streets and highways. According to the Bureau of Public Roads, about half the nation's total motor traffic now moves on roads, highways and expressways that federal money helped to build. The states nominally remain in charge; the federal spending takes the form of grants to the states which build, own and operate the highways.

In truth, the states have been relegated to the role of a construction straw boss. What Washington pays for, Washington controls. The states build roads that are master-planned in Washington, they lay concrete according to "guidelines" set down in Washington, and step by step their progress is reviewed by Washington. The federal government has used the threat of curtailment or withdrawal of highway aid to persuade the states to adopt federal standards for the control of advertising billboards and auto junkyards along roads. Now Washington worries about the annual death toll on the nation's streets and highways and the states apparently are unable to halt the rising tide of casualties. The "solution" may very well be federal drivers' licenses and federal policing of the nation's major traffic arteries, in addition to the federal safety specifications for automobiles that Congress has legislated in the past several years.

Federal road building, the biggest public works project in peacetime history, is a program arrived at in the political arena with precious little concern for what had gone before in transportation and with no regard for what might come after. There is no evidence that the presidentially-appointed National Inter-regional Highway Committee, whose 1944 survey of national highway needs was the basic foundation of the Interstate System which Congress subsequently voted, gave any serious consideration to the relative efficiency or need of rail, water and air, as well as highway, transportation.

To the contrary, the federal highway program is as muddled a product of congressional politics and administrative bureaucracies as the federal waterways program. And, like the Corps of Engineers, the Bureau of Public Roads has powerful special interests on its side. Bureau workers fondly call them "our industries."

The American Road Builders' Association is the major such industry. Its 5400 members are a grass-roots network of highway promoters located in every congressional district in the land. The Road Builders think exactly like the bureau. The association's executive director (a retired Army Corps of Engineers major general) has told Congress, "Our objective is the long range highway program . . . adequate for the growing demands of highway traffic, the needs of an expanding economy and the requirements of the national defense."

The rest of "our industries" don't always see eye to eye with the Bureau of Public Roads but they too help promote the Interstate System. They include the American Trucking Associations, the American Automobile Association and the American Petroleum Institute. Last but certainly not least on one bureau insider's list is the Automobile Manufacturers Association, which gave the Interstate System that final necessary push in Congress in 1956 after it had been defeated in 1955, despite the best efforts mustered by the Bureau and "our industries."

Like the waterways, the federal highway program has been adorned with an economic justification ratio that indicates the nation could hardly afford not to build the Interstate System. It purports to show the system will produce "benefits" of $11.4 billion annually after 1972, but the Bureau of Public Roads' concoction is even more nebulous than the cost-benefits ratio of the Army Engineers. The bureau's calculation of benefits is derived from estimated reductions in car and truck operating costs; an estimated dollar value of time saved; an estimate of the worth of fewer accidents and highway deaths and the value of reductions in the "strains and discomforts of driving."

The highway program is adorned with several more such baubles. One is called the Highway Trust Fund. It looks a little like an industry profit and loss statement: federal excise taxes on gasoline, tires and other highway-use items go into the fund, construction money goes out and income and outgo are to balance off on September 30, 1972, when the Interstate System is scheduled for completion.

The fund might look like a means of transportation coordination and highway justification; if income failed to cover costs, the highway planners presumably would quit or cut back. But it doesn't work that way. The 41,000 miles of Interstate System roads are fixed by statute and when income looks as if it won't cover anticipated costs the government simply jacks up excise taxes. The trust fund and its "user charges" make more fiscal sense than the way the Army Engineers build waterways, but its real significance is as a highway-financing device; with it, highway promoters can be a lot more certain of having 41,000 miles of Interstate System roads under their belts by 1972 than if the program had to go through the traditional annual appropriations mill on Capitol Hill.[2]

Another gem was pinned on the highway program rather after the fact. Congress in 1962 amended the highway statutes to deny federal aid to urban expressway construction in metropolitan areas of more than fifty thousand population, where local planners by July 1, 1965, had not launched "a continuing comprehensive transportation planning process." The congressional intent, which sounded rather like the 1940 preamble to the ICC Act, was to promote "the development of long-range highway plans . . . properly coordinated with plans for improvements in other affected forms of transportation." It's not very meaningful either. The Bureau of Public Roads did not insist on a plan, only on evidence of the beginnings of a "planning process." No matter anyway: the planned 41,000 miles of interstate highways will be built whether or not cities try to coordinate their highway planning with local rail, subway and bus transportation. Cities and states will build more superhighways simply because the federal funds are available to them for highways. If they do not build highways they will lose the funds. There are no comparable federal billions available to the cities and states for rail, subway or bus transportation. Washington, quite simply, has left the cities and states with no practical alternative to building more highways.

In any event, the Bureau of Public Roads is hardly the place in Washington to begin to establish a federal responsibility for coordinated transportation. The highway planners believe in highways no less sincerely than the Army Corps of Engineers believes in waterways. The bureau's chief planner once put it this way: Highways are so obviously popular and essential that "the highway planner is in the unique and favorable position of being able to plan almost without regard to other modes of travel."[3]

Still, as if to embarrass the highway planners where they live, the Federal City is gripped by local controversy over freeway construction. Plans for building $182 million of additional superhighways in and near Washington are fought by residents who place a lower social value on concrete than on the city's great variety of flowering trees that line stately avenues with their traffic circles—circles, with small parks in their centers, that are relics of an age of non-rush. Citizens' associations in the city's handsome and largely white northwest sector battle the highway planners. Blacks in the city's less handsome sectors also oppose the planners and their allies, who include the Washington Metropolitan Highway Users Conference, the chairman of which is the chief Washington representative of Firestone Tire and Rubber Company.[4]

The controversy in Washington is beginning to be repeated with appropriate variations in cities and communities across the nation. But the citizens fight a losing battle, for the controversy in truth is not between citizens and highway special-interest groups but between citizens and citizens. The issue is not whether highways will be built but where they will be built. Federal law providing for the 41,000-mile Interstate System has required the states to hold public hearings on where the highways will go, not on whether they'll be built. The Bureau of Public Roads, at the direction of the Secretary of Transportation who was responding to the growing volume of citizen complaints, in 1968 proposed rules providing for larger state hearings on highway routes. The proposal was vigorously opposed by the American Road Builders Association and the American Association of State Highway Officials.[5] Little matter, for the highways will be built somewhere. Citizens who want no highways at all in preference to ribbons of concrete through their suburbs or ghettos have no recourse except to the courts. The federal courts have found no legal basis for a claimed right of freedom from highways and have left the choice of routes to the expertise of the federal and state planners.[6]

Fears grow in the cities that more highways will not relieve traffic congestion but will increase it more. No matter how rapidly the highway planners build, they seem unable to keep up with a still more rapidly growing population of automobiles and trucks. Lyndon B. Johnson, on addressing himself to the transportation problem, noted that the mileage of paved roads and streets in the United States had doubled since World War II, rising from 1.5 million miles in 1946 to 3 million miles in 1966. That is nearly a mile of concrete and asphalt roadway for every square mile of land, and still, President Johnson observed, there is "no relief from time-consuming, frustrating and wasteful congestion."[7]

The automobile and the truck have never been economical means of transportation. The motor vehicle is a relatively expensive method of going from one place to another. But ever since Henry Ford rolled out his first Model T, the motor vehicle has offered transportation convenience and flexibility in greater measure than are available from so-called common-carrier types of transportation such as the railroad, the bus and the subway. Today, the motor vehicle undeniably offers less convenience and flexibility than once it did because there are so many motor vehicles relative to the available streets, highways and parking spaces. There were about 9 million motor vehicles in the nation in 1920, about 32 million in 1940 and today there are more than 90 million autos and trucks on the streets and highways.

Perhaps the federal highway planners did not singlehandedly create the motor chaos that today faces the nation. The cities and states that now are most bogged down in traffic are those in the Northeast that began massive road-building programs of their own before Washington took almost full charge of highway planning. On the other hand, it is to be doubted that highway construction would have gone so far so fast without federal planning and federal money. Federal law creates a uniformity across the land that does not bend to the varying needs and desires of the states and cities. If Washington had not in 1956 adopted the largest public works program in peacetime history, each city and state predictably would have adjusted highway construction to local needs and would have coordinated highways with other forms of transportation. Washington surely could have been a more modest or less dogmatic highway promoter. The federal government could, for instance, have paid for 90 percent of intercity highway construction and allowed each state and city to decide for itself whether federal aid to be expended inside city limits would be spent for highways or for some locally determined combination of highways, subways, railways and buses. An even larger choice might have been left with the states to decide whether federal transportation grants for intercity transportation would be spent for highways or for a mix of highways, railroads and airport facilities.

But federal transportation planning is not coordinated, nor do the splintered transportation bureaucracies in Washington permit much coordination by the states or the cities. With the $50.6 billion federal Interstate Highway System still some years from completion, the nation already is beginning to feel the effects of an uncoordinated overbuild of urban and intercity superhighways at the expense of other forms of transportation. Just as the federal highway program is unprecedented in size, so too will be the public costs of resuscitating other forms of transportation.

13

Airways

The federal government began to promote commercial air transportation in the 1920's and, predictably, it has never attempted to relate aviation policy to highway or railroad or waterways policies. As a result, the conflict between federal aviation policy and other transportation programs is growing rapidly and consumers are paying the price again, not only as airline passengers, but also as taxpayers.

Washington has played two distinct roles in the development of commercial air transportation. The first relates to aviation safety. The second stemmed from the congressional conviction that commercial airlines were an infant industry deserving of federal promotion, including the paternalism of subsidies. The industry now has come of age and would have done so, if perhaps at a slower pace, without subsidies. But the subsidies have never stopped.

Commercial aviation has benefited probably more than any other private industry from government paternalism, relative to the size of the industry and the time span involved. Since 1926 Washington has spent more than $4 billion to enhance the safety of flying. It has handed to commercial airline companies, in the form of direct subsidies, about $1.3 billion and in addition has protected these companies from price competition and from invasion by outsiders who desired to enter the airline business. Beyond all this largesse, commercial aviation has benefited indirectly from the billions of dollars the government has spent on research and development of military aircraft.

The safety function is a necessary one that probably nobody other than the federal government could perform. Mid-air collisions are clearly not in the public interest. Airways know no state boundaries and the skies are full of not only commercial jet airliners but also thousands of smaller private aircraft and hundreds of military planes. They must be safely separated in the available airspace; the air traffic cop is the Federal Aviation Administration, which is part of the executive branch. The Federal Airways System consists of some 300,000 miles of designated airlanes at varying altitudes. Pilots, whether commercial, private or military, use them as motorists use highway maps. The complex includes radio and electronic navigational aids to assist pilots. Air traffic controllers of the FAA guide flight movements from airport control towers and from ground control stations spotted throughout the nation to police in-flight traffic patterns.

The only substantial policy question raised by the $4 billion the government has spent on air safety involves coordination with other federal transportation programs. In considering FAA's annual appropriations requests, Congress has never attempted to relate air safety and navigation expenditures to highway, waterway or railroad spending or regulatory policies. The air spending has been guided principally by FAA's estimates of the facilities and manpower necessary to ensure the safety of projected quantities of air traffic.

How much commercial airline traffic there is to be is the business of a separate agency, the Civil Aeronautics Board. There is no planning coordination between the CAB's awards of airline routes and the FAA's operation of the airways traffic system. The FAA does not participate in CAB route cases, but merely takes the traffic the CAB generates.

Federal promotion of commercial aviation began with subsidies. The original subsidy program started in 1925 and it was administered by the Post Office Department because the subsidies were included in payments the government made for hauling airmail. No one knows how much the subsidies amounted to between 1925 and 1938, the year the CAB was created, because the government has never calculated how much the airlines were paid above their legitimate cost of hauling the mails.[1]

When Congress created the CAB in 1938, it charged the agency with "development of an air transportation system properly adapted to the present and future needs of the United States . . . the promotion of adequate service at reasonable charges . . . and the regulation of air transportation as to foster sound economic conditions in air carriers." To accomplish these ambitious economic planning goals, Congress equipped the CAB with a full kit of tools: controls over the routes airlines fly and the fares they charge, and subsidies. The board has used this trio of powers in concert. Its general policy of course always has been to restrict severely price competition in the industry. It has taken a similarly conservative approach in awarding routes. Since 1938 the board has mapped out the routes all airlines fly, but it has never drawn up a master plan of the routes. Rather, the CAB planned by indirection—waiting for airlines to come in with route applications and approving new or additional scheduled airline service between individual pairs of cities on a case-by-case basis.

Historically, the CAB's involvement began with so-called trunk lines that were in business in 1938 and gradually expanded their route systems and awarded each of the domestic and overseas lines more subsidies as the route expansion continued. As commercial traffic grew in the 1940's and 1950's, these airlines' need for subsidies declined and by the mid-1950's all the trunk lines were earning sufficient profits on commercial revenues to be cut off the subsidy list. By then the CAB had created a new class of airlines, the so-called local airlines that the board established to bring scheduled airline service to communities too small to support trunk-line service. In addition, the board after World War II began awarding routes and subsidies to groups of airlines operating in Alaska and between the Hawaiian Islands and then it added some helicopter airlines in the New York, Chicago and Los Angeles areas to the subsidy list.[2]

Thus, while the total federal airline subsidy bill has declined temporarily at times, its long-term trend has been forever upward. It declined from $58 million in 1954, when the trunk lines went off subsidy, to $50 million in 1959. Yet by 1964 the taxpayers' total subsidy bill was higher than ever—nearly $86 million. It since has hovered between $50 million and $80 million and there is no reason to predict any substantial decline in the years ahead. To the contrary, airline subsidies predictably will swell as the CAB discovers new areas in which to expand airline service and as general economic recessions create financial difficulties in old areas.

The CAB has not been a brilliantly successful economic planner, despite its full kit of economic tools. For instance, the total airline subsidy bill in 1964 climbed to $86 million partly because of a CAB blunder that landed one of the trunk lines, Northeast Airlines, back on subsidy. The story of Northeast Airlines illustrates the fallibility of government economic planning in the relatively elementary projection of supply and demand.

In 1955, the CAB ordered a hearing to determine whether a new airline route should be drawn between New York and Florida to assure a quantity of service "adequate" to the needs of the public. All the evidence considered was of an economic nature. The board examined population, tourism and industrialization trends in Florida and population changes in New York, Boston, Washington and a number of other northeastern cities. It analyzed these trends, projected their effects on air travel and weighed the ability of Eastern and National Airlines, the two already serving this travel market, to handle the expected increase in traffic.

The CAB issued its decision in 1956, saying that air travel in "this extremely rich market" had grown 300 percent between 1948 and 1954. "There is no indication that this growth has reached a plateau," the five board members unanimously declared. In 1954, about one million airline passengers had flown between New York, Boston and other cities in the Northeast and points in Florida; the board unanimously projected a growth in these markets to three million passengers in 1956. "We are convinced that a third carrier is required," the board said.

Turning then to which airline should get the third route, the majority picked Northeast. That too was a planning decision. Northeast had been a relatively small carrier in New England; the new route would remake the company into a major airline. The majority said, "We recognize we are in substantial measure changing the character of this carrier's operations," and therefore the board after five years would review Northeast's performance. But the board expressed its "confidence" that Northeast would become a "profitable . . . strong, self-sufficient carrier."

By the time the five years ran out in 1961, every one of the board's predictions had proved wrong. Traffic between major northeastern cities and Florida had not reached even two million passengers. Northeast Airlines had indeed grown from a small airline with fewer than a thousand employees to a big one with close to three thousand employees, but Northeast was not profitable, strong or self-sufficient. The $831,000 earned surplus it had in 1956 had turned into a retained loss of nearly $44 million by the end of 1962.

The CAB began its promised review in 1961, and in 1963, after weighing the same supply and demand factors it had considered in 1956, came up with precisely the opposite conclusion: "Public convenience and necessity do not require" three airlines. The board ordered Northeast out of the Florida markets.

The board admitted error. Its 1963 decision said, "The anticipated growth . . . [in traffic to] three million passengers did not, in fact, materialize. Instead of the profitable operations predicted in 1956, Northeast incurred heavy losses each year" since then. Worse yet, Northeast had diverted business from both Eastern and National Airlines, with a "marked economic impact" on Eastern.

Admittedly, the remaking of Northeast into a small New England regional carrier again would be painful. "Northeast has risked its capital and lost millions," the board conceded. "Its management has worked hard and diligently to develop its Florida route. Northeast has greatly expanded its organization and increased the number of its employees. Termination of the Florida route will inevitably have adverse effects on its employees, the New England communities in which those employees reside, its creditors and its stockholders."

Despite its acknowledgment of those dire consequences, the CAB concluded its 1963 decision with an order that Northeast stop flying from New York and other cities in the region to Florida. The airline company decided, however, not to go quietly. It went to the courts for help and eventually the taxpayers also helped. The board graciously decided that, while Northeast was fighting the ouster order and the matter remained unresolved, the airline should have a subsidy, paid of course by the taxpayers, of some $2 million annually.

Northeast filed suit in its home city of Boston with the Federal Circuit Court of Appeals. After the suit to overturn the CAB order was filed, the court ordered the CAB to take another look at its decision, and said further that, while the board was looking, Northeast could continue to operate on the Florida route. The CAB restudied its 1963 decision and twice more voted to oust Northeast. But the court still wasn't satisfied and in 1965 it ordered the CAB to start all over again by conducting a brand new hearing where Northeast and the other airlines could present all their evidence once more. This the board did and finally, in 1966, an examiner recommended to the board that Northeast be given a permanent route license for the Florida route. He said that traffic had picked up and ruled "that the public convenience and necessity require the authorization of a third" airline on the route. Early in 1967 the board accepted the examiner's recommendation and awarded Northeast the permanent license. Thus the CAB's planning venture ended in 1967 with what might be termed a vindication of its 1956 economic projections. The vindication was accidental rather than of the board's making and the tomfoolery that went on in the intervening years certainly cost hundreds of thousands of dollars in lawyers' fees plus more than $4 million of subsidies, for which the taxpayers paid.

The Civil Aeronautics Board's planning talents are not always applied with such maudlin results but the Northeast case also was not a unique example. Because the CAB's economic forecasting has often proved grossly in error, other airlines on occasion have come fully as close to the brink of financial disaster. So desperate was National Airlines' financial condition in 1948 that the CAB proposed to dismember the company. Capital Airlines was so sick in 1961 that the board said it had "no practicable alternative" to approving its merger into United Air Lines. Nor can it be said the CAB has succeeded permanently in creating "sound economic conditions" in the domestic airline industry at large. The major trunk lines as a group in the early 1960's suffered annual losses of more than $34 million.

Airline profits of course recovered magnificently. They had gone down with the general economic recession of the early 1960's and went up in the boom of the mid-sixties. The CAB might, and sometimes does, argue, therefore, that it should not be blamed so harshly for the industry's lows any more than it is lauded for the highs. Yet while airline earnings do rise and fall with the general economy, Congress nevertheless superimposed the CAB on the industry in order to keep profits from going too far in either direction. Basically, Congress' purpose in giving the CAB iron-fisted control over airline routes and rates was to secure the optimum airline service obtainable under sound economic conditions—in other words, to regulate competition. The CAB's job was to measure and project the demands for service between pairs of cities and then meet those demands as fully as possible with a supply of routes distributed among the nation's airlines in a manner to preserve the economic stability of each. Indeed, before the board awards any route it is required by law to find the airline "fit, willing and able" to provide the service authorized.

When, after World War II, the CAB was preparing to draw the *international* route map American companies would fly, it did turn to its professional staff planners. The resulting route structure was based on comprehensive, industry-wide, long-range planning and it has proved to be a generally successful balancing act, insofar as the financial stability of these airlines—principally Pan American World Airways and Trans World Airlines—is concerned. Not incidentally, the CAB also minimized route competition, and eliminated rate competition, for these airlines.

In drawing routes across the face of the United States, however, the CAB has stuck with the case-by-case approach. Its planning has been neither comprehensive nor long-range. To the contrary, in awarding domestic routes, as well as in fixing fares, the board has kept its eyes on the airlines' profit-and-loss statements, handing out many routes when airline business is good and refusing to hand out any when business is bad. This approach has been sharply criticized; James M. Landis, President Kennedy's adviser on the regulatory agencies, asserted it has resulted in a "hodge-podge of routes."[3] The Kennedy Administration's task force on National Aviation Goals criticized the CAB for "lack of thoughtful planning." The Project Horizon task force, looking into a future when a general economic recession in the country will again carry airline earnings downward, saw "some later date [when] the concern is likely to be with keeping alive a mortally ill industry, as the experience of the railroads clearly indicates."[4]

To draw parallels between the effects of government planning on the railroad industry and the airline industry may seem, at first blush, to border on the ridiculous. The railroads are old, the airlines young. Nobody rides the railroads, everybody wants to fly the jet airliners. The parallels are inexact, even in a planning sense; government has minimized price competition and the number of competitors in both industries but only the airlines have had access to direct government subsidies. Indeed, the commercial airlines' access to the United States Treasury is sufficient guarantee that, in any time of future financial distress when the industry becomes mortally ill, the airlines will be kept alive. The trunk lines, which are the backbone of the industry, have not required subsidies in recent years but, as the experience of Northeast Airlines demonstrated, the funds will be available when needed. Several times Congress has rejected proposals to write a law saying that the big domestic and international trunk lines are henceforth ineligible for subsidies. These companies thus remain eligible to fall back on the taxpayers.

But despite the differences between railroads and airlines, there remains room to wonder whether the government paternalism they have shared has not had some parallel effects on management initiative and technological innovation. There is some evidence that airline initiative and innovation have been affected, to the detriment of flying consumers, although the evidence at this stage of economic inquiry remains largely circumstantial.

The subsidies that airline companies have received from the Civil Aeronautics Board have never been designated specifically, as have merchant marine subsidies, for the purchase of new equipment and for day-to-day operations. Rather, the CAB has generally allowed airlines to buy new aircraft of their own choosing and it has given the companies ample operating freedom; it then has awarded subsidies year by year simply to help cover whatever aggregate losses an airline has suffered. The CAB does not stay entirely away from airline management matters but certainly it does not involve itself to the extent that the government controls management discretion in the merchant marine industry.

Airline management decisions on the types of aircraft to be bought from airframe and engine manufacturers, on the other hand, have been tremendously influenced by other offices of government. The Federal Aviation Administration and the National Aeronautics and Space Administration, for instance, both have contributed to advances in the design and operation of commercial airliners, primarily to improve air safety. Far and away the largest contributor to technological progress has been the Defense Department. The Pentagon has spent billions of dollars on military aircraft programs—in metals research, aerodynamics study, engine development and airframe design. The military's billions have advanced the construction of commercial airliners immeasurably.

Does airline progress have to be tied as closely as it has been to the military's apron strings? Or have airline managers been so well protected by the CAB that they lacked the initiative to innovate on the military advances? There is indeed evidence that, from the consumer's point of view, the airlines have been tied too closely to the apron strings of both the CAB and the military.

The primary emphasis of the military program almost always has been on greater speed. That is a natural military objective, but the primary emphasis of airline progress also has been on greater speed, and that is not quite so natural. The emphasis on speed in the development of new passenger transports never has been greater than it is today in the government's development of a supersonic airliner. Yet speed is expensive, both in the design and the operation of aircraft. Greater speed can be attained at the sacrifice of greater passenger-carrying capacity which, theoretically, would make possible lower fares per passenger. Airline managers always have tended to buy faster and more luxurious planes, rather than to invest in aircraft that potentially offer reduced fares.

There is at least some evidence that the airlines in the past could have adapted military progress to civil aircraft that, with a relatively minor sacrifice in speed, would have carried more passengers more cheaply. One bit of evidence was offered by Howard Hughes who, before he became the world's wealthiest recluse, controlled Trans World Airlines. In his day he certainly was the most controversial and probably the most brilliant airline manager ever. The primary source of his wealth was Hughes Tool Company, a major military aerospace contractor. Mr. Hughes's big hobby was flying and almost a quarter-century ago he designed, built and briefly flew a huge wooden plane that could carry 750 passengers. Mr. Hughes and his plane were viewed dimly by the Civil Aeronautics Board and airline executives.[5] As things are turning out, he was a prophet in his time, insofar as 750-passenger airplanes are concerned, although not insofar as cheaper fares also are concerned.

Today, a 750-passenger "airbus" is on the horizon. The Defense Department in 1965 decided it needed a transport aircraft that emphasized capacity rather than speed. So it proceeded to contract for the C-5 transport, at a cost of $3.2 billion for research, development and production of the first fifty-eight aircraft. In 1968 the first C-5 Galaxy rolled out of Lockheed Aircraft Corporation's plant at Marietta, Georgia—the world's largest military aircraft, only eighteen yards shorter than a football field, rolling on twenty-eight wheels and capable of a cruising speed of about 500 miles per hour. Lockheed plans to adapt the Galaxy to civilian use with a plane capable of carrying 750 passengers. There have been some theoretical calculations that a civilian version would be capable of flying its 750 passengers across the Atlantic at $75 a person, or half the price of the cheapest ticket on a transatlantic jet that today carries up to 150 passengers at about 600 miles per hour. But flying consumers have no reason to believe that the fare reductions will be anything more than theoretical. International and domestic airlines will put into service in the early 1970's, several years before the civilian Galaxies, jumbo jets or airbuses capable of carrying up to five hundred or so passengers. The International Air Transport Association has said that it is "idle speculation" to hope for "tremendous fare reductions" on the airbuses.[6]

The high-capacity airbuses and later the Galaxies will mark a new departure in commercial aviation. On the other hand, the development of a supersonic airliner will advance the speed of flying and sacrifice capacity. The high-capacity aircraft offer no hope of fare reductions and the supersonic plane almost certainly promises fares substantially higher than present prices of airline tickets. All three are products of military research and development, adapted to civilian uses within the framework of an essentially noncompetitive airline industry. Those who would compete on the basis of fares or technological innovation not so closely tied to the military—the nonskeds or the Howard Hugheses—have gone. Civil aviation technology of course can and will advance with military research and development, but IATA fixes even the number of seats and inches of leg room on aircraft operated by the international airlines.

It is not unreasonable to conclude that the absence of competition in domestic and international commercial aviation has unnecessarily stifled innovation. The Project Horizon task force acknowledged commercial aviation's progress in the speed of flight and recognized the necessarily large influence of military research and development. It also concluded that government aid in general and the Civil Aeronautics Board in particular had "inhibited managerial ingenuity" in the industry. Decrying the absence of "business incentives and competition" in the airline business, the study asked "whether a regulatory philosophy developed initially for twin-engine piston aircraft does not require adjustment to the jet age."[7]

The irony of 600-mile-an-hour jets today and of Galaxies and supersonic planes tomorrow is that all the taxpayers have helped to pay for them, but only a minority of them reap any benefits as consumers. No more than 30 percent of the American people have flown, according to estimates usually accepted inside the airline industry and by the Civil Aeronautics Board. The Project Horizon study found this estimate too high, saying that "probably no more than 10 percent to 15 percent of the population" had flown. Whichever estimate may be correct, the fact is that probably more than 100 million Americans have helped to pay for airline progress but have received no benefits. There seems to be no major disagreement among industry people, the CAB and Project Horizon concerning the principal reason most Americans have never flown. Some still may fear air travel and others find automobile travel more convenient. But the major reason relatively few have flown probably is that they feel they cannot afford the price of airline tickets, as fixed by IATA and the CAB.

The Resultant Chaos

There is no law which says that the waterway, railway, highway and airway planners together cannot, by means of administrative action and legislative recommendation, attempt to begin to bring some measure of coordination to federal regulation and promotion of transportation. Indeed, the possibilities of informal gatherings, where the planners could get to know one another and swap ideas, occurred to President Kennedy. He decided not to attempt to call all the planners together at once but, for a modest beginning, to bring together only the Interstate Commerce Commission, the Civil Aeronautics Board and the Federal Maritime Commission. He "requested" the chairmen of these three agencies "to meet at frequent intervals to discuss regulatory problems affecting the various modes of transportation and to seek coordinated solutions in the form of legislation or administrative action."

The chairmen began in 1962 to meet monthly and continued to do so after Lyndon B. Johnson became President so that their chitchats promised to become permanent. They talked about many things, but what seemed to engage their most serious attention was something the President never dreamed of. It was the Hovercraft, an exotic vehicle being developed to travel over land or water, propelled by and floating on jets of air. Now here was a dilemma!

A special committee was established and the Coast Guard, Federal Aviation Administration, Maritime Administration, Customs Bureau and State Department were called in for consultation. The three chairmen finally decided that it was too early to decide whether a Hovercraft was a bus, a boat or an airplane. They agreed "jurisdictional conflict" should be avoided, but "should jurisdictional problems arise" Congress might have to decide which among them should promote and regulate such vehicles. The Hovercraft determination, preliminary though it was, seems to have been the most substantial accomplishment of the informal get-together approach to transportation coordination.

Theoretically, there is still another avenue for coordination within the existing framework of transportation laws and bureaucracies. Each of the commissions, boards, bureaus and offices must, by law, hold public hearings before it decides route, rate and subsidy matters. The Civil Aeronautics Board could, therefore, utilize the public forum of a Federal Maritime Commission hearing to expose the ocean shipping planners to the necessities of planning overseas air transportation. The Interstate Commerce Commission could appear at a CAB hearing to demonstrate the availability of passenger train service between, say, New York and Washington; the CAB then would weigh the train service against the necessity or desirability of additional plane service between the two cities. The CAB and the ICC could appear before the Bureau of Public Roads, and vice versa. The possibilities are endless.

They remain wholly theoretical. For one agency to appear before another is unheard of, perhaps in part because it has been tried on a lower level and the results have been discouraging. On occasion, a company or a whole industry regulated and promoted by one agency has appeared before another agency. Railroads, for instance, have appeared before the CAB. Such appearances admittedly constitute something less than sincere attempts by public officials to coordinate public policy. Companies and industries naturally argue their own points of view. Nevertheless, a railroad can expose the CAB to different approaches. Invariably, the exposure has come to nought. Consider the experience of a large segment of the intercity bus industry when it presented to the CAB a highway point of view.

The National Trailway Bus System in 1963 and again in 1965 went to the CAB to oppose a proposal of twenty airlines to slash their fares by 50 percent for military personnel on leave. The airlines told the board that the fare reduction would not only fill otherwise empty seats but also would "promote air transportation by introducing young servicemen to air travel for the first time." Moreover, the airlines said, they could save young Americans from "the risks of highway travel." The indignant bus operators told the CAB the reduction "discriminated" against bus travel and against airplane passengers who paid full fare. The board upheld the reduction on the grounds it would increase airlines' annual profits by an estimated $13 million and would serve the national interest by giving young servicemen the "morale" boost that the board said comes with air travel.[1]

In practice, there is no coordination among the transportation bureaucracies and there cannot be any meaningful cooperation within the existing framework of divided responsibilities and loyalties. Indeed, given its legislative mandate, the Civil Aeronautics Board would be violating the law if it failed exclusively to promote the airlines, as would the Federal Maritime Commission if it failed to promote steamships, and the Bureau of Public Roads if it devoted itself to anything other than superhighways. Uncoordinated planning serves the interests of industries and of members of Congress who are allied politically, geographically and emotionally with particular transport industries. The airlines prefer to be promoted by an independent and isolated CAB because coordination would diminish the single-mindedness of government promotion and it might also diminish airline subsidies. The isolation of ocean transportation planning is similarly sustained by ship operators, maritime unions and members of Congress from the nation's port cities. Even the railroads figure they are better off with an independent Interstate Commerce Commission than with coordinated federal planning. Independence and uncoordination are thus maintained throughout all the planning bureaucracies.

In evaluating the effects of uncoordinated federal planning, on consumers who use transportation facilities and taxpayers who pay for them, it is well to recall original purposes. Not since 1920, when it abandoned its original purpose of keeping railroad fares and rates low, has the government purely and simply regulated any transport industry. Promotion of waterways, which began long before 1920, and promotion of railroads, airways and highways each was occasioned by a particular conviction at a particular time that the public interest required the construction or maintenance of a particular type of transportation. If all the planners had started at the same time and if America still lacked capacity in all four types of transport, there would be no conflict today. Railway, highway, waterway and airway facilities all are necessary and the planners each could proceed independently to promote a greater supply of services for the public. But today America has an abundance of facilities and services and, because each form of transportation was planned without reference to the other, it has an over-all excess of transportation capacity and, at the same time, a misallocation of transportation resources. It has invested billions of public and private dollars in transportation but now it often does not have the right kind of transportation in the right place at the right time.

The economic waste that flows from creation of excess capacity is visible enough when the Army Engineers build waterways with a formula based on the amount of freight that barges can take away from railroad tracks that run along a riverbank. The tracks fall into disuse, their maintenance becomes a financial burden on the railroad company and eventually the Interstate Commerce Commission allows the railroad to contract or tear up the river tracks to preserve the financial integrity and operating stability of the company as a whole. Or it allows two ailing railroads to merge and abandon some of the trackage of each. Yet, perhaps one-quarter of the total mileage of railroad tracks in the United States still is surplus, insofar as it represents transportation capacity that once was necessary and today is used so lightly as to constitute an economic burden. The freight has moved to waterways and highways and the ICC has allowed railroads to shrink their trackage from some 430,000 miles that spanned the nation in 1930 to roughly 340,000 miles today. But excess capacity persists.

Uncoordinated planning assignments have given rise to many similar conflicts between government agencies and offices. The Maritime Administration has subsidized the operation of ocean passenger liners at the same time the Civil Aeronautics Board has subsidized overseas airliners. Today, the ships sail with far less than full capacity of passengers and the Maritime Administration still subsidizes their operations while the CAB promotes the airlines, though no longer with subsidies. Airlines operating within the United States, including those that do receive subsidies from the CAB, perennially fly with less than 60 percent of their seat capacity occupied. The chief competitor of the airlines is the highways built by the Bureau of Public Roads. Highways have taken business from railroad passenger trains, which today run at only 30 percent of capacity despite the drastic curtailment of train service which the ICC has authorized in recent years. Intercity buses, which also are regulated by the ICC, operate at about 50 percent of capacity.[2]

The decline and disappearance of older forms of transportation are commonly accepted as natural consequences of the forward march of technology and affluence. The buggy whip and the automobile are the usually cited analogy. The parallel is inexact, because there was no federal commission to foster and preserve the buggy, and it is ridiculous to accept transportation trends today as simply the consequence of natural economic forces. The transportation problems that the nation today faces are, in very large part, the consequences of uncoordinated government planning and undisciplined government spending. The problems, moreover, are not simply those of conflicts among bureaucracies. Larger problems have grown from the historic commitment of government to the maintenance of common-carrier transportation and the modern provision by government of rights of way for private transportation.

Government has eroded the financial integrity and operating stability of the common carriers by providing do-it-yourself transportation alternatives for passengers and for shippers of freight who choose not to pay the high prices or to utilize the services of the common carriers. Highways, airways and waterways built with the tax monies of individuals and corporations, of course, were never intended to be barred to use by individuals as travelers or by corporations as shippers. Travelers and shippers thus have availed themselves of the alternatives of private transportation, by purchasing some eighty million private automobiles, perhaps ten million private trucks, 85,000 private airplanes and probably more than ten thousand private barges and ships.

The conflict that arises from this dual commitment begins with the Interstate Commerce Commission and the railroad industry. The railroads represent the sole form of transportation for which the government has not, in any contemporary sense, provided rights of way and the ICC has no subsidies to give to the railroads. The ICC has, of course, attempted to redress this slight. In addressing itself to the railroads' loss of freight business to the waterways built by the Army Engineers, the ICC has attempted to utilize its powers over the rates of both railroads and barge lines. Still, the distressing fact is that the ICC today can reach only about 10 percent of the barge traffic on the nearly 19,000 miles of inland waterways built or improved by the Engineers. Only that small share of river traffic is carried by the common-carrier barge lines that the ICC regulates. The other 90 percent represents traffic that is unregulated, either because it consists of ICC-exempt bulk commodities or because the barges are owned by haul-it-yourself grain processors, chemical companies, steel mills and giant oil companies.[3]

A similar conflict, with yet larger public meanings concerning both intercity and intracity transportation, exists between railroad and other common-carrier forms of transport, on the one hand, and highway transportation on the other. This conflict, insofar as it involves passenger transportation, is not only a conflict between privately owned railroads and public highways; it is also a conflict between publicly owned subway and other urban mass-transit systems and public highways. Washington did not alone create the paradox of clogged highways and unused rail and other mass-transit facilities; the cities and states that now fear most for the future of their common-carrier transportation grids are those in the Northeast that began massive road-building programs before Washington took over. But it is also no coincidence that the beginnings of chaos date from 1946 when federal road spending began to turn up sharply.

The decline in surface and subway mass transit in the cities, in commuter trains to the suburbs, and in intercity passenger trains began in the 1920's when the private auto and truck started their rise. Between 1920 and 1940 motor vehicle registrations in the nation increased from 9 million to 32 million. At the same time, mass-transit riders decreased from 15 billion to 13 billion and the number of train commuters decreased from about 400 million to 200 million. This loss of business wasn't painless for the railroads and the mass-transit companies of the day, but it did not constitute a national problem either. The older forms of transportation contracted, but it was not until after World War II that railroad and mass-transit companies began wholesale abandonments, with state and federal regulators' permission, of services and facilities.

This cumulative effect of the highway steamroller all across the nation is demonstrated by a Philadelphia story.[4] The Pennsylvania–Reading Seashore Lines, whose tracks connect Philadelphia with Atlantic City and many other points in southern New Jersey, once upon a time hauled millions of passengers to New Jersey shore resorts at a one-dollar excursion fare. In 1926 Philadelphia's city fathers cut the ribbon that opened the first vehicular bridge across the Delaware River between Philadelphia and Camden, New Jersey. The year the bridge, now called the Ben Franklin Bridge, was opened, the railroad carried two million fewer passengers than the 18 million it had carried in 1925. Not so good for the railroad, but no particular public problem. Even by 1946 when the railroad's business was down to about 8 million passengers, the trains still kept running, though not as frequently. The business still was worth preserving and the company immediately after the war dieselized its engines and air-conditioned its cars. In 1951 the New Jersey Turnpike was opened and in 1955 the state cut the ribbon on the Garden State Parkway. In 1956 the railroad's business was down to 1.6 million passengers, but still the trains ran. It wasn't until 1959, when business barely topped 1 million, that Seashore Lines decided the jig was up. In that year some 56 million autos, buses and trucks streamed across the three bridges in the Philadelphia area. The company decided to abandon passenger service and wouldn't be enticed to stay even with a $277,000 annual subsidy from the state of New Jersey.

The same decline and fall of older forms of transportation has made the streets of Manhattan a huge traffic jam. New York City and Nassau and Suffolk counties and the Triborough Bridge and Tunnel Authority spent $2.7 billion on highways and other vehicular facilities in the half-dozen years between 1957 and 1963. The federal government's share of the $2.7 billion was $532 million. Total federal spending under the Interstate System program in the New York metropolitan area will by 1972 top $4 billion.

New York, before the highway-building binge started, was served by an abundance of common-carrier transportation—commuter trains, subways, buses and ferries across the Hudson. The railroad-owned Hudson River ferries in 1930 carried 94 million passengers between the Manhattan and New Jersey shores. In 1947 they carried 38 million passengers and in 1956 about 19 million. Motor traffic over and under the Hudson numbered 52 million vehicles in 1930 and 206 million in 1956.[5] The tremendous growth of vehicular traffic caused the New York Central Railroad to abandon its ferries, as well as its commuter trains that ran along the west shore of the Hudson. Further curtailments of service have since been made.

New York's ailing subway system, which long ago passed out of private ownership and into the public hands of the Transit Authority, has barely held its own. The subways carried about 1.4 billion passengers in 1957 and roughly the same number in 1965.

Most of the commuter railroads that connect New York with the suburbs in New Jersey, Long Island and Connecticut haven't even held their own. Riders on the Central Railroad of New Jersey, which accepted a subsidy from the state, declined from about 10 million in 1957 to about 6 million in 1964. New Jersey's Erie Lackawanna Railroad accepted subsidies but nevertheless asked the state to let it abandon commuter service. The Long Island Rail Road, the most heavily traveled commuter line in the nation, as early as 1954 became the recipient of government aid under a special New York state statute. Even after it was rehabilitated with state help, the Long Island could not attract enough new passengers to break even financially; it carried 76 million passengers in 1955 and 77 million in 1964. Thus the Long Island, incorporated in 1834, became publicly owned in 1966; the Pennsylvania Railroad, which for many years had owned the Long Island, was delighted to sell it to the New York Metropolitan Commuter Transportation Authority.

The cause-and-effect pattern of the New York traffic jam is splendidly illustrated in the plight of the New York, New Haven & Hartford Railroad. The New Haven possesses what would seem a priceless asset: a broad, clear right of way that runs from the center of Manhattan to the center of Boston through the richest suburbs and the most densely populated part of the Northeast megalopolis. Still, the New Haven went into bankruptcy, and passenger service on its rail throughway will survive only with tens of millions of federal dollars.

The New Haven, once a rock-solid New England institution that sold at $200 a share, carried 86 million passengers in 1922. In 1957 it still carried 45 million and in that year New Haven freight trains ironically were weighted down with tons of supplies with which the Connecticut Turnpike was being built. The turnpike opened in 1958 and the New Haven's fate was sealed. The turnpike is but a few yards from the railroad right of way from New York City through much of Connecticut. New Haven's tracks quite literally went to rust. Its passengers dropped to 39 million the year the turnpike was opened, to 30 million in 1960 and in 1961 the New Haven went into bankruptcy despite an emergency infusion of more than $30 million of federal loans that will never be repaid.

The New Haven's passenger business fell off to 25 million in 1964 and continued to drop as new sections of the federally financed

Interstate System were opened, paralleling both the New Haven and parts of the Connecticut Turnpike. The court-appointed trustees who ran the New Haven after 1961 wanted to abandon all passenger service. The deteriorating service was saved, temporarily, from extinction with state subsidies atop the federal loans. And then, in 1968, the ICC forced the New York Central and Pennsylvania Railroads to promise to take over the New Haven as a condition to government approval of the merger of the Central and Pennsylvania. The two agreed, with the understanding that massive transfusions of federal and state money will continue to flow into the prostrate New Haven.[6]

Over the nation, more railroad passenger service has been crushed by the highway onslaught than has been saved. In the megalopolis that runs along the southern rim of Lake Michigan from Milwaukee through Chicago to South Bend, a commuter railroad that once was a prized possession of utilities magnate Samuel Insull has abandoned its entire line. The Chicago, North Shore & Milwaukee Railway abandoned its line between Chicago and Milwaukee in 1963 in the dust of Chicago-Milwaukee expressway construction. The Chicago, South Shore and South Bend Railroad, which also sprang from the Insull empire, didn't quit but dropped forty-seven trains in 1964, sharply curtailing service as a result of competition from the new Calumet Expressway and the Indiana Toll Road.

And so it goes. Illinois Terminal Railroad, which once hauled commuters to and from St. Louis, now hauls only freight. Chicago Great Western Railway got completely out of the passenger business in 1965 when it dropped its last two trains between Omaha and Minneapolis. The St. Louis–Southwestern Railroad has abandoned the passenger business. The ICC allowed Chicago & North Western Railway to curtail its passenger service between Chicago and Minneapolis as new sections of the Interstate System were opened all over the upper Midwest served by C&NW. Louisville & Nashville Railroad dropped trains between New Orleans and Pass Christian, Mississippi. Southern Pacific curtailed passenger service between Oakland, California, and Portland, Oregon.

The Bureau of Public Roads' highway program is affecting even the airlines and the Civil Aeronautics Board. The Federal Interstate Highway System will not, to be sure, bury any airlines because the

CAB has subsidies which the ICC does not have. Nevertheless, completed sections of the Interstate System have caused curtailments and some abandonments of service by the regional, or local service, airlines that the CAB created after World War II. These lines were created to offer consumers air service on short hops to smaller cities but the Interstate System is offering people a convenient alternative and many are driving instead of flying. The CAB, which isn't accustomed to concerning itself with any form of transportation other than flying, has said in rather startled tones that "as the Interstate Highway System further develops, the adverse impact on [air] carriers grows in importance."[7]

A fine example of the kind of transportation the CAB was trying to provide was the route between Chicago and Rockford, an industrial city of 135,000 population in northern Illinois. The CAB assigned the Chicago-Rockford route to Ozark Air Lines. Rockford by 1957 was a busy point on Ozark's midwestern system. That year an average of eighty passengers each day boarded Ozark planes at Rockford. Ozark flew six flights daily each way between Rockford and Chicago, and for the year 1957 Rockford generated almost $300,000 worth of ticket sales for the airline. Then the Northwest Tollway was opened between Rockford and Chicago, enabling travelers to drive the seventy miles in approximately one hour. The tollway, state-built but designated Interstate 90 in the federal system, happens to pass close by Chicago's O'Hare Field and, to make matters worse, in Ozark's view, the Rockford Chamber of Commerce supported the inauguration of a new bus service between downtown Rockford and the trunk-line terminals at O'Hare. Ozark's business nose-dived and eventually the airline curtailed service 50 percent, to three flights each way daily. On an average day in September, 1965, only twenty-two passengers left Rockford on Ozark flights. Annual revenues were down to about $76,000 from the $300,000 of 1957.

What a highway did to Ozark Air Lines and to the CAB program at Rockford, other highways are doing to regional airlines all over the country. Central Airlines on an average day in 1959 picked up two or three passengers at Lubbock, Texas. Lubbock got new highways; Central's business by 1963 averaged less than one passenger daily, and the airline quit serving Lubbock. Highways have cut into Central's business at other cities, too, like Topeka, Kansas, and Muskogee, Oklahoma. Mohawk Airlines back in 1957 picked up on average about thirteen passengers a day at Worcester, Massachusetts. As new highways, particularly into Boston, were opened, Mohawk's business at Worcester declined to about four passengers daily.

To the extent that highways take business from airlines, highways built by the Bureau of Public Roads tend to increase the size of the subsidy bill paid by the Civil Aeronautics Board. Airline service can be curtailed, but not rapidly, and it cannot easily be abandoned. There is no reason to believe that the conflict between highway and airway policy will, in the long run, be resolved other than by more federal highway construction and larger federal subsidies for airlines. Similarly, history offers no assurance that highway planning will be cut back because of the automobile's conflict with railroad transportation or urban transit. To the contrary, the solution to these conflicts already is being charted: more federal subsidies for the railroads and for urban mass transit.

In the mid-1950's the federal government began to draw the conclusion that more highways, airways and waterways would not alone suffice and that the nation's future transportation needs in addition required direct federal assistance for railroads and urban transit systems. The Senate Commerce Committee held its hearings on the "deteriorating" railroad situation and then, in 1958, Congress enacted a law to help the railroads. Its two main features were somewhat contradictory, from a public point of view. One encouraged railroads to modernize, by authorizing the ICC to guarantee repayment of railroads' borrowings; the government guarantee enabled railroads to borrow from private lenders at lower rates of interest than their own credit ratings allowed. The guarantees became subsidies when some railroads, such as the New Haven, could not repay and the government had to pay off the lenders. Secondly, the 1958 law conferred on the ICC the authority to allow railroads to discontinue individual passenger trains when the states refused and the commission felt that continued losses of the trains endangered the survival of a railroad's remaining passenger and freight service. In the decade following 1958, railroads applied to drop 258 trains and the commission approved most of the applications.

If the two programs seemed contradictory insofar as public

railroad service was concerned, Congress intended both to help railroads to preserve at least some service. The law may have helped to stem the further deterioration of some of the nation's weaker railroads, but it did little to modernize trains or create additional services. In 1961, the ICC told Congress that the railroads were heading for a "plunge to disaster" and urged outright federal subsidies for passenger trains and other legislation to help the railroads regain freight business.[8]

Congress in 1961 was not prepared to go that far and President Kennedy came to office with proposals covering a wide range of inconsistencies in existing federal transportation spending and regulation and of needs for the future. As a result, Congress in 1961 enacted a program of grants and loans to modernize existing bus, subway and commuter railroad operations and to explore new mass-transit service techniques. It was a modest beginning, authorizing $75 million of federal spending, but it was the start of federal efforts to save the nation's remaining urban transit and commuter services and to start rebuilding them. In 1966, Congress extended and enlarged the program, authorizing $675 million of federal spending over the next four years.

Between 1961 and 1968, some $375 million was obligated to stabilize and improve local public transportation systems in the United States. Kenner, Louisiana (population 17,000), received a $49,000 grant to buy two new buses and build a garage and many other smaller communities also received aid. But most of the federal funds were channeled to the largest cities with the biggest automobile and truck traffic jams. The Long Island Rail Road, for example, received a $30 million grant to extend electrification of its commuter lines and a total of $98 million was given to subway, bus and commuter train operations in the New York metropolitan area. Grants ranging from $4 million to $60 million were given to improve or build subway and other facilities in Boston, Chicago, Cleveland, Philadelphia and San Francisco.

Urban transit and commuter operations thus were accorded first priority, but in 1965 Congress embarked on a program to revitalize railroad transportation between cities. The lawmakers voted $90 million to begin a research and development program in the Commerce Department looking toward more modern, higher-speed rail passenger trains. The program was directed first toward the development of high-speed service in the northeastern megalopolis that extends from Washington through Baltimore and Philadelphia to New York and Boston. The task was to improve the track roadbed of the Penn Central between Washington and New York and of the New Haven between New York and Boston and to design and build a train capable of running safely and smoothly at up to 125 miles per hour on the improved roadbed. It proved more difficult than the research and development people first thought.

A train had not run at 125 miles per hour in regular service in the United States since 1905 and the technology of doing so apparently had been lost. So Washington sent delegations of government and railroad officials to Japan (one was headed by an ICC commissioner) to study the new Tokaido train that runs between Tokyo and Osaka at up to 130 miles per hour. The planners met further delay when they could not find among U.S. railroad equipment manufacturers the desired train developmental talents and had to turn for help to companies experienced in aircraft technology. The government committed $11 million and Penn Central added more than $30 million to the Washington–New York portion of the megalopolis railroad project. By 1968 a new train was produced and this portion of the roadbed was upgraded.

But the initial $375 million for urban transportation and $90 million for intercity passenger trains were only beginnings. Seven years after the urban transit and commuter program was begun, the mayor of Seattle, speaking for the National League of Cities, complained that the federal spending was only "minimal" and that cities "are approaching chaos in the area of public transportation."[9]

Another expert on city problems asserted that a $10 billion federal outlay over the next ten years might fall far short of improving urban public transportation sufficiently to alleviate the auto traffic jams, present and future.[10]

Similarly, the $90 million for the redevelopment of intercity passenger transportation was but a drop in a very large bucket. In the first place, the more than $40 million of federal and Penn Central funds spent on the Washington–New York part of the megalopolis railroad by the end of 1968 did not magically convert the roadbed or service into the public surface transportation of the future. The start even of limited, 125-mile-per-hour service was delayed repeatedly by mechanical and technical problems that arose essentially because not nearly enough was spent to straighten and strengthen the old roadbed for high-speed trains. The real train service of the future that the planners foresee is a turbine-driven train running on an entirely reconstructed roadbed, or perhaps in a tube, at speeds up to 400 miles per hour, and it will cost billions of dollars. And if the supertrains are successful in relieving highway congestion between Washington, New York and Boston, there will be demands upon the United States Treasury for equal treatment elsewhere. Federally subsidized supertrains will be demanded for service between Chicago and Milwaukee, San Francisco and Los Angeles, Chicago and St. Louis and other pairs of cities where passenger train business has been crushed by the superhighways of the Bureau of Public Roads.

There is no longer any serious doubt that Americans will demand and need more and better passenger trains as well as urban transportation facilities in the 1970's and 1980's. The number of automobiles on the nation's streets and highways, according to the highway planners, will grow from 80 million now to 115 million by 1975. The number of trucks will grow to 20 million and each will be heavier and longer than today's trucks. Federal highway construction thus far has not been able to keep pace with traffic growth and there is little reason to believe highway building will relieve traffic congestion in the future, unless more motorists ride buses, subways and trains. Air traffic, at least at some times and places, also seems to be outdistancing the government's ability to enlarge airports and the air traffic control system. In the summer of 1968, the glut of air traffic above some large cities was such that incoming and outgoing flights at times were delayed for several hours and the Federal Aviation Administration ordered restrictions on the number of flights at the Kennedy, LaGuardia and Newark airports in the New York area, at Chicago's O'Hare Field and Washington's National Airport.

Even the Interstate Commerce Commission in 1968 seemed to be nearing the conclusion that highway and airway congestion were such that the commission should put a halt to the railroads' discontinuance of passenger trains. An ICC examiner, John S. Messer, charged in a formal opinion that the commission in allowing railroads to abandon trains since 1958 had "adopted the passive role of moderator with absolutely negative results." He recommended that the commission require railroads to provide dining service, restore sleeping cars and operate passenger trains at "not less than [the average speed] of the most expedited freight train."[11] The commission reacted by refusing to allow Southern Pacific Company to drop its Los Angeles–to–New Orleans Sunset Limited, charging that Southern Pacific had deliberately downgraded service to discourage passengers, and also by asking Congress to study the need for preservation of a "national rail passenger system."

If, then, common-carrier urban and intercity passenger services are to be preserved and expanded by federal direction and with federal monies, two questions remain. The first is whether the government and its taxpayers will be willing and able to pay these billions of dollars in addition to billions for highways and airways. The second and related question is whether uncoordinated federal planning in the future will be any more successful than it has been in the past.

There has been no taxpayers' revolt against transportation spending thus far—there only have been the revolts of citizens who don't want more highways or bigger airports in their neighborhoods. But there is evidence of a recognition, at local, state and national levels of government, that tax treasuries are not bottomless and some amount of coordination in transportation planning is essential. A number of large cities have created metropolitan area transportation authorities to coordinate bus, subway and commuter train service— although not highway construction, yet. At the federal level, the Department of Transportation was created to coordinate transportation programs.

But coordination, which must begin at the federal level, is not a fact because the Secretary of Transportation has very little influence over highway and airway spending and none over rivers spending or ocean shipping subsidies. So the questions of willingness to pay for more and better transportation and of the effectiveness of future federal planning remain unresolved issues that pit the public interest in coordination against private interests in a continuation of uncoordination. The fight is on and the public is not winning. Highway industry lobbyists in Washington, for example, have successfully opposed efforts to divert some Highway Trust Fund monies to mass transit and commuter train uses. Maritime industry and labor lobbyists are so much opposed to coordination that they successfully urged Congress to pass a bill taking the Maritime Administration out of the Commerce Department and making it a separate unit in the executive branch, with the semi-independent status enjoyed by the National Aeronautics and Space Administration. The bill, which was addressed only to the threat of coordination rather than the possibility, since the Maritime Administration was not in the Transportation Department, did not become law only because President Johnson in 1968 vetoed it. But these and other battles are only beginning.

The Regulation of Energy

No government planning for private enterprise is as old, as large, as convoluted and as conflicting as transportation planning, but all government economic planning shares some of the traits of transportation planning, for instance, the planning of the economic distribution and consumer use of energy.

There was a time, long ago, when the generation of electricity and the manufacture of gas from coal were matters involving local utilities and state regulators. Federal regulation in an embryonic form began in 1920, not for the purpose of regulating the nation's major energy supplies but because conservationists feared that construction of hydroelectric projects by local electric utilities was despoiling navigable streams and rivers that were under federal jurisdiction. It was those fears that in 1920 resulted in a federal law requiring the licensing of utility-owned dams and other projects on navigable waters. Prior to the New Deal, Washington had little interest in the price consumers paid for electricity or gas. The New Deal was vitally interested. Congress in 1933 created the Tennessee Valley Authority, which was and still is a novel experiment in government ownership of a means of production, and President Roosevelt by executive order in 1935 established the Rural Electrification Administration within the Department of Agriculture to help finance construction of public power lines in rural areas. But most of America still was supplied with electricity by privately owned utilities and Congress in 1935 enacted the Federal Power Act to place those companies under the surveillance of the Federal Power Commission, an independent agency of five commissioners. The FPC picked up the old authority to license hydroelectric projects on navigable waters and it was given new authority to police the accounting methods and securities issues of utility companies that, by reason of their location on navigable waters, were deemed in interstate commerce and thus subject to federal regulation.

The ability of the FPC in 1935 to hold down consumers' bills was severely limited, as a practical matter, because most of the electricity and gas produced by utility companies was made locally and it did not move in interstate commerce, or across state lines, on its way to the consumer. The commission thus had little control over rates. But in the 1930's, industry technology was beginning to alter the localized nature of utility companies and, in its wake, the nature of regulation. Transmission of electricity over longer distances was becoming feasible with the development of high-voltage electric power lines and movement of natural gas with the development of large-capacity gas pipeline systems. Congress responded to the latter development in 1938 by voting broad powers for the FPC to supervise the construction of natural gas pipelines from wells in the Southwest and to regulate the rates the pipelines charged big city utilities that bought natural gas for distribution to consumers. The gradual replacement of manufactured gas by natural gas has given the FPC significant powers indeed over consumers' gas bills, even though the states and cities nominally regulate consumer gas rates. So also with electricity: extra high voltage lines now make possible the interconnection of many local utility companies in vast power pools, the lines crisscrossing state boundaries, thereby broadening the FPC's authority over the electric rates ultimately paid by the consumer.

Today, Americans pay more than $6 billion annually for electricity, not only to light their homes but also to operate air conditioners, can openers and toothbrushes. Residential sales of natural gas amount to more than $4 billion annually for home heating, gas air conditioning and gas appliances. And today the federal government is deeply involved in the regulation of production and transportation of electricity and natural gas.

Federal regulation of the production of electricity and of natural gas began with the purpose of assuring consumers of cheap, abundant and dependable supplies of energy. But, as with rail, highway and other forms of transportation, the attainment of objectives is no longer so simple a matter. The Federal Power Commission still is responsible to the nation's consumers who purchase their electricity and gas from private utility companies and within the last decade the FPC has become far more involved in planning for these companies. The commission, however, does not alone bear the federal responsibility for cheap, abundant and dependable energy supplies. The government, meaning principally the Tennessee

Valley Authority and the Department of the Interior, now is a large supplier of electricity to some regions of the nation. The government, meaning the Department of Agriculture, assists local people to form electric cooperatives which supply electricity to many towns. And the government, meaning the Atomic Energy Commission, has spent billions of dollars to subsidize the development of nuclear electric power plants and other civilian uses of atomic energy.

The multiplicity of federal involvement raises a number of questions which could, in the not-distant future, loom as large as the problems now posed by uncoordinated transportation planning. Perhaps the major point of conflict ahead will relate to the AEC's development of atomic power plants for the use of private industry, and the FPC's commitment to the maintenance of a natural gas industry adequate to the nation's future needs, as well as a healthy private electric utility industry. Nor is this the only question posed. The public question most immediately at hand involves no particular conflict among government agencies but rather the Federal Power Commission's excursion into planning that bears a resemblance to what the Interstate Commerce Commission attempted in the 1920's; the ICC tried unsuccessfully to apply utility-type regulation to multiple numbers of railroads and the FPC is attempting with results still unknown to apply roughly similar patterns of uniform national planning to electric and gas companies that may be local or regional utilities but that constitute no national monopoly. One result, however, is quite well known: the great Northeast blackout of 1965 was not wholly the FPC's fault but its planning certainly was not unrelated.

The FPC for years has exercised rate and route powers over certain of the interstate aspects of the electric and natural gas industries, not unlike the powers of the Interstate Commerce Commission and the Civil Aeronautics Board in the transportation area. The FPC has a mandate also. Congress directed it in the Federal Power Act of 1935 to assure "an abundant supply of electric energy throughout the United States with the greatest possible economy and with regard to the proper utilization and conservation of natural resources." A similar policy underlies the Natural Gas Act of 1938. Under its first mandate, the FPC licenses the construction by private electric utilities of hydroelectric dams on navigable waterways, but it has only limited authority over such projects built by federal agencies such as TVA. Within its jurisdiction of investor-owned electric utilities, the commission long applied an essentially conservative type of regulation, licensing the construction of dams, case by case, without great involvement in the detailed operations of the industry.

Early in 1962 the FPC, with the cooperation of the industry, stepped off anew. It began the National Power Survey, the avowed purpose of which was to chart the future growth of the industry. More specifically, its major purpose, the FPC said, was to encourage and guide bigger and better "interconnection and coordination" of electric generating facilities. Local electric utilities all over the nation for years had been expanding their generating capacities with the growth in demand for power. Individual utilities as far back as the 1920's also had begun interconnecting their generating and distribution systems with other nearby local utilities. A utility that tied into another with surplus capacity could thereby obtain power, to help meet, say, seasonal peak demand or reserve requirements, without having to build still more capacity.

The potential advantages of larger local and regional interconnections had been long recognized by the industry and by the FPC. Pooling of generating capacities through bigger connections among utilities was obviously more efficient than construction by each individual utility of all the capacity it needed to meet peak demand. Moreover, larger interconnections could provide access to giant hydroelectric dams, such as those on the St. Lawrence and Columbia rivers, for many local utilities far distant from the dams. However, the growth of interconnections from simple ties between two local nearby utilities to regional grids has come only as industry technology has produced transmission equipment capable of safely carrying huge loads of electricity.

The Federal Power Commission had been encouraging bigger interconnections ever since the 1930's. In 1935 it complained of the "relatively haphazard" growth of the electric power industry and said more interconnections would serve "the highest public interest." But its "efforts in the past have been directed principally to interconnection studies of local electric systems," the FPC said in 1962, when it ordered the National Power Survey. "There has been no program to carry out these important responsibilities on a nationwide basis."[1] The survey, subtitled "Guidelines for Growth of the Electric Power Industry," was published in October, 1964. It was a master plan for industry progress through 1980, charting bigger interconnections "covering broad areas of the country" and looking eventually to a time when "all the electric systems in the entire nation may be joined in a single interconnected network."[2] The National Power Survey assured the nation that the power grids it proposed were safe. "Large networks can be operated in parallel with a high degree of operating stability," the survey declared. The survey dismissed the possibility that an entire regional grid could be blacked out because "it is unlikely that maximum outages of units on all systems will occur at precisely the same times."

A year plus one month later, maximum outages on systems in the Northeast power grid did occur at the same time and what happened was the most massive power failure in history. As dusk was gathering in the early evening of November 9, 1965, the lights went out in Rochester, three minutes later in Boston and seven minutes after that in New York City. Within minutes, an inconceivable power failure plunged into darkness thirty million people in an area that stretched from Lake Huron to the Atlantic and from Canada into Pennsylvania. A relay device at a hydroelectric plant near Niagara Falls had failed, and the utilities in the Northeast that were tied to it by miles of extra high voltage cable failed in chain reaction.

The Northeast power failure was no quirk. It was a demonstration of what could happen and has happened on a smaller scale in other places, when interconnections outdistance technological advances with a proven capability of handling the bigger loads. That, essentially, was the diagnosis rendered by the FPC itself, which was ordered to the scene of the disaster by President Johnson within two hours after the lights went out in New York. The commission reported back to the President that "outages of the November 9 magnitude" could recur in the Northeast or elsewhere, but "there is no reason why equipment and techniques cannot be improved to the point where the likelihood of recurrence would be . . . remote."

Power failures of relatively limited impact continued to occur. Then, in midmorning of June 5, 1967, another massive power failure occurred. Millions of consumers in the East who largely had escaped the 1965 blackout were without electricity when another power pool failed. That failure covered a 50,000-square-mile area, including portions of New Jersey, Delaware, Pennsylvania and Maryland, that was served by five utility companies tied together in the Pennsylvania-Jersey-Maryland Interconnected system. It added a new technological wrinkle to the FPC's puzzlement over why interconnections fail. A sagging high-voltage transmission line in southeastern Pennsylvania had touched another line, causing a short circuit on one line. But the commission didn't know, said its chairman, "why the loss of this one line brought about the service interruption throughout the four-state area."

Service was restored within hours after both the 1965 and the 1967 blackouts and perhaps the blackouts were a blessing in disguise, if they slowed the development of the even larger interconnections projected by the National Power Survey. On the other hand, the failure of the grids had an effect that to some degree negated the commission's basic purpose of encouraging a more efficient electric power supply. After the blackouts, many manufacturing companies, hospitals and even communities that had relied totally on the utilities to keep their lights burning invested in expensive stand-by emergency generators, just in case it happened again.

The blackouts illustrate, again, the great difficulty that the supposedly expert federal regulatory agencies universally have had in dealing with tremendously complex matters of industrial economics and technology. Interconnections of electric utilities are desirable from the consumer's point of view but pursued too rapidly they are a public inconvenience and could be a public disaster. The Federal Power Commission could not be accused of stifling technological progress in the electric power industry; its sin was trying to go too fast on the basis of technical evaluations of the safety of interconnections that proved faulty. The 1964 National Power Survey was produced at a time when the FPC was headed by a man more expert in his field than most regulators. Joseph C. Swidler, whom President Kennedy named FPC chairman in 1961, for some years had been an official of the Tennessee Valley Authority. But four years after the survey was published—and after more FPC studies of the causes and cures of blackouts—the FPC said "the growing complexity of equipment and the increasing use of electric power make blackouts more probable all the time." Indeed, power failures that the commission classed as "major" were slowly increasing to an annual rate exceeding 100.[3] And Swidler's successor, Chairman Lee C. White, was saying, "The day of predicting that it won't happen is gone."[4]

Under Joseph Swidler, who resigned from the FPC late in 1965, the commission also moved rapidly ahead under the second of its mandates, which relates to natural gas. In 1961 President Kennedy and Mr. Swidler told the nation that the FPC had failed miserably to meet its responsibility under the Natural Gas Act of 1938, of assuring consumers an abundant and cheap supply of gas. So the commission in 1961 began to make plans to assure a cheap supply. In so doing, the commission under Swidler left behind a new question for consumers: Will we also, in years to come, be denied an abundant supply of natural gas?

With the original Natural Gas Act of 1938, Congress attempted to help consumers by placing under regulation the interstate pipeline companies that transport gas from the production wells in the southwestern states to cities throughout the nation, where local utilities buy the gas for distribution to consumers. The federal government did not attempt to regulate the wholly intrastate local utilities and thus it did not directly control the consumer price of natural gas. But the theory in 1938 was that the FPC indirectly could control the consumer price by regulating the interstate pipeline companies and the prices at which they sold gas to the local distribution systems. Thus Congress gave the FPC the authority to regulate the prices charged by the pipelines and the lawmakers said no pipeline could be built or abandoned without the FPC's permission.

As early as 1940, it appeared to some that federal control over the price at which the pipeline companies delivered gas to local utilities was not enough to assure the lowest possible consumer prices. The pipeline companies were, after all, only the conduits between local intrastate utilities and gas producers. Local utilities were regulated by the states and thus were not the problem. On the other hand, gas producers were not regulated and the price pipelines paid for gas in the Southwest had a direct bearing on the price they charged local utilities in metropolitan areas throughout the nation. Pipeline companies in the United States generally have produced only a small part of their gas requirements; most gas is brought out of the ground by so-called independent producers, including many of the country's largest oil companies that produce gas as a by-product from oil wells.

The issue of whether federal regulation should be extended to independent producers began to come to a head after World War II, particularly as independent producers raised their prices and pipelines sought to pass the increases on to local utilities by posting at the FPC one price increase after another. A number of states in the large gas-consuming areas in the North argued that the commission should assume control over producers' rates and could do so under the Natural Gas Act. Some local utilities in the North took the same view. Southwestern states took the opposite view. The FPC sometimes seemed close to asserting jurisdiction but it wavered, unable to make up its mind. Congress, Presidents and politics became deeply involved. Leland Olds lost his job. But neither the FPC, Congress nor the White House settled the issue.

The Supreme Court did. The wavering FPC had ruled, in a case involving Phillips Petroleum Co., the nation's largest natural gas producer, that the Natural Gas Act did not give it authority to regulate producers' rates. The state of Wisconsin took the FPC to court and in 1954 the Supreme Court ruled that independent producers selling gas to pipelines for interstate transmission were subject to FPC rate regulation.[5]

Thus ended the confusion of indecision and began a confusion of delay and backlogs. The FPC spent the six years following the Supreme Court's 1954 decision in an attempt to decide how to regulate gas producers. There were thousands of them and they obviously were not utilities in the usual sense.

First, the commission assigned to an experienced and trusted hearing examiner, Joseph Zwerdling, the job of figuring out how to regulate producers' rates. Zwerdling held hearings within the context of the Phillips case which the Supreme Court had remanded to the commission and eventually wound up with a hearing record ten thousand pages long. Finally, in 1959, Examiner Zwerdling came up with a traditional utility-type of formula for regulating producers' rates based on production costs plus a fair return on investment. (The formula, incidentally, as applied to Phillips, required that its rates be increased!) Meanwhile, following the Supreme Court decision, thousands of producers began to comply with the High Court's edict by filing their rates with the FPC. These cases, atop the backlog of pipeline rate increase cases the commission had accumulated, added up to probably the biggest logjam in the history of the regulators.

The commission studied Examiner Zwerdling's recommended decision for a bit longer than a year, all the while watching its backlog grow bigger and bigger. In September of 1960, the commission issued its decision: it threw in the towel on any attempt to regulate each of the thousands of producers' rates on a case-by-case basis. "Producers of natural gas cannot by any stretch of the imagination be classified as traditional public utilities," the FPC decided. "The traditional . . . method of regulating utilities is not a sensible, or even a workable method of fixing the rates of independent producers of natural gas." Even if its staff were tripled, the FPC said, it would not become current in regulating producers with the case-by-case approach until the year 2043.

The decision of the Republican-led commission in 1960 was to divide the nation's gas-producing wells into twenty-three geographic areas and then set uniform prices for all producers within each area. Soon after President Kennedy took office, he drubbed the FPC for its "incredible backlog" of some four thousand gas rate increases adding up to more than $500 million a year.[6] The new President's adviser on regulatory agencies, James Landis, slapped hard at the FPC for taking six years in deciding how to regulate producers' prices, claiming, "The recent action of the commission in promulgating area rates . . . has come far too late to protect the consumer. The Federal Power Commission," Jim Landis added, "without question represents the outstanding example in the Federal government of the breakdown of the administrative process."[7]

Mr. Swidler then arrived and the FPC moved like a gazelle. The new commission cleaned up the backlog of suspended pipeline rate increases by negotiating settlements. The FPC split the difference. Of some $420 million of annual rate increases then pending, the pipeline companies for the future were allowed to retain $205 million and roll back their rates to the tune of $215 million a year. Of the nearly $1 billion by which the pipelines revenues had been increased up to 1960 by the annual rates hikes, the companies refunded $658 million to their local distributing and industrial customers and they kept a roughly equivalent sum.

The fixing of uniform ceiling prices for all future gas deliveries in each of the twenty-three producing areas proved more difficult. It was longer than four years after the arrival of Swidler that the FPC finished the first of the twenty-three area price proceedings. In August, 1965, the commission fixed prices for the big Permian Basin area of western Texas and southeastern New Mexico. The FPC transcript in the Permian Basin proceeding ran to some thirty thousand pages, but even that was not the end of it. A number of Permian Basin producers, including large oil companies such as Phillips, Standard Oil Company (New Jersey) and Texaco, Incorporated, went to court asserting that the ceiling prices the commission had fixed were too low. The appeal was settled finally in 1968 when the Supreme Court upheld the FPC's Permian Basin rates "in full."[8] The Supreme Court could hardly have done otherwise, inasmuch as it had started the whole thing. But the fact is that fourteen years passed from the time the court directed the commission to regulate natural gas producers and the time regulation became effective, in 1968, in the first group of the twenty-three production areas. Roughly two decades may well have passed before the FPC effectively regulates producers in all twenty-three areas and thus before the promise made to consumers by the Supreme Court in 1954 becomes reality.

But there is more to be said about promise and reality. The FPC, despite its earlier reluctance to regulate gas producers, has applauded its achievement in protecting consumers from upward spiraling gas prices. It is true that the commission prior to 1968 halted, at least temporarily, the upward trend of prices. It also is true that Swidler, before he resigned, talked many state regulatory agencies into requiring local gas utilities to pass on to gas consumers much of the $658 million the FPC-regulated pipelines had passed down to the utilities.

There are, however, at least two reasons why consumers might restrain their adulation. The first is that all gas producers' rates in the twenty-three production areas are not coming down. Some producers were charging rates somewhat below the ceilings the FPC fixed for the Permian Basin and will fix for other areas. These laggards have raised or will raise their rates, probably up to the maximum levels. Some other producers were charging rates that apparently were substantially below the maximums, and for these the FPC fixed and will fix minimum rates. For instance, when the

Supreme Court made the Permian Basin rates final in 1968, the FPC estimated that Permian producers as a group would then be required to reduce their rates by $16 million annually. But, the FPC added, this reduction would be "offset" by lesser millions of dollars of rate increases to be allowed producers charging less than the fixed rates. Another way of stating the matter is that the commission, in the course of fixing maximum gas producers' rates to lower consumer prices, at the same time employed its power, long familiar in the regulation of passenger and freight transportation, also to fix minimum producers' rates—presumably on the theory that low rate competition would be unhealthy for the majority of producers who were charging maximum rates.

The second reason for consumer restraint is that neither the Federal Power Commission nor anyone else can know for some years what effects the fixing of area-wide uniform maximum and minimum natural gas rates will have in the future on individual producers and on total gas production.

In arriving at the rates that producers in each area uniformly must charge, the commission did not begin with actual costs of all individual producers or prevailing field prices but instead relied on average, composite and historic cost and price data. The Supreme Court upheld this method as the only practical means of fixing uniform rates for thousands of producers. But, in fact, "no single producer's actual costs, actual risks, actual returns, are known," Justice Douglas commented in dissenting. William O. Douglas, more experienced in regulatory affairs than any of the other sitting justices in 1968, objected of course not to the FPC's purpose of protecting gas consumers but to the imprecision of its method. He was concerned with the fact that the application of average and composite costs had unknown results on individual producers and on the "level and feasibility" of total area production.[9]

In fixing uniform prices for current gas production in the Permian Basin and other areas the FPC has recognized that it might stifle initiative and thus has attempted to provide an incentive for exploration and production of new gas wells. Indeed, Chairman Swidler once said he recognized that "regulation suffers . . . from the risk of discouraging management enterprise."[10] The question left behind was whether, recognizing that risk, the FPC was successful in avoiding it. If time proves the commission was not successful, the decline of the natural gas industry could mean for millions of consumers in some future year higher gas prices and a bone-chilling shortage of natural gas.

The use of natural gas in the United States in the years since World War II has increased more rapidly than the consumption of other forms of energy. By 1964 natural gas was supplying about 30 percent of the nation's total residential and industrial fuel requirement. The United States has always had vast reserves of gas in the ground but they were of no practical meaning until they were located and pipeline technology advanced from wood to steel capable of transporting the gas in vast quantities from the Southwest to major metropolitan areas all over the country and delivering it to local utilities at prices competitive with manufactured gas, coal and oil.

As natural gas transmission companies, under FPC regulation, stretched their pipelines ever farther from the producing areas, natural gas exploration and production kept pace. In 1940, for instance, only about 3 trillion cubic feet of natural gas was produced and the nation's estimated reserves in gas fields that had been located and proved stood at only 85 trillion cubic feet. In 1950 production was up to 7 trillion feet and estimated proven reserves were up to 185 trillion feet.[11]

Natural gas consumption, production and reserves all have continued to increase in the years since 1950. In 1965 production was up to 16 trillion feet and proven reserves were 286 trillion feet. But two things have happened in the years since the Supreme Court told the FPC to regulate producers' rates and the commission began to comply. First, gas exploration activity has declined sharply. Secondly, proven reserves have declined relative to production and consumption, even though reserves in absolute terms have continued to increase. There are a number of influences behind both trends, but the FPC would appear to be a major one.

Exploration activity began to decline in 1956, two years after the Supreme Court decision. The number of exploratory wells completed in the United States in 1965 was roughly one-third less than the number of "wildcat" wells completed in 1957.

The decline in the ratio of proven reserves to annual production is a longer-term trend that began immediately after World War II as natural gas consumption climbed. In 1945, proven reserves were more than 30 times production in that year. In 1954, the year of the

Supreme Court decision, reserves were equal to 22.5 times annual production. At that time, the FPC seemed to take the position that the country needed proven reserves of at least 20 times annual production to be on the safe side; at least, the FPC would not approve a pipeline construction project unless the transmission company was assured of enough gas to supply the project for a minimum of 20 years.

By 1963 reserves were down to 19 times annual production, in 1964 the ratio of reserves to production was 18.3 to 1, and in 1965 the ratio fell to 17.6 to 1. The significance of this decline as a statistic is debatable. Gas producers claim the FPC's area price ceilings were wiping out "the incentive necessary to explore for and produce the tremendous new reserves of natural gas that will be necessary to provide fuel for the warmth and convenience of thousands of American homes in the next decade. The public will go cold!"[12] The FPC, even though it now was approving pipeline construction projects with an assurance of only nine to twelve years' supply of gas, preferred to look on the more positive side of national gas reserves. Proven reserves were indeed continuing to increase, to 286 trillion cubic feet at the end of 1965, even though the ratio of reserves to production was declining.

The FPC also shared Chairman Swidler's feeling that regulation can discourage management initiative. Exploration is a risky business; the rule of thumb is that only one out of every eight or nine wildcat wells completed proves to be a producer. Recognizing all this and declaring that "a strong exploration program which will discover and develop gas reserves in ample time to meet the increasing demands is vital," the FPC tried to keep down producers' prices and at the same time not discourage exploration. Its method was to fix one ceiling price on gas from existing wells and a higher price on gas from new wells. In the Permian Basin, the commission set a ceiling price of 16.5 cents per thousand cubic feet of gas delivered from new wells and 14.5 cents on gas from old wells.

Only time will tell whether that attempt to avoid the recognized risk of regulation will succeed. The FPC believes it will. On the other hand, even some local utilities that originally argued for federal regulation of producers' prices are no longer so sure; they worry that the decline in exploration eventually will threaten their supply of gas to sell to consumers.

The United States is not running out of natural gas. Geologists believe, as the FPC recently said, that "the remaining volumes of gas yet to be discovered and economically produced in the United States range from 500 trillion to 2,000 trillion cubic feet." But that gas will be of no practical use to the nation until and unless new gas fields are discovered and added to the nation's proven reserves.

The Federal Power Commission can, of course, in the future adjust the field price of natural gas upward in an effort to stimulate greater exploration activity. However, raising prices to accommodate a production objective and, on the other hand, keeping prices down to serve the consumers' interest is a highly uncertain kind of balancing act, as the Interstate Commerce Commission's experience has demonstrated. Moreover, ICC experience suggests that the FPC's assumption of planning responsibility for natural gas, from the wellhead to the city gate, comes at a particularly unfortunate time. Quite by accident, the FPC has taken over at precisely the time when the billions of dollars with which the Atomic Energy Commission for years has been promoting the nuclear generation of electricity apparently are beginning to pay off. It does not require a great deal of imagination to see the FPC in a few years laboring to defend the natural gas industry against an indirectly subsidized electric utility industry, much as the ICC has tried to protect railroads from the onslaught of other transportation industries which are indirectly subsidized by other government agencies.

America's fascination with atomic energy began, of course, when two atomic bombs were dropped on Japan in 1945. The United States had a monopoly of the military applications of atomic energy and the civilian applications appeared no less overwhelming. We tended, in fact, to rationalize our creation of the bombs with our expectations of the great good that atomic energy would bestow on mankind. Congress was quite convinced that atomic energy would "cause profound changes in our way of life."

Almost immediately, the United States faced the issue of military versus civilian control of this new form of energy. It decided on civilian control and in 1946 Congress placed the nation's trust in a commission of five. The AEC was and still is unique, in several ways. It is the only major government agency with both military and civilian responsibilities and it is the only multimember government agency with operating as well as regulatory functions. The commission assumed ownership of major production and laboratory facilities, such as those at Oak Ridge, Los Alamos and Hanford. Since 1947, it has spent more than $40 billion on development of nuclear weapons, nuclear generation of electric power, nuclear propulsion of ships and submarines and a wide assortment of other projects.

The expectations that brought forth the Atomic Energy Act of 1946 were, as it turned out, a bit too large. Nuclear research and development produced results, such as the United States' fleet of nuclear-powered submarines and warships, where construction and operating costs are irrelevant. But the AEC was not able to promote, with the same degree of success, a civilian nuclear industry. Congress therefore amended the 1946 Act in 1954. The original law had created an absolute government monopoly of commercial uses of nuclear energy. Although most of the AEC's research and development operations were conducted by private contractors, principally very large corporations such as General Electric Company, all of the processes and products were the property of the government. Private patents generally were not allowed and the AEC regulated the use of those that were permitted. In 1954, Congress amended the law to loosen the monopoly in order to attempt to induce industry to contribute more to the development of civilian uses of nuclear energy. Inventions produced in work on a government project continued to be the property of the government. But somewhat greater latitude was permitted private patents of civilian applications and the commission was authorized to license private construction and ownership of atomic power plants and nuclear fuel.

Nuclear energy has not yet profoundly changed our way of life because the AEC has not demonstrated that nuclear energy performs a great number of tasks better or cheaper than conventional ways of doing things.[13] The N.S. *Savannah*, a nuclear-powered merchant ship built by the AEC and the Maritime Administration, remains a very large and handsome white elephant because she has not shown that nuclear propulsion of a commercial vessel is competitive with oil as a ship fuel. But the AEC is licensing private electric utilities to build an increasing number of nuclear electric generating plants. Thus far, all are being built under developmental licenses, rather than commercial licenses. (Before the commission may issue a commercial license, it is required to find that a nuclear generating plant is economically practical and competitive with conventional electric generating plants, and this, according to the AEC, has not yet been established for any type of nuclear generating plant.)

The nuclear plants now built or under construction are very large and extremely costly. Consequently, they have been constructed by joint ventures of a half-dozen or so private utility companies. The joint ventures, promoted by the AEC, already are causing concern among two other agencies of government, the FPC and the Department of Justice's antitrust division.[14] Their concerns are that the big joint ventures may freeze smaller electric utility companies out of the nuclear power business and that the nuclear plants are being constructed with little reference to the nation's existing power supplies and hydroelectric projects and water resources. These concerns have not yet reached the potential conflict between nuclear generation of electricity, as promoted by the Atomic Energy Commission, and the resource of natural gas, as regulated by the Federal Power Commission. But this state of affairs, predictably, also will be reached one day.

The Master Plan for Television

Money and technology. These are the twin pillars of many a modern enterprise. Together, scientists and businessmen have created vast new industries, employing millions of workers and giving us marvelous products undreamed of a few years ago—industries like electronics, or aerospace, or modern medicine. And television.

In television the worlds of science and business come into conflict. The basic fact is that not everyone can start a television broadcasting station, no matter what his bankroll. There is a mathematical limit to the number of signals that can be put on the radio spectrum. If there are too many, you get static or interference. The radio spectrum is a resource not unlike natural gas in that it was there all the time but commercial exploitation awaited technological development. Usable spectrum space continues to grow with greater technological sophistication, but it remains a precious resource, relative to demand, in part because a large portion of the radio spectrum has been set aside in the United States for exclusive military and defense uses.

The Federal Communications Commission, established in 1934, gave consumers a single agency to regulate commercial communications by radio and by wire. Congress transferred to the FCC the authority that since 1910 had been vested in the Interstate Commerce Commission to regulate telegraph, telephone and cable companies. The FCC also acquired the authority, which under the 1927 Radio Act had been exercised by the Commerce Department, to license commercial radio broadcast stations. Commercial television broadcasting became a technological reality in the early 1940's and the commission had an unusual opportunity to mold the new medium. It experimentally set aside certain portions of spectrum space and granted some licenses for commercial station operations, but in 1948 decided this untidy approach would not do. So it placed a temporary freeze on new TV station franchises and proceeded to work on a master plan which not only would determine how many commercial and educational TV stations the nation would have but would pinpoint their locations.

The master plan unveiled on April 11, 1952, consisted of two hundred pages of fine print and was unimaginatively titled the *Sixth Report and Order on Television Allocations*. It is difficult to imagine how economic planning could have been more wrong, by the standard of what the FCC said should be and what television in fact is today. Newton N. Minow, the young Democratic lawyer from Chicago whom President Kennedy appointed FCC chairman in 1961, summed it all up when he termed television a "vast wasteland."

Fewer than half of the commercial television stations promised by the 1952 master plan have in fact come on the air. Instead of becoming the local voices of self-expression that the FCC envisioned, the television stations are dominated by an oligarchic television network industry. Instead of the diversity and competition the FCC promised, there is a sameness geared to the networks' idea of the lowest common audience denominator. In his heyday at the FCC Minow claimed, "Too many local stations operate with one hand on the network switch and the other on a projector loaded with old movies."[1] Yet, with five years of the term given him by President Kennedy still ahead of him, Mr. Minow departed the FCC,[2] and it would seem that the most obvious change since 1961 has been the network appropriation of old movies.

The FCC in 1952 was not required by the laws of science or the laws of Congress to master-plan television the way it did. It could have followed the essentially free-enterprise approach to TV that had been taken to radio. There was no master plan for radio. The Commerce Department and, after 1934, the FCC, fixed operating and engineering standards and anyone who could shoehorn a new station onto the map within those standards and without causing undue interference to other stations could have a license. The scheme provided a highly flexible commercial radio industry of powerful "clear channel" stations serving wide areas, less powerful regional stations and hundreds of local stations, many of which would be on the air only from sunrise to sunset. All told, the scheme did a reasonable job of eliminating the static and interference that government regulation initially was created to eliminate. Today it accommodates more than five thousand stations that air a diversity of noises. The only substantial complaints come from radio broadcasters who grumble at the amount of competition.[3]

Some sort of allocation of spectrum space was necessary for television in 1952. But the master plan which the FCC adopted was not grounded essentially in engineering or economic data. It began with four fundamental FCC policy decisions. The commission made its first policy choice when it rejected the essentially free entry concept, used in policing radio station signals, in favor of its down-to-the-last-detail master plan. The commission specifically rejected any "fortuitous" distribution of TV stations patterned after what it termed the "demand" method of radio allocations.

Its second policy decision was to set aside for television a very large portion of spectrum space—far more than commercial and educational stations ever have used. The commission in 1952 set aside twelve very high frequency channels plus seventy ultra high frequency channels of spectrum space for commercial and educational stations, although the lion's share of the available space has been used by commercial stations.

Third, the commission decided as a matter of policy that it would not disturb, by moving to new channels, the 108 commercial TV stations that already were on the air. These stations had begun operating, under interim FCC authority, prior to 1948.

And fourth, the commission—again, at least partially in the interest of stations that were on the air in 1948—decided that the commercial television industry should consist of a single, standard size of stations. It rejected the approach, used for radio, of three classes of stations—small, medium and large—which had fostered competition among a multiplicity of stations in every city. The FCC's plan for a standardized television industry dictated a large and well-protected operating area for each station and uniform transmitter powers and antenna heights. Each station would be separated from other stations broadcasting on the same channel by the very liberal distance of not less than 155 miles.

Having decided the policy questions, the commission handed to its staff engineers the task of drawing up the geographic master plan. The commission gave the staff these rules to follow: Every consumer household in America, no matter how far removed from an urban area, was to be within receiving range of at least one TV station; every city and town in America was to have at least one station of its own, insofar as the supply would last; and third, as many households as possible should have access to two or more stations.

The staff planners got out their maps, their 1950 census tables and their slide rules. The twelve very high frequency (VHF) channels—numbers 2 through 13 on the TV dial—could accommodate a total of over five hundred stations, given the minimum of 155 miles the commission said should separate stations on the same channel. All of the 108 stations already on the air were on choice VHF channels and the engineers had to plan around them. So they tried to spread the remaining four hundred or so VHF stations among larger cities but they also made sure that every state was assigned at least one VHF station.

When the VHF channels were used up, the planners turned to the not-so-choice seventy ultra high frequency (UHF) channels—numbers 14 through 83 on the TV dial—which, they calculated, potentially could accommodate upward of fifteen hundred stations. They alloted several hundred of these to larger cities that also had been assigned VHF stations. Then the engineers scattered the remaining UHF station assignments over the hinterlands, biggest towns first and generally one to a community as far as they went. Junction City, Kansas, was allotted one UHF station; Cincinnati got three VHF's and three UHF's and New York City got seven VHF's and two UHF's. In the final count, close to 80 percent of all the stations in the master plan were to operate on UHF.

The resulting master plan looked perfectly fair and fairly perfect. No fewer than 1250 cities and towns, beginning with New York and ending with Goldfield, Nevada, in the population scale, were allotted television stations. No state was assigned fewer than a half-dozen stations. A few large cities got as many as ten, but many communities with populations of less than four thousand got stations too. "There should be few, if any, people of the United States residing beyond the areas of television service," the planners said in the *Sixth Report and Order*, and they were certain they'd built the framework of a national competitive television industry, a system wherein all national TV networks could compete in all markets.

A dozen years and as many studies later, there were only 273 cities and towns with operating television stations. Of the 2216 commercial and educational stations allocated in a slightly updated master plan, only 628 were on the air.[4] Not a single commercial station was operating in New Jersey, which the planners said should have eight, or Delaware, which was assigned three. Of the 273 cities that did have stations, only 102 had at least three stations and thus could accommodate all the offerings of the three national television networks. Those 102 cities, of course, included the country's largest population centers. But it was estimated that 16 million American families, or about 28 percent of the population, lived in areas where television sets could not pick up all three networks.[5]

This end result of government planning was absurd. Perhaps the FCC's original mistake was to reject the "demand" method of station allocation and believe it could accurately weigh all the economic, geographic and population considerations essential to a successful television master plan. But the commission committed that error and then proceeded on to others. Certainly the largest error of the master plan was the mixing of UHF and VHF stations in the same communities. The FCC knew full well in 1952 that there is a technical difference between a VHF signal and a UHF signal and that the difference has large economic implications. The master plan tried to make them equals but the UHF signal is higher in the spectrum and does not travel as far as a VHF station signal. The economic consequence is quite simple. Commercial TV stations live on advertising revenues; TV stations' advertising rates are based, like newspaper ad rates, on the size of the audience. The farther a station's signal travels, the larger its audience, the higher its rates and the bigger its revenues.

All this the FCC knew. But it said, "We are convinced that the UHF band will be fully utilized and that UHF stations will eventually compete on a favorable basis with stations in the VHF."

That prediction, bearing a United States government seal, encouraged the establishment of more than one hundred UHF stations that subsequently went dark, most of them soon after starting up in 1953 and 1954. The experiment cost the would-be broadcasters an estimated $20 million worth of wasted investment in equipment and operating losses. Some went bankrupt. By the end of 1964, about 82 percent of the VHF commercial stations that the planners had allocated were on the air. Even a respectable 53 percent of the educational stations assigned VHF channels were operating. But in UHF's bleak desert, only 7 percent of the commercial allocations and 13 percent of the educational assignments were on the air.[6]

There were several reasons for this unforeseen result. First, it is more expensive to build a UHF station than it is to build a VHF station of comparable range. Taller antennas and more powerful transmitters cost money. Many businessmen refused to increase the size of their gamble in an already costly undertaking.

Second, the uniform geographic coverage of station signals without regard to population made little economic sense. A New York City station, according to the 1950 census data used by the planners, had within reach of its signal an audience potential of 14,332,829. With precisely the same service area, the Goldfield station would reach 3715 souls. The New York station could charge $3750 an hour for prime time advertising. The technically equal Goldfield station, if it based its rate on a similar evaluation of audience potential, would have a rate of $0.97 an hour.[7]

Third, the planners failed because they ignored almost completely the crucial effect of the networks on TV station economics. Network affiliation for most TV stations is necessary for economic survival.[8] Except in the country's largest cities, even some VHF stations have difficulty surviving without affiliation and many UHF stations haven't survived. The networks are an affiliated station's primary source of programs; stations without access to network programs must produce their own or buy them from independent producers. In either case, their costs can be substantially higher than the programming costs of affiliated stations. Network programs are an important source of revenues for an affiliated station, but they're more than that. Because network programs are popular, an affiliated station may build a loyal audience that out of habit will tune in even its non-network shows, meaning a higher advertising rate and more revenues from local advertisers. But each network normally affiliates with only one station in a city. By 1952, NBC and CBS in particular, since they'd had long experience in radio networking, had already picked their affiliates in many of the country's biggest and most lucrative television markets. All were VHF stations. Consequently the networks were then and still remain highly enthusiastic about VHF and distinctly cool toward UHF.

Allen B. DuMont Laboratories, whose DuMont Television Network was a relative newcomer to broadcasting in the 1940's, foresaw what the result would be. As the FCC in 1950 and 1951 neared the conclusion of its master plan studys, DuMont urged that all major metropolitan centers be assigned at least four VHF stations. Thus the NBC, CBS, ABC and DuMont networks would all be on equal footing in at least the biggest cities. This would take VHF channels from smaller cities but the great majority of cities still would get the same number of VHF and UHF assignments the FCC planners had proposed.

DuMont claimed that if fewer than four VHF stations were assigned to major markets, its network would have to rely on UHF stations and thus have a severe handicap in competing with the other networks. Its plan was absolutely essential to the promotion of network competition, DuMont asserted. The FCC wouldn't listen. To concentrate even a few more VHF stations in big cities would deny some other communities "the opportunity of enjoying the advantages that derive from having local outlets that will be responsive to local needs," the FCC planners said. And anyway, they added, "The commission is of the view that healthy economic competition in the television field will exist within the framework" of the FCC's own plan. DuMont's national television network died in September, 1955.

Many economic, political and technological consequences have flowed from the failure of the 1952 master plan to do what the FCC said was required in the public interest. One obvious consequence has been to create an artificial shortage of economically viable television stations. The artificial shortage of course means high profits and high values on VHF stations, particularly in large cities. A larger, network-affiliated station today carries a price tag of more than $20 million, and a large part of the price represents the piece of paper which the broadcaster received free of charge from the federal government. A Pittsburgh station, to cite an example, not long ago was sold for $20.4 million. Of this total price, only $3.9 million represented the worth of its transmitter, antenna and other physical assets. Most of the remainder reflected the value of the station's FCC license and its network affiliation contract. The inordinate and unearned worth of FCC licenses has at times given rise to "trafficking" in licenses—the acquisition and sale of licensed stations for profit by persons who have no intention of or interest in broadcasting.[9] FCC licenses, network contracts and high profits have made wealthy men of the fortunate owners of many television stations. These same elements also have brought immense political pressures on the members of the FCC.

These pressures always are, and must be if they are to be effective, secretly applied. But the public once was treated to an inside view of what can happen. The unfortunate subject of public inquiry was Richard A. Mack, a Florida Democrat whom President Eisenhower appointed to the FCC in 1955.[10]

Mack's qualifications for appointment to the FCC were that he had served on the Florida Railroad and Public Utility Commission and he was recommended to the President by Florida's two senators, George Smathers and Spessard Holland. He was sworn in as a member of the FCC on July 7, 1955, and could not have arrived at a worse time. Pending before the commission was a case involving a license to operate a new television station on Channel 10 in Miami. Four Miami applicants were competing for the franchise, worth perhaps $10 million. One was WKAT, Incorporated, a company owned by Frank Katzentine, an old friend who had helped Richard Mack get into a fraternity back at the University of Florida. Second was L. B. Wilson, Incorporated. Third was North Dade Video, Incorporated. And fourth was Public Service Television, Incorporated, a concern owned by National Airlines which at the time had its headquarters in Miami.

Station WKAT had applied for the Miami Channel 10 license in 1948. The other three had applied for the same channel in 1953. An FCC examiner had considered the four proposals and recommended, in March of 1955, that the license be awarded to Frank Katzentine's company, WKAT. Eleven days after Richard Mack was sworn in, the commission heard oral argument on the case. Mack could have, and should have, abstained from participation in the decision. He apparently intended to do so, for he did not sit in on the oral argument. On December 21, 1955, the six commissioners who did sit took a straw vote. Three votes were cast for Public Service Television, two for WKAT and one for L. B. Wilson.

Such preliminary votes, on the basis of which regulatory commissions begin to draft their formal opinions, are supposed to remain secret, but knowledge of this one leaked and, as a result, the pressures began to build on Mack. If he participated in the final vote, his vote for Frank Katzentine's WKAT would mean a deadlock which would block award of the license to Public Service Television. If he voted for Public Service, that company would have four votes and clearly be the winner.

The final vote was not taken until February 7, 1957, a bit longer than a year after the straw vote. During the year, Katzentine sought the aid not only of Senators Holland and Smathers but also of Senator Kefauver of Tennessee. A former mayor of Miami, Perrine Palmer, Jr., came into the picture at the suggestion of Senator Smathers. Palmer and Katzentine made at least two trips to Washington to talk with Commissioner Mack. Jerry Carter, another old friend from Miami, twice saw Mack to urge him in the final vote either to vote for Frank Katzentine or to abstain again. Carter also talked with another FCC commissioner, George McConnaughey. Senator Holland recommended Katzentine to both Commissioners Mack and McConnaughey. Senator Smathers spoke to Mr. Mack. It remains unclear why Senator Kefauver was interested or what action he took, but Richard Mack later complained of "too much Kefauver."

National Airlines heard of the presentations that were being made to Mack on behalf of Frank Katzentine. So it decided to hire someone to "neutralize the pressure of the opposition." It hired Thurman Whiteside, a Miami lawyer who had been a friend of Richard Mack since they were youngsters. What National Airlines apparently did not know was that Thurman Whiteside had been lending money to Richard Mack since their college days. Whiteside spoke to Richard Mack several times to obtain his favor for National's bid for the TV station. In addition, according to records disclosed later, Mack while he was a commissioner placed more than two dozen long-distance telephone calls to Whiteside in Miami.[11]

North Dade Video began to hear, too. It employed a Washington lawyer named Robert F. Jones "to try to neutralize the pressures." Jones, a former congressman and FCC commissioner, did not talk with Mack. Instead, he attempted unsuccessfully to interest Congress in a law that would have made it illegal for an airline to own a television station.

When the final vote was taken, four votes were cast for National Airlines, one for Frank Katzentine's WKAT and one for L. B. Wilson. (The seventh commissioner, T. A. M. Craven, was a new arrival who abstained.) The four votes for National Airlines were those of Commissioners Mack, McConnaughey, Doerfer and Lee.

The story might never have been told publicly, had Frank Katzentine called it quits. Instead, he submitted to the House Legislative Oversight Subcommittee, through the good offices of Senator Kefauver, an affidavit which alleged that Richard Mack had sold his vote to Thurman Whiteside for the benefit of National Airlines. The subcommittee aired the affair at public hearings, at which Richard Mack testified that his old friends from Miami had him "over a barrel." The congressional investigators learned that Mack, while a member of the FCC, received checks totaling $2600 from Whiteside. He was forced to resign from the FCC in 1958 and with Thurman Whiteside then was indicted by a federal grand jury for allegedly having conspired to arrange the award of Miami Channel 10 to National Airlines.

Whiteside was tried and acquitted. Seven months later, he shot himself to death in his Miami office. Mack's trial in 1959 ended in a hung jury and in 1961 the government dropped its charges against him. He returned to Miami and became a chronic alcoholic and psychiatric patient. On November 26, 1963, Miami police were called to investigate a complaint about a loud radio in a rooming house near the city's skid row. They found the body of Richard Mack.

As for the great prize, the FCC eventually awarded the Miami Channel 10 license to the L. B. Wilson Company, purely and simply because its hands were the cleanest of the four pairs that had been outstretched. All the technical and financial findings upon which the commission finds all TV license awards to be "in the public interest" played no more part at the dismal end of the Miami Channel 10 case than they had at the beginning.

It is impossible to know the extent to which similar pressures were and are applied or what they yield. Presumably the pressures are not so great nowadays because the FCC has given away all of the valuable VHF station licenses that are permitted by its restrictive master plan. Whatever the extent of covert political pressures on commissioners for valuable TV franchises, they were but a part of far larger political, economic and technological problems spawned by the 1952 plan.

The FCC has not been unaware of the plan's failings. Indeed, the agency from time to time since 1952 has proposed drastic revisions but each time it has withdrawn its proposal because of intense opposition exerted by television broadcasters through key members of Congress. In 1956 the FCC proposed to shift all or most all commercial TV stations to the UHF channels, and thus place the industry on an equal competitive footing, in order to encourage more UHF stations to come into operation. But VHF stations raised a howl and nothing came of it. Later, the FCC spent $2 million on another study of the "UHF problem." Then "deintermixture" became the slogan. The idea was to unscramble VHF and UHF stations by converting all the stations in particular cities to one or the other. Senator John O. Pastore, a Democrat from Rhode Island who is one of the few key members of Congress who retained an independence of judgment on the matter, said, "At long last, a partial solution." But very little happened because entrenched TV station owners again objected vehemently. Nine bills were introduced in the House to stop the unscrambling process and, though no law was enacted, the FCC quit.

Then, in 1962, Congress enacted the All-Channel Receiver Act, which put the blame for UHF's failure on the manufacturers of TV receivers and consumers who bought them. The law required all U.S. manufacturers and importers to equip all new sets with the capability to receive all seventy UHF channels as well as the twelve VHF channels. Manufacturers since the 1940's had been making all-channel receivers but production had declined because there was little to see on the UHF channels and consumers were not buying the sets. The new law gave consumers no choice but to buy all-channel sets and to pay the added cost, which variously has been estimated at $3 to $5 per receiver. For their investment, consumers in some cities are seeing a few more commercial and educational UHF stations. It remains extremely doubtful, however, that the All-Channel Act will succeed in its stated purpose of rescuing the FCC's master plan by attracting to the air hundreds of additional commercial UHF stations. By the end of 1968, only about 100 commercial UHF stations were operating, out of the more than 600 channels reserved; about 95 educational UHF stations were broadcasting, compared with more than 500 channels reserved.

The master plan, its failure and the repeated rescue attempts have combined to produce strange consequences indeed. Because the plan has not provided all Americans with all the television fare they want and are willing to pay for, two new industries have sprung up. One is cable-TV, or community antenna television (CATV). The second, which exists more in theory than in fact, is subscription television, or pay-TV. The continuing battles of these two industries for the right to survive, despite repeated political setbacks, are evidence enough that the All-Channel Act has not succeeded.

Cable-TV is a relatively simple commercial enterprise. An individual or company puts up a high master antenna to serve a town that has no TV station of its own or is too distant from the nearest station for good reception, or a town or city where people want more or better TV fare than is delivered by the local station or stations. The master antenna picks up TV stations' signals from one or more distant cities. The signals are amplified and distributed locally by wire into the homes and apartments of people who pay a monthly fee for the service. By 1964, when FCC restrictions began to have an effect, more than 1.2 million American families were paying on average sixty dollars yearly for CATV service.[12] Or, put another way, Americans were paying $72 million yearly to purchase television fare that the FCC's master plan was not providing.

The FCC and the commercial television industry didn't pay much attention to CATV in the beginning in the early 1950's when enterprising individuals first erected master antennas in the mountains of Pennsylvania and the Far West to import television signals into the small towns in the valleys. Their attention and hostility mounted in the 1960's as CATV spread to smaller cities with one or two TV stations of their own and then threatened to move into New York and the nation's other large cities. The agency, openly and frankly fearful that CATV would take audiences and advertising revenues from existing TV stations and diminish further the commercial attractiveness of unused UHF station assignments, several times asked Congress for authority to regulate CATV systems. The Senate Commerce Committee voted out a bill providing the authority but no bill was enacted. Apparently the CATV industry's lobbying efforts against the FCC and the broadcasting industry succeeded in stalemating Congress.

In asking Congress for legislation, the FCC had said it had no power to control CATV either under its authority to regulate use of the airwaves or its authority to regulate wire transmissions by telephone and telegraph companies. Nonetheless, in 1962 it employed its authority over airwaves to place certain restrictions on CATV systems that utilized microwave links in their antenna-to-TV-set distribution of imported signals. Then, in 1966, the commission went all the way, claiming jurisdiction over all CATV systems. In so doing, it ruled that CATV systems henceforth could not expand in any of the nation's hundred largest commercial TV markets—meaning generally the hundred largest cities—without a prior commission finding that the expansion would not threaten the "healthy maintenance of television broadcast service in the area." Cable-TV companies appealed to the Supreme Court, which in 1968 upheld the FCC's assertion of jurisdiction. The High Court acknowledged Congress' failure to act, but held that FCC regulation of CATV was a reasonable extension of powers Congress had given to regulate the airwaves and wire communications. "The commission," the court said, "has reasonably concluded that regulatory authority over CATV is imperative if it is to perform with appropriate effectiveness certain of its other responsibilities."[13]

Pay-television has not gotten even as far as community antenna television. Pay-TV proposals differ from CATV in that pay-TV originates its own programming rather than picking up commercial TV stations' programs. Pay-TV permits a consumer to sit in front of his home receiver and, usually by inserting coins in a little black box attached to the set, watch events which do not normally appear on commercial TV, such as Broadway plays, sporting events and symphony concerts. There are basically two kinds of pay-TV systems. One utilizes an FCC-licensed television station to transmit its signals over the air into subscribers' homes. The second avoids the FCC, or tries to, by transmitting its programs not by way of the airwaves but by leased telephone lines or other wires.

The FCC has kept an extremely tight rein on pay-TV by airwave. It has allowed the use of licensed TV stations only on a limited, experimental basis and only one significant pay-TV venture found the FCC's rules sufficiently acceptable to go on the air. That experiment was the one conducted in Hartford, Connecticut, by Zenith Radio Corporation and RKO General, Incorporated. The Hartford experiment ended early in 1969, shortly after the FCC resolved its indecision concerning the service pay-TV should be allowed to render to the American public. The FCC, seventeen years after beginning its first study of pay-TV, decided to authorize on a permanent basis the use of one television station in each large city for pay-TV. But the commission prescribed various restrictions to protect "free" TV from pay-TV competition; several, for example, absolutely barred pay-TV outlets from "siphoning" sports events and other programs usually broadcast by regular commercial stations.

Ventures in pay-TV by wire have gone absolutely nowhere in the United States and the FCC has not had to decide whether to assert jurisdiction. A successful pay-TV system would require a very large investment in programming not now on the networks or in the acquisition of programming, such as professional baseball and football games, that are now on the advertiser-supported networks. The only well-organized and adequately financed attempt to establish a permanent pay-TV system in this country was one tried in California. Its backers were prepared to invest $25 million to end-run the FCC by using wires to distribute their television fare.[14] Presumably the FCC could have stretched its Supreme Court–approved jurisdiction over CATV to the California pay-TV system. But the system was stopped cold by California TV broadcasters and movie-house owners who got out the votes in a state-wide referendum that was held in November, 1964. The referendum vote held pay-TV to be illegal. Subsequently, the courts held that the pay-TV referendum was unconstitutional. But the organizers of the venture meanwhile went into bankruptcy proceedings.

In sum, pay-TV and CATV are intruders on the FCC's master plan and its industry of commercial television stations and networks. The competitive potential of each has been demonstrated; elements of both could be combined (as they recently have been, on a small scale, in New York City) in a national subscription television service that would originate and re-transmit a great variety of TV fare and that would revolutionize television, as we know it. The FCC has responded to the existing and potential threats of pay-TV and CATV as the CAB earlier reacted to the intrusion of the nonscheduled airlines: by attempting to carve out for the newcomers a small role within which they will supplement but not compete with the established companies in the industry. Yet, the established commercial TV broadcasters and their friends in Congress opposed even these small roles and consequently the future of pay-TV and CATV may be no brighter than that of the supplemental airlines.

There is a final comment to be made about the FCC and its television master plan. The FCC's fundamental task is to preserve the public interest in private use of the frequency spectrum, which by law is a public resource which commercial interests use but to which they do not acquire legal title. It is for this reason that the government does not "sell," or make a charge for, station licenses and that a license is, at least in theory, revocable.[15] By reserving vast quantities of spectrum space for UHF broadcast stations that have never come on the air, the FCC has squandered the very resource it was created to husband.

Commercial broadcasting is the spectrum usage with which the public is most familiar, but it is not and never has been the most vital use. Long before the FCC came along, radio was used in the rescue of distressed ships at sea, and the first police use of radio was in 1916 when the New York City Police Department began operating a station to talk with its harbor patrol boats. The Radio Act of 1912, which marked the beginning of federal allocation of the spectrum and licensing of users, did not anticipate commercial broadcasting and in 1925, when Herbert Hoover as Secretary of Commerce was helping to rewrite the act, he complained about the fledgling broadcasting industry's "naked commercial selfishness." When the FCC came along, some fifty thousand radio users, including 623 commercial radio stations, were under federal license. Today, more than 1.4 million licenses are outstanding, covering more than 4 million fixed and mobile transmitters. Hundreds of thousands of licenses have been issued for marine and air navigation, fire and police protection, taxicab and truck and railroad communications and many other industrial uses. United States Steel Corporation, for example, holds more than 3500 licenses for fixed and mobile radio transmitters. Its eight planes and sixty-nine Great Lakes ore boats and river vessels are licensed for communications and navigation purposes; it uses radio for control of locomotives, bulldozers and overhead cranes; radio coordinates activities of personnel operating over large areas in ore, coal mining and steelmaking operations; it is used by plant foremen for materials handling and by plant guards for dispatching fire equipment and ambulances.

Demand for frequencies has been heavy since the 1920's and technology has increased usable spectrum space. Since World War II, however, demand from police, industrial and broadcasting users has outdistanced the increase in usable space and, in spite of the development of transistors and other devices that have made usage more efficient, the FCC has had to ration frequencies and require large numbers of users to share them. The arrival of commercial television broadcasting after the war created an enormous demand for spectrum space. A single TV station's picture and sound transmissions require about two hundred times the spectrum space occupied by a standard AM radio station; the single TV station needs about six times the spectrum space assigned to all AM radio stations as a group. Stated another way, when the FCC in 1952 set aside eighty-two channels, or groups of frequencies, for television broadcasting, it reserved 492 megacycles of spectrum space. Only 4 megacycles of space can accommodate 160 separate business or industrial radio users in each metropolitan area of the country.

The reservation of unused space for UHF broadcasting represents a waste of frequencies and a denial to business and industry of a useful production tool. The National Association of Manufacturers has asserted that many business concerns have discontinued use of radio and others have not started because of interference due to congestion on the frequencies assigned to business and industrial use. With as many as thirty business users assigned to a single frequency, as in the Los Angeles area, "a substantial number have been forced to discontinue the use of radio because of their complete inability to establish even a reasonable standard of communication," said the NAM.[16] The unavailability of more spectrum space has concerned the New York City Police Department, caused congestion in communications between aircraft and control towers at some major airports and prevented the full development of telephone service in family automobiles.[17]

There also appears to be evidence that the FCC's reservation of space for UHF broadcasting has tended to discourage research looking toward broader and more efficient use of the spectrum. A highly placed committee of industry and university spectrum specialists recently wrote that the radio spectrum is a resource that "neither precedents nor pressures should be allowed to waste." Too often, the statement continued, allocations of spectrum space are made not so much on technical grounds as on "rather drastic social-political type" grounds. As a result, it added, the coordination of radio system design with spectrum usage "has not been consistently good. Dependence on 'squatters rights' has often made the introduction of improvements in the art woefully slow."[18]

The complexities of frequency allocation and licensing undeniably are great and perhaps are greater than those with which the other federal regulatory agencies must deal. Government regulation of the frequency spectrum, moreover, is a matter of necessity, required by the limited nature of this public resource; regulation in other areas has come into being by political choice. The FCC owes its duty to the people, no less than any other agency. Congress created it to "make available . . . to all the people of the United States a rapid, efficient, nation-wide and world-wide wire and radio communication service." The annals of the FCC suggest it could manage the complexities to the reasonable satisfaction of the people, if it were allowed to be truly independent and expert. Instead, the political pressures and industry self-interests have combined to repress CATV and pay-TV and increase the prices consumers pay for TV sets, all in the name of saving the television master plan. In television, the regulatory maelstrom is most turbulent because here politicians and broadcasters are one in the same.

Lyndon Baines Johnson was the most illustrious of them. He was a broadcaster for almost as long as he held political office. He arranged for the purchase of an Austin, Texas, radio station that was the beginning of the family's interest in a chain of radio and television properties. The stocks were held by Mrs. Johnson, but Mr. Johnson's attention to operating and financial details never waned. The broadcasting stations built the family fortune that enabled him to concentrate on his political career. Mrs. Johnson placed her stocks in trust after he became President in 1963 and removed them when he left office in 1969.

The tale of the LBJ radio empire begins in 1942, when Lyndon Johnson was a thirty-four-year-old Texas congressman with five years in the United States House of Representatives already to his credit.[19] He had just finished an active duty stint in the Navy, during which time Mrs. Johnson had kept shop at his House office. At that time the Johnsons were intrigued to hear that KTBC, an Austin radio station serving his constituents, might be for sale.

It was just before Christmas, 1942, and young Congressman Johnson, back home in Texas for the holidays, learned that a local group already had an option to buy the station. Johnson approached a member of the group whom he knew rather well, E. G. Kingsbery. According to the Kingsbery version of what happened, as told many years later, Johnson reminded Kingsbery that the year before he had appointed Kingsbery's son to the United States Naval Academy and then announced that the Johnson family would like to have the station. Kingsbery put the congressman in touch with the group's lawyer and the result was that Mrs. Johnson purchased KTBC.

She bought it in early 1943 and the purchase was approved by the FCC, after she had recited her qualifications: service on Capitol Hill; experience in administering her personal inheritance; a balance sheet showing assets of $64,332, partly liquid and partly in real estate; and a pledge of "full time and energetic efforts" to be a broadcaster.

Station KTBC had been headed by a Texan named Robert B. Anderson, a man whose financial genius was sufficient to lift him later to the post of Secretary of the Treasury under President Eisenhower, but insufficient then to keep KTBC out of the red. The outfit had lost $7231 in 1942, on revenues of $26,795. The basic reasons for the station's financial trouble, according to A. W. Walker, one of the former owners, were that "we did not have a network affiliation and couldn't operate at nighttime." As a matter of fact, KTBC had only leftover hours of broadcasting, because all that the original owners had been able to win from the FCC after a long struggle was the right to share a transmitting wave length primarily assigned to Texas A&M College.

Mrs. Johnson paid $17,500 for KTBC. She quickly asked the FCC to grant the station unlimited broadcasting hours and to quadruple its 250-watt transmitting power. Permission was granted for both; the former required FCC allocation of an entirely different wave length. She also pursued network affiliation. An NBC executive, who was a friend of Congressman Johnson at the time, said later that, regretfully, Lady Bird Johnson's request for his network's programs had to be turned down because of the objection of a San Antonio affiliate. But she rapidly won affiliation with CBS.

In August, 1943, KTBC achieved its first profit, $18, and the Johnson good fortune improved constantly thereafter. The $17,500 investment, by the most conservative estimate, grew more than two-hundredfold; assets of $4,315,828 were shown on the balance sheet for the family company's fiscal year ended June 30, 1964. Experts have estimated that the actual market value of the enterprise might be more than $7 million. The company's profit and loss statements disclose that operating profit for the 1964 fiscal year (the last year for which figures are publicly available) was $338,079; net profit, including dividends and other income, was $685,157.

The LBJ careers in broadcasting and in politics grew side by side, with their branches intertwining. A number of noted men assisted the growth of both careers, serving at times on Mrs. Johnson's broadcasting staff and at other times on Mr. Johnson's political staff. One was John B. Connally, later Secretary of the Navy and governor of Texas and always Lyndon Johnson's closest political and personal confidant. Another was J. J. "Jake" Pickle, who was elected to Congress from Johnson's old Austin congressional district after the Kennedy assassination in 1963. Still another was J. C. Kellam, who back in the 1930's had been with the National Youth Administration when Johnson was NYA director for Texas and who rose to become president of the Johnson broadcasting company. A fourth was Walter Jenkins, who for many years served simultaneously as Mr. Johnson's administrative assistant in Washington and as Mrs. Johnson's corporate treasurer in Austin. After Johnson became President, Jenkins moved into the White House, occupying the old office once occupied by Sherman Adams; only then did Jenkins relinquish his role as corporate treasurer and place his relatively small holding of Johnson company stock in a trust.

Lyndon Johnson himself at no time held office or stock in the broadcasting enterprise. The FCC's public records contain but one letter from Johnson, although the agency's files on KTBC since 1942 contain many license renewal and other applications, as do the files on all stations. Records of House and Senate floor debates similarly show no participation by Representative or Senator Johnson in debate on broadcasting industry matters, although Congress of course involved itself time and again in industry and FCC affairs over the years of the Johnson stations' greatest growth. Johnson was elected to the Senate in 1948, and promptly moved to a seat on the Commerce Committee; this was the year the FCC began its study of national television allocations. By 1951 he had in addition become Democratic whip, thus holding his party's number two power position in the Senate. The following year, the FCC unveiled its TV master plan and from then until 1961, when Johnson left the Senate to become Vice President, the commission and Congress engaged in a more or less constant dialogue over the master plan's failings.

Quite apparently, there was no need for Senator Johnson to write letters to the FCC or engage in open floor debate. The family interest in broadcasting was no secret. Mrs. Johnson's stock holdings were a matter of public record at the FCC. Indeed, the name of the company was changed in 1956 from Texas Broadcasting Company to the LBJ Company. Senator Johnson was well known to the commissioners as well as to broadcasting industry executives. The KTBC stations since 1943 have been affiliated with the Columbia Broadcasting System and Johnson's friends of prominence long have included CBS President Frank Stanton. Among those less well known was Frank Russell, who for many years was NBC's Washington vice president. One day in 1962, when a testimonial luncheon honoring Russell was held at the Mayflower Hotel in Washington, Vice President Johnson sat next to him at the head table and rose to deliver ten minutes of reminiscences about their long friendship. Among the more than one hundred guests present were all the members of the FCC, the president of NBC, other network executives and key members of Congress including Chairman Oren Harris of the House Commerce Committee.

The Johnson broadcasting properties grew not because Johnson asked favors but, as one FCC official has remarked, because Mrs. Johnson was consistently "lucky." In 1952, when the FCC unrolled the master plan and lifted the freeze on new television station grants, Austin was allocated one very high frequency channel and two ultra high frequency channels. With a population of 132,459, according to the 1950 census, that apparently is all Austin deserved. But it also is to be noted that Austin was and still is one of the largest cities to receive a single VHF channel; FCC experts have said it is "among the top four or five single-station markets" in the nation.

The commission announced publicly on April 14, 1952, that Austin had been allocated VHF Channel 7. The Johnson company had applied for precisely that channel one month earlier. On July 1, the FCC began processing 716 applications then on file for new television stations. Ten days later it issued its first group of permits to eighteen fortunate applicants, among them the Johnson company. By October, KTBC-TV was putting TV pictures on the airwaves in Austin.

There are those at the FCC who believe to this day that the commission made great haste in processing that stack of 716 applications to get to the one signed by Claudia T. Johnson. In the opinion of one veteran FCC staff aide, "they hurried without being asked," in due deference to the senator from Texas who then was number two Democrat in the Senate and a member of the Commerce Committee.

No rival applicant had contested Mrs. Johnson's application, and her record in radio left no doubt of her broadcasting qualifications. The financial statement her company submitted to the FCC, to demonstrate its capability of building and operating a television station, showed that the property purchased not a decade earlier for $17,500 in 1951 had assets of $488,116 and a net profit for the year of $57,983.

As a footnote, it must be observed that there were other people who did want to televise from Austin. Applications for both of the UHF stations were filed with the FCC and granted in the summer of 1952. Why did these two groups not seek the choice VHF allocation? The recipient in 1952 of one of the two UHF channels, a Dallas television broadcaster named Tom Potter, has supplied an answer: "Lyndon was in a favorable position to get that station even if somebody had contested it. Politics is politics." In fact, the two groups that received the Austin UHF permits within less than a year handed the permits back to the FCC, as did many other UHF licensees throughout the country. Consequently, the Johnson station for many years enjoyed a television monopoly in Austin and was affiliated in one way or another with all three national television networks, although the KTBC stations' primary affiliation always has been with CBS.

The Johnson broadcasting interests also began to expand beyond Austin in the early 1950's. The company first looked ninety-six miles northward to Waco, Texas, and it was in connection with this venture that Senator Johnson wrote to the FCC, although the letter at the time gave no indication that the Johnson fortune ultimately was to be advanced. The letter was written in February, 1952, at a time when video had not reached Waco and shortly before the FCC lifted its freeze on new station assignments. The Senator asked for information on the status of a TV application which had been filed by KWTX Broadcasting Company, operator of a Waco radio station, explaining that he was asking on behalf of a constituent who held stock in the KWTX company. Competing applications filed for the VHF channel assigned to Waco had delayed an FCC award. In April of 1953 Johnson again wrote to the commission, this time on stationery of the "Office of the Democratic Leader," inquiring about the Waco TV situation and urging "serious consideration to this problem, based on its merits."

On December 2, 1954, the commission awarded KWTX Broadcasting Company the Waco VHF permit and almost simultaneously it became apparent that the Johnson company also had been watching the Waco TV situation. Indeed, Waco's new KWTX-TV almost immediately found itself subjected to what it later claimed was a two-pronged Johnsonian invasion.

First, the FCC on December 1, 1954, authorized the Johnson company to purchase for $134,000 a debt-burdened UHF television station which had started broadcasting in Waco the previous year. The new KWTX-TV, which had been seeking network affiliation without success, told the FCC it was dismayed to observe that after the Johnson company took over, the Waco UHF station obtained both CBS and ABC affiliations.

Second, in March of 1955 the Johnson station in Austin asked the FCC for a large increase in transmitting power, to 247 kilowatts from 100. At this point Waco's KWTX-TV, just getting into operation, exploded in violent opposition. It complained to the FCC that Austin's Channel 7 broadcasting arc, which hitherto had overlapped only the southern fringe of the KWTX-TV audience range by 91 square miles, would with such an increase in transmitting power multiply the overlap to 740 square miles. The Waco VHF station protested to the commission that the Johnson company was violating antitrust law through ownership of the Austin VHF station and the Waco UHF station and their network contracts. Stronger transmitting power for the Austin station, KWTX-TV continued, would not only increase the Johnson station's strength in bidding for advertising revenues in the overlap area but also would enable it to "strengthen and solidify its monopolistic activities" in the enlarged area it alone would serve.

The Johnson company replied to the FCC that these accusations were "entirely without substance." And then, surprisingly, the Waco company suddenly seemed to agree. In mid-May of 1955, KWTX-TV tersely told the FCC it wished to withdraw its objection, "certain facts having been brought to the attention" of its executives. The regulatory agency permitted the withdrawal the same day, although it was given no further explanation and apparently sought none. Then the commission granted the Johnson company's Austin station its requested transmitting power increase. (This has been permitted to rise since, to 295 kilowatts, almost thrice the original wattage.)

What happened to cause KWTX-TV to withdraw from the fight? According to sources that were intimately involved, the Waco company, lacking confidence that the FCC would heed its complaint, had prepared a private antitrust suit against the Johnson company and was ready to file it in a United States district court in Texas. But the lawsuit served, at most, as a catalyst. It never was filed. Instead, the dispute resolved into a fast-breaking deal. The Johnson company, paying no cash, received 29 percent of the stock of Waco's KWTX Broadcasting Company, and KWTX-TV received the CBS and ABC network affiliations it never before had been able to obtain. The ABC affiliation agreement was dated May 16, the same day KWTX withdrew its objection to the power increase sought by the Johnson station in Austin. Finally, ownership of the UHF station in Waco, so recently acquired by the Johnson company, was transferred to KWTX Broadcasting Company—which by the end of 1955 simply shut down this previous competitor.

Thus, the Johnson company had succeeded both in expanding its audience and advertising market in Austin and in becoming the largest single owner of what was converted into a single-station Waco TV operation. The value of the former feat is difficult to calculate, but industry experts have figured that the 29 percent stock interest in the Waco company is worth roughly $600,000.

After its successful excursion to the north, the Johnson company turned southward to Weslaco, Texas, a town less than ten miles from the Gulf of Mexico. There KRGV-TV, owned by O. L. Taylor, had gone on the air in 1954 but had not been able to obtain network affiliation and had sunk into financial difficulty. Two groups in 1956 wanted to come to the rescue of KRGV-TV. One was the LBJ Company and the other was a Texan named H. C. Cockburn. The FCC dismissed the Cockburn bid and approved the LBJ intervention. The Johnson company paid $5000 for 50 percent of Weslaco Television Company and promised to lend $140,000.

Within months, KRGV-TV in Weslaco gained FCC permission to increase its transmitting power to 100 kilowatts from 28.8 and signed network contracts with NBC and ABC. In 1957 the KRGV radio station, owned separately by Taylor, was transferred to Weslaco Television Company. The following year, the Johnson company with FCC approval purchased from Taylor the remaining 50 percent of the Weslaco Television Company stock, paying $100,000. Having gathered everything into one basket and tidied it up, the Johnson Company in 1961 sold the whole works. Taylor later figured the LBJ Company had put about $600,000 into the venture, including assumed debt and loans forgiven. The Johnson company sold out for more than double that amount: $1.4 million.

Thus did the Johnson family fortune grow. Mrs. Johnson's contributions as a businesswoman are not to be underrated, nor are Mr. Johnson's as a businessman. She has said publicly that LBJ Company executives in Austin dispatched to Washington weekly reports of such detail that they recited every call made by the Austin stations' advertising salesmen, including "the pitch he gave them, the response he got from the merchant." A broadcasting executive who is an old family friend has said privately that these weekly reports were studied assiduously in Washington by Lady Bird, Lyndon and Walter Jenkins. Other facets of the tale will never be known in full. For example, during the 1964 Senate investigation into the business affairs of Robert Baker, the freewheeling secretary to the Senate's Democratic majority during the 1950's when Johnson was majority leader, Baker refused to answer whether he had urged national advertisers to buy time on the Johnson stations.[20] But a Washington insurance agent, Don Reynolds, told the Senate investigators he had sold $200,000 worth of insurance on Johnson's life to the LBJ Company and, in exchange for getting the insurance business, had bought time on the Johnson stations in Austin and also had made a gift of a hi-fi set to the senator in Washington. Then there was the matter of the house at 1901 Dillman Street, the Johnsons' residential address in Austin for many years while he was in Congress. A number of the Johnsons' friends, some of whom at one time or another were employees of the Johnson stations—John Connally, Walter Jenkins, Willard Deason, Jesse Kellam, Edward Clark and J. J. Pickle among them—applied to the FCC for a new radio station license in Austin, using the 1901 Dillman address. The

FCC could not have assumed that the Johnsons were seeking a second Austin radio station, for it is illegal for the owner of one radio outlet to have any interest in a second one in the same city. The FCC granted the license to KVET, apparently without bothering to check on the coincidence of the address.

It was not until Johnson became President in 1963 that Mrs. Johnson resigned as chairman of the board of the LBJ Company and placed her broadcasting stock in trust. The name of the company also was changed back to Texas Broadcasting Corporation. These details were handled by Leonard Marks, the Washington lawyer who was counsel to the Johnson stations, and Abe Fortas, the attorney in Washington who for many years handled the Johnsons' personal legal matters. Named as trustees of Mrs. Johnson's stock were A. W. Moursund and J. W. Bullion, very old Texas friends of Lyndon Johnson.

The stock remained in trust while Johnson remained in the White House. During those years, the profits of the broadcasting properties continued to accrue to Mrs. Johnson and the stations continued to do business with the FCC, obtaining license renewals, purchasing a CATV system in Austin and so forth. Whether the trusteeship in fact made any difference is questionable. A Republican FCC commissioner said privately it "means nothing. The Johnsons retain beneficial interest. They'll get the management of the stations back when Lyndon leaves office." Said a Democratic commissioner: "Of course, every commissioner and every member of the staff is aware" of the presidential family's continued interest. He termed the trusteeship "a halfway measure that does not divorce the family from the stations." In practice, the Johnsons did not permit the trusteeship to insulate them from contact with executives of the family broadcasting company. Jesse Kellam, who remained president of the company, made trips to Washington and slept at the White House. When the Johnsons were home on the LBJ Ranch near Austin, they frequently saw their neighbor, Judge Moursund.

But the Johnson Presidency paid a certain price for the accumulation over many years of private wealth in an industry regulated by the federal government and the family's unwillingness to disassociate itself totally even after Johnson was President. Lyndon Johnson as President was never able to rid himself of the wheeler-dealer image that stemmed in large part from public disclosure, by many newspapers and magazines in 1963 and 1964, of the many facets of the family broadcasting enterprise's past. The public image was reinforced by President Johnson's appointments to high federal offices of a number of his old broadcasting associates—of Willard Deason to the Interstate Commerce Commission, Edward Clark to the post of ambassador to Australia, Leonard Marks to head of the United States Information Agency, and of Abe Fortas whom Johnson named to the Supreme Court but whom the Senate would not permit him to elevate to Chief Justice. Cronyism was not the whole of President Johnson's unpopularity that in 1968 denied him another term in office. Yet, cronyism, ironically, contributed to his retirement to Texas and to the dissolution of the Texas Broadcasting Corporation trusteeship.

PART FOUR

Dispensing Consumer Justice

The Regulation of Banking and Investment

The presidential appointees who regulate business conduct in the commercial and investment banking industries, in the labor markets and in the wholesale and retail trade are fortunate. They have no subsidies to give away, they build no rights of way and do not become involved in details concerning natural gas pipelines, television towers and diesel locomotives. They are not immune to political pressures, as was publicly demonstrated during the Eisenhower Administration, but the pressures are not so constant or crude.

All federal regulators of industry have planning functions of one sort or another and all also have policing roles, but the emphasis varies. In the transportation, communications and energy resources areas, the planning function is dominant and the related policing tasks—the overseeing of railroads' rate-fixing conferences, the monitoring of television stations' public service programming, and so forth—are inferior indeed. In the banking, trade and labor areas, on the other hand, the policing of industry to ensure consumer justice is the superior assignment. These regulators are charged by law with some planning functions, in controlling entry into the commercial banking business, in regulating monetary policy and regulating stock exchange commission rates, for instance. But, whatever Congress originally intended, the emphasis in general now is on the policing assignments of these regulators.

Perhaps because the political pressures are not as large, regulation of banking, trade and labor practices unquestionably has attracted more able regulators. The Federal Reserve Board and the Securities and Exchange Commission are the most prestigious of the federal regulatory agencies. The paraphernalia of cases, hearings and formal opinions surely are more adapted to the policing function than to industrial planning. For all these reasons and more, federal regulation of banking, trade and labor practices has served the people better than federal regulation in general. A certain occupational hazard attaches to any police function, a federal regulator must have the initiative to seek out wrongdoing and the intestinal fortitude to pursue the wrongdoers; a planner, by way of contrast, can wait for industry to bring him mergers, rate increases and all manner of other requests. Federal policing of banking, trade and labor practices has produced an uneven record of pursuit and retreat.

Federal regulation of commercial banking has grown over a century and today there are three independent agencies that guard the safety of consumers' bank deposits: the Office of Comptroller of the Currency (created in 1863), the Federal Reserve Board (1913) and the Federal Deposit Insurance Corporation (1933). There is a reasonable division of labor among the three. The Comptroller charters and supervises national banks, which are national not in the scope of their operations (federal law says state laws are determinative in the extent to which national banks may geographically spread their branches) but in that their charters are granted by the national government, not by the states. The Federal Reserve Board was created over the initial opposition of the banking industry for the dual purpose of establishing a central banking system and enhancing the safety of the people's bank deposits, through regulation of banking practices. The United States had had no central bank since the demise of the second United States Bank in 1836, although Congress subsequently had enacted certain laws to expand commercial banking services. After the turn of the century, Congress, in effectuating its constitutional power "to coin money [and] regulate the value thereof," felt the nation needed a more centralized and flexible commercial banking system that would respond to the changing money needs of industry and consumers. Many argued, moreover, that the nation's basic system of privately owned banks was dominated by a "money trust" of New York banks that contributed to the country's periodic financial panics. The Federal Reserve Act of 1913 created a partnership system of government and bankers. It established twelve regional federal reserve banks, members of which are all national banks and larger state banks that hold the reserve banks' capital stock. The reserve banks are empowered to issue currency and the Federal Reserve System is supervised by seven members, or governors, who compose the

Federal Reserve Board. The Federal Deposit Insurance Corporation supervises insured state banks that are not members of the reserve system, but it also has authority to make special examinations of any insured state or national bank.

Today the nation is served by about 14,000 commercial banks, of which nearly 5000 are national banks and the remainder state banks. About 1500 state banks are members of the Federal Reserve System and thus are subject to federal supervision. Another 7400 state banks, roughly, are not members of the system but are insured by the FDIC and subject to its regulation. The layers of state and federal regulation are quite confusing and members of Congress and bankers themselves sometimes get lost in the maze.

The dual system of state and national banks has not grown from a rational determination that the consumer or the nation is best served by duality. Its historic roots are in the federalism of governmental powers divided between the states and Washington and its contemporary preservation is due in large part to the competitive preference of some bankers for state regulation and others for federal regulation. Federal regulation now dominates, of course, but state regulation remains a significant factor in some areas of bank operation. The federal regulators in general do not view with alarm the expansion of big banks, through acquisitions or the opening of branch offices; state regulators in general try harder to protect the neighborhood or community hegemonies of small banks from competitive invasion by big banks. Because state law still controls the branching privileges of national as well as state banks, big bank lobbies and little bank lobbies perennially battle one another before state legislatures over geographic limitations on branch banking.

There are conflicts aplenty between the three federal banking agencies, in spite of their general accord on the matter of bank size. The three agencies have tangled on a long list of other matters, such as whether banks can underwrite municipal revenue bonds and whether subordinated notes and debentures can be counted as part of a bank's capital stock and surplus. Discord was so great for a time that the Comptroller refused to attend meetings of the FDIC. The Comptroller is by law the ex officio third member of the FDIC board of directors but James J. Saxon, who served as Comptroller between 1961 and 1966, was so outspokenly opposed to FDIC positions that he sometimes would not meet with the other two directors. These discords seem like esoteric matters from the consumer's point of view, but millions of dollars ride on the resolution of the issues.

There is a serious question as to whether the division of authority among the three federal bureaucracies hinders the effectiveness of federal bank supervision. Bank failures in the United States have been infrequent in the prosperity of the post–World War II era, ranging generally between one dozen and two dozen liquidations and suspensions yearly. But one of those failures illustrates the reason for questioning the effectiveness of divided responsibility for bank supervision. That example was the failure in September, 1964, of the Crown Savings Bank of Newport News, Virginia.[1]

Crown Savings, a state bank insured by the FDIC, failed after it had helped to finance a small loan and money order operation covering parts of Virginia, New York and Georgia. After the failure, the president of the bank and several individuals operating out of Atlanta were indicted in connection with the money order operation.

In July of 1963, some months after Crown Savings had begun to lend money to the Georgia-based operators, the bank was examined by Virginia state examiners. But their report "evidently" was not passed on to the FDIC, according to the House Banking subcommittee that subsequently looked into the case. In March of 1964, FDIC examiners in Virginia suspected trouble, but did not make a formal examination until June. At the same time, the Federal Reserve, presumably because of the widespread nature of the small loan and money order operation, also suspected trouble at Crown Savings, but did not inform the FDIC of the information it had. Prior to March, 1964, FDIC examiners in Georgia knew of the money order operation because one of the operators had become a director of an FDIC-insured bank in Georgia; but the FDIC in Georgia was not in communication with the FDIC in Virginia.

Crown Savings was closed in September, 1964, after FDIC examiners discovered losses aggregating about $946,000. "It is clear," the House subcommittee staff said, that if the FDIC had acted in July, 1963, after the state examination, or even in March, 1964, "it could either have prevented the failure of Crown Savings Bank or greatly minimized the losses to the public, to depositors and to the insurance fund." The staff deplored the "lack of communication between the FDIC in Georgia and the FDIC in Virginia; between the FDIC in Virginia and the Federal Reserve in Virginia; and between the FDIC and the Virginia banking authorities. Because of this break-down in communication, the action taken by the FDIC was too late."

J. L. Robertson, a member of the Federal Reserve Board who had been a bank regulator for more than thirty years, first on the staff of the Comptroller and then as a governor of the Reserve Board, has concluded that "overlapping powers and conflicting policies, ineffi-ciencies and inconsistencies" are not in the public interest and can "impair Federal bank supervision," as certainly was true in the Crown Savings Bank case. That is to state the obvious but "the evil goes much deeper," Mr. Robertson continued. "The result could be to create doubts about the integrity of all government agencies and to diminish the confidence of the people of this country in our commercial banks."[2]

There also are elements of conflict among the three banking agencies relative to their planning functions. If all three in general go further than state regulators in supporting a banking industry comprising fewer and bigger banks, the Comptroller's support has gone beyond that of the Federal Reserve Board. The states control bank expansion through branching but the federal government regulates expansion by way of merger. The Reserve Board of course has gone along with the Comptroller in approving hundreds of bank mergers in recent years. But the board has sided with the Depart-ment of Justice in opposing some mergers of very large banks in New York, Philadelphia, San Francisco and elsewhere that have been approved by the Comptroller. There is no conflict among the three agencies insofar as planning of monetary expansion and contraction is concerned, because the Federal reserve Board does not share this task. The conflict is elsewhere and shall be discussed later.

When times are good, the most blundering of government policies tend to be ignored and the most wanton of private enterprises frequently go unchallenged. Warnings to the effect that flawed public policies or undisciplined private actions might contribute to the demise of public prosperity are difficult to heed, and Congress does nothing until crisis comes in one form or another and it is forced, or perhaps enabled, to act.

It was this kind of history that led to federal regulation of the investment banking and securities business in 1934. In the roaring twenties, hundreds of ᵗhousands of people who had no business in the stock market participated in the orgy of speculation and market professionals took full advantage of the public participation. By 1929, market pools and other forms of manipulative activity were being directed at more than 100 issues listed on the New York Stock Exchange, interest rates on loans to carry securities rose above 10 percent and there was standing room only in many brokerage house board rooms. The market crashed, the little investors lost a great deal of money and Congress created the Securities and Exchange Commission so that another Great Crash would not again send waves of economic demoralization across the nation. The SEC cannot guarantee absolutely that such a disaster will never happen again because it cannot protect people from their own foolish hopes of making a fast dollar in a ever rising market. But there were many things the SEC could do to dampen speculation and to protect the more than twenty million Americans who today own shares in what has been called people's capitalism.

Congress created the SEC with the Securities Exchange Act of 1934, which gave to the commission the power to control entry into the stock exchange business and to regulate the rates and practices of stock exchanges. Congress also transferred to the SEC administration of the Securities Act of 1933, the "truth in securities" law which required companies wishing to sell new stock issues to the public to first disclose to the SEC financial and operating information that potential purchasers needed to properly evaluate the worth of the offering. The 1934 law also expanded the disclosure principle by requiring companies with outstanding securities listed for public trading on a stock exchange to disclose financial and operating data on a continuing basis. In 1935, Congress enacted a third and more specialized law, the Public Utilities Holding Company Act, which gave the SEC rather drastic powers to require the reorganization and simplification of those electric and gas utility holding company empires that had fallen like houses of cards in the Great Crash.

The results of these laws have been a mixture of successes and failures in policing and planning. The Holding Company Act required planning and Congress was quite precise about what it wanted. As a result, the SEC planned very well. It forced the old holding companies to separate their electric and gas operations and simplify their corporate structures and, as a result, the financial well-being of the electric and gas distribution industries was enhanced. On the other hand, the SEC as planner has failed to foster competition among more stock exchanges. It has become the defender of the right of members of the New York Stock Exchange and each other exchange to fix commission rates among themselves. And it has been an ineffective regulator of the rates so fixed; indeed, in 1968 it encouraged the Big Board and other exchanges to reduce their commission rates for big investors, through a type of quantity discount for large blocks of stock, and thereby gave exchanges a new argument for raising the commissions charged small investors.[3]

The uneven performance of the SEC as the policeman of Wall Street is illustrated by the personal conduct of a chairman who left the commission some time ago, not because he was disciplined for sloth but for political reasons. It was the pleasant habit of this individual to take a leisurely luncheon and then return late but relaxed to the gray temporary building, unfondly known as the "tar paper shack," that for thirty years was the SEC's headquarters on Washington's Second Street.

Not infrequently he went straight to the big second-floor conference room, sometimes to hear a half-dozen staff lawyers present a case against an errant brokerage house, or sometimes to listen to a delegation from the New York Stock Exchange. He would extend cordial greetings to the visitors gathered, working his way to the head of the conference table, then lower his robust frame into a soft, high-backed brown leather chair and the meeting would begin. The chairman would lean back, listening closely, and after a time his eyes would close in deep concentration. They flickered open when he asked a question or two and then there would be no questions from the chair for two, three, four minutes at a time. The chairman was napping.

Literally and figuratively, the SEC slept for most of the decade of the 1950's while a classic Wall Street stock market manipulation was being carried out on the American Stock Exchange, the nation's second largest exchange.[4] Certain exchange members, who held pivotal positions in the handling of public orders to buy and sell securities, were using their positions to unload thousands of shares of stock at rigged prices. Much of the stock had not even been registered with the SEC, as is required under the corporate disclosure laws. The management of the exchange in the 1950's was at fault, but the final responsibility for detecting and stopping manipulation rested with the SEC. Conceivably the SEC during the 1950's was misled into believing that the American Stock Exchange was in good hands because the exchange's $75,000-a-year president at the time, Edward T. McCormick, had been an SEC commissioner.

By the time the SEC in 1961 caught up with the American Stock Exchange and with the manipulators, a father-and-son team of exchange specialists named Gerard A. Re and Gerard F. Re, investors probably had been done out of at least a million dollars.

The SEC staff that finally uncovered the mess said in a marvel of understatement that the case showed that regulation "in the public interest has not worked out in the manner invisioned by Congress." If it wasn't to happen again, "the commission's performance of its supervisory role must be strengthened."[5]

The Securities and Exchange Commission had fallen into the lazy, sleepy ways that are an ever present danger for any bureaucracy. The SEC's staff people during the 1950's were never seen on the trading floor of the American Stock Exchange or any other exchange. The commission had no other means of maintaining an adequate surveillance of trading in the $30 billion of securities that were listed on the American Exchange or, for that matter, of the $400 billion of securities that were listed on the New York Stock Exchange. The need for watching apparently never occurred to the watchdog; the exchange market was in the hands of people the commissioners knew and liked. The SEC by the time the 1950's rolled around had settled back pretty much into a pencil-pushing routine. It is true that when market speculation boomed in the late 1950's the commission spent some of its time cracking down on flamboyant peddlers of cheap uranium stocks. It closed some "boiler rooms," those floating stock shops that pop up in cheap rooms in lower Manhattan to hard-sell blocks of worthless stock, usually by way of a battery of long-distance telephone lines, and then disappear into the woodwork until a new block of merchandise comes along. But policing of the obvious crooks only farther obscured the SEC's failure to police the stock exchanges, which are far, far more important to America's twenty million investors.

The American Stock Exchange scandal was so disturbing to Congress that the lawmakers in 1961 passed a resolution directing the SEC to conduct an investigation of the adequacy, "for the protection of investors," of stock market regulation. The congressional resolution calling for an investigation of the SEC by the SEC initially raised the possibility of a whitewash or worse. But, as it turned out, the investigation was highly objective and it produced in 1963 the most thorough study of the stock market that had been made since Congress in the 1930's enacted the original securities laws. The commendable study can be credited largely to William Cary, the Columbia University law professor who served as SEC chairman during the Kennedy era. Congress appropriated $950,000 for the study and Professor Cary set up a special staff of sixty-five persons to conduct it. Many of them were experienced lawyers and economists, who came to the SEC to make the study and who left when it was finished. Cary thus assured that the study staff would operate independent of prior or subsequent commitment to the commission.

It did. The 1963 report to Congress of the SEC's Special Study of Securities Markets was a five-volume bible of what was wrong in the stock market and its regulation.[6] The report contained more than 175 recommendations for righting the wrongs. Some of the recommendations could be put into effect by the SEC under existing law, others called for new legislation.

It would be inaccurate to say that the Special Study was fruitless. The SEC disassociated itself from some of the more than 175 recommendations and it is doubtful that a single member of Congress read all or most of the five volumes. But Congress in 1964 did extend to some 2700 companies with outstanding securities that were publicly traded in the over-the-counter market—which comprises all trading that does not take place on a stock exchange—the disclosure and other requirements that since 1934 had applied to companies whose securities were listed for trading on an exchange. Congress in 1964 also authorized the SEC to prescribe entrance qualifications for certain groups of aspiring securities salesmen who were not covered by the requirements established for their member firms by the exchanges or the National Association of Securities Dealers, which oversees the over-the-counter market under SEC supervision. In addition, the commission, without the need of new legislation, adopted regulations putting into effect some of the Special Study recommendations. The commission in 1964, for instance, adopted the rule that sharply restricted (but did not eliminate) trading on a stock exchange floor by exchange members for their own accounts. And in 1968 it persuaded the New York Stock Exchange and other exchanges to alter their fixed commission rates to the extent of allowing discounts for large transactions.

However, in the half-dozen years following publication of the Special Study, Congress refused to act on other reforms, such as a proposed law to assist the smallest investors by reducing management fees and sales charges of mutual funds. The SEC, with abundant legal authority under existing law to force exchange commission rates down and to require more rate competition among exchange members, did little on its own for the smallest investors and did nothing to encourage the private antitrust suits that challenged exchange commission rates. Unquestionably the SEC was a more watchful policeman under Professor Cary and his successor, Chairman Manuel F. Cohen, than it had been in the 1950's. It secured the indictments on charges of manipulation or other securities law violations of many fly-by-night stock sellers and of several quite prominent Wall Street figures. It tried to erect new barriers to the use of inside, nonpublic financial and operating data by corporate officers and Wall Street professionals, bringing suit successfully against executives of Texas Gulf Sulphur Company and then taking administrative action against Merrill Lynch, Pierce, Fenner & Smith, Incorporated, the largest securities firm in the nation.

Yet, the SEC remains a timid watchdog in many respects. Merrill Lynch, for instance, was punished by being ordered to suspend operation of several of its departments for a number of days; small violators time and again are given severe punishment that in effect puts them out of business. The SEC's position—that closing of a large member firm of the New York Stock Exchange would inconvenience too many investors—may meet the test of logic, but hardly of justice. The SEC in the fifties and sixties has not been effective in curbing "hot issues" and the other manifestations of rampant speculation. Its leadership in the complex matter of improving corporate financial accounting and reporting has been inconsistent, although its legal authority is great and uniformly accurate accounting is fundamental to meaningful public disclosure. More than three decades after the SEC was created, the senior partner in one of the largest accounting firms still could assert, "My profession appears to regard a set of financial statements as a roulette wheel for investors —and it's their tough luck if they don't understand the risk that's involved in interpreting any accounting report."[7]

The generalization made by the SEC's own Staff Study in 1963 remains valid: "The commission's concepts and mechanisms . . . have been essentially of a passive kind, rather than of an active and continuous character."[8] The study also described the dangers, for individual investors and for the national economy, inherent in federal regulation that promises more public protection than it delivers. Public understanding of the stock market is "clouded by many illusions and misconceptions," the study asserted. "It is an excellent thing to aspire toward high standards . . . but an entirely different thing to encourage the investing public to believe that the aspiration is the fact. Mere lip service or exaggeration may do more harm than good, because the investing public may be led to expect too much in the way of certainty and protection, may fail to appreciate the risks inherent in investment and may not exercise the vigilance and care required of the investor."[9]

18
The Labor Market

Regulation of the national labor market is, by comparison with regulation of commercial banking, a relatively new federal undertaking. Regulation, in the modern sense of deep federal involvement in the relationships between thousands of companies and their employees, dates from 1926. Before 1926, Congress enacted certain labor laws such as those circumscribing the use of child labor (which the Supreme Court first held to be unconstitutional intrusion on states' rights and later upheld). These and more recent statutes, including laws prescribing minimum wages employers must pay, have clear and definite meanings. Congress therefore assigned them to the Department of Labor for administration. But in 1926 as Congress began to write labor laws that were more ambitious and that left more to the discretion of the administrators, it set about creating independent administrative agencies. There are now four such agencies that in fact or in practice are independent of the Labor Department.

The federal government, by interposing itself as a third party in the process by which a worker bargains for his services with an employer, has tended to increase the prices consumers pay for the goods and services of industry. Government traditionally has intervened, as by imposing minimum wages and enforcing the right of employees to organize, to redress the unequal bargaining power of workers. It may safely be assumed that the increased cost of labor has not in its entirety been absorbed by either the generosity of employers or the increased productivity made possible by more mechanization and automation. Some part of the increased costs of labor has been passed on to consumers in the form of higher prices. But higher consumer prices are paid, willingly and ably, for the social as well as economic benefits derived.

There is another side of the coin. Federal intervention is no longer motivated by the single purpose of assuring the rights of workers as against those of employers. Labor is finding that government is increasing its role as regulator. Moreover, the contemporary scale of intervention poses a question concerning the bargaining freedom of unions no less than of management. Modern regulation began in 1926 with labor-management relations in transportation, and in 1963, for the first time in this nation's peacetime history, government in effect dictated the settlement terms of a transportation labor dispute. The question, obviously, is whether this bridge, once crossed, will be crossed again, perhaps many times, to resolve disputes in transportation and other industries.

That law enacted in 1926 was the Railway Labor Act. It banned employer interference with the right of railroad workers to organize and created the National Mediation Board to help railroads and the brotherhoods of rail workers to settle their disputes. The board in time acquired the authority to hold elections where railroad employees could vote on whether they wanted to be represented by a union and, if so, which union. A union that received a majority of the votes was certified as the legal bargaining agent with which the railroad was required to negotiate on wages and working conditions. The board also was empowered to mediate contract disputes and delay strikes, but it was not empowered to force railroads or unions to accept any settlements recommended. The three-member National Mediation Board now exercises all these powers in the airline industry as well as in railroad labor disputes.

It would appear that the Congress which sat in 1926 was under the impression that the agency it created would suffice forevermore. In naming its creation the National Mediation Board (the name initially was the United States Board of Mediation, changed in 1934 to National Mediation Board), the 1926 Congress apparently thought either that the government would not mediate other than transportation labor disputes or that whatever additional disputes were mediated would be handled by the board. But subsequent Congresses did not share that understanding.

In 1935 the New Deal created the National Labor Relations Board. The NLRB was made to guard the people's rights as wage earners rather than wage spenders and to ensure workers in general the same right to organize that in 1926 had been given railroad employees. But it was cast in the mold of the old ICC. And, like the Federal Trade Commission, it was created not to regulate conduct within a particular industry but to supervise certain matters in all industry. The states and Congress over many years had enacted various laws to protect employees, such as laws that restricted child labor and that limited the number of hours a day that railroad employees could be required to work. But the National Labor Relations Act of 1935 went far beyond the federal government's earlier attempts to better the lot of the wage earner.

The NLRB grew out of an earlier New Deal experiment, the National Industrial Recovery Act of 1933. That law, among many other things, guaranteed workers the right to organize in unions and provided for improvements in both wages and hours of employment. But "the nine old men" who sat on the Supreme Court had declared major portions of it unconstitutional, so President Roosevelt and Congress picked up some of the pieces and put them together in a new package in 1935. Two years later, the Supreme Court upheld the constitutionality of the so-called Wagner Act. The law and the National Labor Relations Board, an independent agency of five members, are no longer so one-sidedly pro-labor as they were in 1935, but the NLRB still enforces the right of a wage earner to join a union and requires companies to bargain with unions.

Then, in 1947, Congress created another agency, the Federal Mediation and Conciliation Service, to mediate labor-management disputes in general. This agency attempts to persuade companies and unions (other than railroads and airlines) to settle their disputes without strikes or lockouts. And, in 1964, Congress faced a new labor problem and created still another agency. The creation of the Equal Employment Opportunity Commission by the Civil Rights Act of 1964 marked the assumption by the federal government of the responsibility to Negroes and other minority groups to eliminate discrimination in employment, whether the discrimination appeared in the membership clauses of union constitutions or in the hiring practices of employers.

This evolutionary growth of laws and agencies has greatly enlarged the powers of the federal government over labor-management relations. The enlargement has had effects on the right of workers to organize, the obligation of management to bargain and and on the mediation of disputes between managements and unions. In order to assure bargaining rights across the nation, the NLRB has grown into a bureaucracy with regional offices throughout the nation and an annual budget of some $30 million. It holds

8000 representation elections annually and investigates ten thousand complaints, filed by unions, employees and employers, alleging all manner of unfair labor practices. Its work has settled down to a routine that, inevitably, sometimes involves the board in trivial matters. The board ruled in 1966, for example, that Westinghouse Electric Corporation was guilty of an unfair labor practice when it refused to bargain with a union over some price increases Westinghouse posted for food served in three plant cafeterias in Baltimore. A major issue involved a penny-a-cup increase in the price of a cup of coffee. The two dissenters to the board's 3-to-2 decision declared that "collective bargaining is healthy, but if bargaining over a penny-a-cup increase in coffee becomes mandatory to the menu on the bargaining table, the result is liable to be acute indigestion." In 1966, to cite another example, the NLRB ruled that an employee of an Indiana gear manufacturer, who had been fired for drawing nasty cartoons of his boss, was not guilty of an unfair labor practice and therefore was entitled to his old job, plus back pay.

These examples illustrate the breadth and depth of government involvement in the rights of workers and the rights of employers. But with the growth of government power there also has been a change in government attitude. Congress has amended the National Labor Relations Act to oblige unions also to refrain from unfair practices against employers and it has conferred certain rights on workers who choose not to belong to unions. Consequently, the courts have found, for instance, that a dissident union member has the right to picket union headquarters carrying a placard disparaging union officers.[1] And the NLRB has ruled that a union cannot overcharge a nonmember worker for use of the union's hiring hall.

Perhaps more significantly, from the point of view of organized labor, Congress has decided that the time has come for government to regulate the business of unions. Congress in 1959 enacted the Labor-Management Reporting and Disclosure Act, which is administered by the Department of Labor. "Congress finds," the law began, "that there have been a number of instances of breach of trust, corruption, disregard of the rights of individual employees and other failures to observe high standards of responsibility and ethical conduct." To cure these ills, Congress said that labor union locals must elect officers no less frequently than every three years, "by secret ballot among the members." The law provided that union members aggrieved of election procedures could complain to the Labor Department and that the Secretary of Labor, if he found that an election was unfairly conducted, could order a new and fair election held.

The growth of government involvement in the settlement of strikes and lockouts also has been accompanied by a change in government attitude. Washington is ever less willing to tolerate strikes or, put another way, to allow unions full freedom in the exercise of their ultimate weapon. Despite many years of mediation effort, by the National Mediation Board in the transportation industries and the Federal Mediation and Conciliation Service in other industries, strikes are more frequent. The total number of work stoppages in American industry has grown from an annual average of about 2800 in the 1930's to more than 3500 annually in recent years.[2] Certainly, there are many reasons for the increase but, whatever they may be, Washington is impatient with strikes that disrupt a significant segment of the nation's economy.

One manifestation of its impatience was the enactment by Congress in 1947 of a law that permits the President, through court order, to enjoin for eighty days and investigate a strike which he believes would constitute a national emergency. A second and certainly more ominous display of increasing government unwillingness to tolerate strikes was the compulsory arbitration law of 1963 to stop a national railroad strike. Labor lost and management won in this particular instance of government compulsion but there is no reason for management, labor or government to take satisfaction from what happened. Indeed, government least of all was entitled to satisfaction, for the last resort of compulsory arbitration was an unspoken admission of the failure of forty years of federal effort to assure labor-management peace in the railroad industry.

The federal program established under the Railway Labor Act is not identical to the mediation machinery with which government has sought to secure labor-management peace in other industries. The problems in railroad labor-management relations also are not precisely the same as those in other industries. But there are similarities.

The Railway Labor Act program is older and more elaborate, providing successive levels of government mediation and fact-finding up to a presidential board and for injunctions to temporarily prevent work stoppages while the settlement efforts continue. In industries other than the railroad and airline industries, government can temporarily enjoin only those strikes which the President says constitute national emergencies. None of the mediation laws permit government to force a settlement which, of course, is why Congress decided it had to enact a compulsory arbitration statute to head off a nation-wide railroad strike. It is accurate to say that railroad managements and unions today are incapable of settling their differences without government mediation. It is not outlandish to inquire whether government intervention is similarly stultifying bargaining in other major industries. If free bargaining is rendered futile by the hopes of each side that government intervention eventually will work to its benefit and if government is increasingly unwilling to tolerate the end result of unsuccessful mediation, then government in the future will be forced increasingly to dictate settlement terms.

The problems of railroad labor-management relations that urged compulsory arbitration resolution basically involved mechanization and automation. These are basic problems in many American industries today. Labor contracts in the railroad business are based on an astonishingly complex system of "work rules" governing rates of pay, job assignments, distances that train employees travel and the like. The rules, which evolved over many years, were based on the speed and other operating characteristics of steam locomotives. After World War II, the railroads spent more than $17 billion to replace steam locomotives with diesel-electric locomotives and for related facilities. The diesels, because they could haul freight trains faster or could haul longer trains, made some of the work rules obsolete. Moreover, they eliminated the need for the firemen who stoked the boilers on the steam locomotives. For a dozen years after World War II, the railroads, the unions and the federal mediators went through the motions of attempting to revise the work rules. Apparently, neither the companies nor the unions really expected to negotiate a settlement, but each instead hoped that delay and federal intervention eventually would work to its benefit. By the late 1950's the focus of the dispute had shifted from serious mediation to serious public relations. Both sides were running expensive publicity and lobbying campaigns to convince the public and Congress of the righteousness of their positions. The unions were claiming that the firemen still were needed to help the engineers operate trains safely, even though the firemen's jobs on steam locomotives had disappeared. The railroads were running newspaper advertisements asserting that firemen were featherbedders and that obsolete work rules were costing the industry some $600 million a year.

Presidents Eisenhower and Kennedy tried unsuccessfully to use their personal powers of persuasion to get the railroads and the unions back to the bargaining table. That failing, President Kennedy appointed a special commission to investigate and it reported to the White House in 1962.[3] But the railroads and the unions did not accept the commission's report as a basis for a negotiated settlement and finally, to prevent a national strike, Congress in 1963 passed a law dictating a method of settlement. Under the compulsory arbitration award, the unions were forced to accept the elimination of more than ten thousand firemen on diesel locomotives before the arbitration award expired in the summer of 1967. It might be said that collective bargaining in the railroad business has become a charade. Sometimes the federal mediators eventually can bring about a settlement and other times, when they cannot, there are strikes on individual railroads. Congress has not yet forced the end of a local or regional railroad strike or lockout. But the idea of government-dictated compulsory arbitration is no longer foreign to legislative thinking in Washington. During the prolonged strike in the summer of 1966 against some of the country's major airlines, the lawmakers gave serious consideration to compulsory arbitration to restore airline service.

No one in 1964 knew precisely the extent of racially discriminatory covenants and practices in employment, but Congress in creating the commission accepted an assumption they were widespread. The commission subsequently produced evidence confirming the assumption. One of its surveys, for instance, found that Negroes in 1966 made up only 2.6 percent of the "white-collar" headquarters staffs of the hundred major New York City–based corporations, a group that accounted for nearly 16 percent of the gross national product and that included some of America's largest employers. "Those who should be the leaders in this crucial area of local and national concern are, in fact, the laggards," the commission said.[4]

The passage of the Civil Rights Act of 1964 and the creation of the Equal Employment Opportunity Commission have not been without effect. The mere enactment of the law constituted a pressure on companies and unions to cease overt discrimination and some additional job opportunities in production-line and other "blue-collar" employment have been opened to Negroes. Yet, the progress of the EEOC since 1964 has been painfully slow. In four years, the commission's investigations of allegedly illegal discrimination had resulted in the filing of a mere handful—fewer than two dozen—federal suits to stop discrimination by employers or by unions. Most of the suits were against small companies or union locals. It was not until mid-1968 that a suit was brought against the nation-wide operations of a larger employer. The director of the Congress of Racial Equality complained that the commission's progress was so meager that "before an aggrieved person can get a remedy, he may have found another job or starved to death." And a leading Negro authority on job recruitment and employment wrote of "equal job opportunity: the credibility gap."[5]

Denial of equal job opportunities is only one form of white discrimination against blacks. The blacks who rioted in Detroit, Newark and other industrial cities in America didn't carry placards denouncing the Equal Employment Opportunity Commission. But employment discrimination was one of the root factors involved in black discontent. The basic cause of the riots, the U.S. Riot Commission Report said, "is surely the continuing exclusion of great numbers of Negroes from the benefits of economic progress through discrimination in employment" as well as in education and housing.[6] Government, meaning particularly Congress and the Supreme Court, has made many promises of equality to Negroes, in employment and education and housing, and it has not for various reasons come close to fulfilling those promises.

The reasons for the EEOC's poor performance have been many. Congress initially in 1964 appropriated about $2 million to enable the commission to start up. But President Johnson did not name the commissioners until well into 1965. Then he named as chairman Franklin D. Roosevelt, Jr., a seemingly appropriate choice. But Roosevelt after a few months resigned to run for political office. So roughly two years passed before the commission settled down to business. When it did, it found the administrative machinery provided by Congress to be slow and cumbersome. It could only investigate complaints that unions limited or barred blacks from membership or that employers failed to recruit Negro employees or confined those they did hire to menial jobs. The commission on finding such illegal bias could only try mediation; it had to recommend to the Justice Department that suits be brought. The EEOC had no authority to hold administrative hearings on its complaints and issue cease and desist orders against illegal union or employer discrimination. Authority to hold such proceedings is a basic part of the powers of other regulatory agencies and is a fundamental adaptation of law to the expertise of the agencies and the tremendous volume of their work. The EEOC has asked repeatedly for the authority and Congress has refused to grant it. Perhaps a commission is a singularly inefficient method of attempting to achieve employment equality for Negroes, but certainly Congress has abetted the contrast between promise and performance.

19

The Regulation of Trade

Flanking the Federal Trade Commission building, a triangular-shaped structure set between Constitution and Pennsylvania Avenues in Washington, are two larger-than-life statues, each depicting a swarthy man restraining an unruly and rather unnaturally muscular horse. The man who designed the statuary in the 1930's, an employee of the defunct Works Project Administration, had in mind an FTC restraining industrial giantism. Had the WPA sculptor accepted Congressman Emanuel Celler's animal symbolism, he perhaps would have depicted the FTC restraining a goat labeled the consumer. But he apparently took his inspiration from what Congress intended in 1914 rather than what the FTC has become.

The Federal Trade Commission is today a study in contrasts. It refers to itself time and again as the consumer's agency, suggesting that presidential assistants for consumer affairs are Johnny-come-latelies. The commission indeed for many years has been a law-enforcement agency with direct responsibility for policing specific consumer-oriented statutes. It is supposed to make certain that woolen mills, such as the ones Bernard Goldfine operated, do not mislabel the blankets, coats and other items consumers buy. It is supposed to keep advertising truthful and recently it has established an office in Washington to which the Capital City's poor can bring their grievances against ghetto merchants.

Congress in 1914 did not intend the FTC to be a law-enforcement agency of the type the commission has become. At least Congress did not intend the commission to be primarily a cop policing individual little sellers of everything from aluminum storm windows to television sets to baldness balms. It intended the commission primarily to be an economic planner on a national scale, investigating in expert manner and in economic depth the causes and consequences of the trust problem and all other problems of industrial concentration. Its responsibility to the consumer in an industrial economy was indirect, in the same sense that the Sherman Act serves ultimately the interests of consumers. Hindsight suggests that

Congress erred in the beginning by assigning the commission a dual role. But Congress in more recent years has multiplied confusion, first by heaping on the FTC one distinct and narrow consumer-type enforcement statute after another and, second, by telling the commission in the Robinson-Patman Act to protect small business. The FTC, like its peers, illustrates once more the penchant of Congress for specific laws addressed to specific problems at specific times.

Burdened by conflicts, the FTC cannot or will not perform any of its functions satisfactorily, except perhaps that it administers the Robinson-Patman Act to the fair satisfaction of small businessmen. It cannot, as a practical matter, police the entire nation to prevent consumer deceptions and frauds by retailers. The commission itself has conceded that its staff of about one thousand and its annual budget of about $13 million are wholly inadequate to police false advertising and other consumer deceptions throughout the nation. On the other hand, the commission addresses itself to larger matters of industrial concentration by now and then acting to stop a merger. But its total performance as the economic planners envisioned in 1914 is grossly inadequate. And thus, unraveled by conflicts that have pulled and tugged for many years, the commission has acquired a reputation as an ineffectual agency that spends most of its time on matters that, by any rational standard of governmental priorities, are trivia. It was in the course of remarking on the conflicts within all the regulatory agencies and between the agencies and the other branches of government, that Mr. Justice Jackson in 1952 said, "the perfect example is the Federal Trade Commission."[1] The conflicts and the trivia are the reasons that the FTC long ago acquired a Washington reputation as "the old lady of Pennsylvania Avenue."

The creation of the Federal Trade Commission in 1914 was not a frivolous act.[2] President Wilson, Congress and popular opinion felt that the Sherman Act of 1890 was not a sufficient answer to the problems of industrial concentration. The old antitrust act punished business conspiracies and monopolies, but suits brought by the Justice Department and decided by the courts had not proved entirely effective in ridding the nation of business trusts or in halting the trend toward industrial concentration in ever bigger businesses. The courts often were slow and their ultimate decisions could not always be predicted with certainty.

President Wilson proposed a commission as "an indispensable instrument of information, as a clearing house for the facts by which both the public and the managers of great business undertakings shall be guided, and as an instrumentality for doing justice to business where the processes of the courts . . . are inadequate." The legislative history of the FTC's creation leaves little doubt that Congress agreed with the President's description of what was intended. The intention, quite apparently, was to create a permanent agency that would in the future be continually alert to new trends toward greater business concentration, that would conduct penetrating investigations of the public meanings of concentration and advise the President and Congress of whatever additional antitrust laws would be needed.

This reading of history is supported by various precise actions that Congress took in creating the FTC. One was to transfer to the new commission the Bureau of Corporations, which had been set up within the Department of Commerce in 1903 to collect business growth data. Congress in addition conferred on the commission unusually large powers to look into the books and records of private corporations. It said in the Federal Trade Commission Act, the commission's enabling law, that the FTC was empowered to "investigate any corporation." The FTC's inquisitorial powers today are broader in their reach than those of any other agency of government that oversees business conduct. And Congress in 1914 established clear lines of communication between the commission, on the one hand, and Congress and the President, on the other. The FTC Act said the commission was to report to the legislative and executive branches whenever it concluded from its investigations that additional antitrust or other economic legislation was necessary. The FTC was to use its powers of investigation and its public hearing procedures to explore and air issues of industrial concentration, in particular industries or in the economy at large. It could probe corporate records and require the presidents of the nation's largest corporations to appear before it, to testify on matters relating to an industry at large or to a single corporation. On the basis of its findings, the commission could advise the President and Congress or, to test its conclusions, it could bring a formal complaint against a particular company. It could, under the FTC Act, charge a company with "deceptive practices" or with "false advertising." It also could, under the Clayton Act that Congress also passed in 1914, charge a company with "discriminatory" pricing or it could charge that a company's acquisition of the stock of another company illegally lessened competition. Indeed, Congress in 1914 seemed to be giving the FTC an array of all the alternatives of power and procedure that the lawmakers could contrive.

The division of responsibility intended in 1914 between the commission and the Justice Department was appropriate and constitutional. The Justice Department then and now is solely responsible for administration of the Sherman Act. The department is the law-enforcement arm of the executive branch. The Sherman Act provides criminal as well as civil penalties for price-fixing and monopoly. The department brings Sherman Act suits which are decided by the courts. Congress in 1914 gave both the FTC and the Justice Department authority to administer the Clayton Act, a civil statute. The difference was that the FTC did not go to court nor could it hand out criminal penalties. It was prosecutor and judge, it could bring a formal complaint against a company for violation of a specific provision of the FTC Act or the Clayton Act or both, and then hold a public hearing on the complaint and, if it found the company guilty, order it to cease the illegal activity. But this law-enforcement authority surely was ancillary to the commission's unique powers to investigate companies or industries for the purpose of advising the President and Congress on the need for additional antitrust or other economic legislation. This advisory function was the classic role of an agency that constitutionally was an arm of Congress.

Congress, it would appear, heaped too much on the FTC even in 1914. As early as 1924, a commentator who was sympathetic to the FTC's purposes but not to its choice of tasks wrote that the commission had been created "to deal with the trust problem. Time should not be wasted upon petty squabbles and dishonesties."[3] Nonetheless, it would appear that the FTC as a younger agency performed generally in the manner Congress had intended. In the 1920's and early 1930's it conducted notable investigations of such matters as grain marketing, tobacco pricing and securities trading, and a number of its reports to Congress and the President served as a basis for new legislation.

Even today, the FTC does not spend all of its time policing petty squabbles and dishonesties. In 1966, for instance, it conducted an economic investigation of the cement industry and probed in depth the effects on competition of the large number of acquisitions by cement manufacturers of local ready-mixed concrete companies. It used in concert its powers to investigate an industry and its authority to bring formal complaints against individual companies and it halted the national trend of increasing concentration in the cement and concrete businesses.

Another recent example of accomplishment was a formal complaint charging that the acquisition by Procter & Gamble Company of Clorox Chemical Company was illegal. Procter & Gamble is a huge manufacturer of soaps and other consumer products. Clorox was a smaller company but a leading manufacturer of household bleach. Procter & Gamble bought Clorox to add bleach to the P&G line of products, achieving what is termed a conglomerate merger, involving two companies that are not direct competitors. The FTC complaint was noteworthy not simply because Procter & Gamble is a very big business but more because antitrust law traditionally had been applied, by both the Justice Department and the commission, to mergers of direct competitors, such as two soapmakers. The FTC ruled this conglomerate merger to be illegal and new antitrust case law was made in 1967 when the Supreme Court upheld the commission's decision.[4] The commission and the court said, in effect, that Procter & Gamble's huge promotional resources might create so overwhelming a consumer preference for Clorox brand bleach that all other bleach makers would fall by the wayside. Procter & Gamble was ordered to divest itself of Clorox and, if Proctor & Gamble so desired, to get into the bleach business on its own and thus add to the number of competitors in the business rather than subtract from competition.

FTC accomplishments of the magnitude of the cement investigation and the Procter & Gamble case are few and far between nowadays. Congress since 1914 has heaped additional law-enforcement responsibilities on the agency and the commission's principal concern has indeed become the elimination of petty disputes and dishonesties.

The Clayton Act was amended in 1938 with the Robinson-Patman Act. It was amended further in 1950 with the Celler-Kefauver Act, which banned not only stock acquisitions but also acquisitions of assets that "may substantially lessen competition or tend to create a monopoly." Congress authorized the FTC and the Justice Department to administer these two wholly dissimilar amendments. The department has left the Robinson-Patman Act almost entirely to the commission. The Celler-Kefauver Act certainly is not petty and the department and the commission have a good working arrangement so that both do not bring antimerger actions against the same acquisitions.

The powers that Congress voted for the FTC alone and that are petty in a relative sense include the 1939 law by which the commission was directed to guard against the misbranding of wool products. In 1951 the lawmakers told the FTC to "protect consumers against misbranding [and] false advertising of furs." In 1953 the commission was directed to guard against use of highly flammable fabrics in the manufacture of clothing and other consumer goods. And in 1967 the FTC began to enforce a portion of the Fair Packaging and Labeling Act, which Congress passed to protect consumers against food and other boxes and packages that may contain less than appears.

Whatever the intentions of these laws and amendments, each has added to the FTC's burden, and under it the commission bogs deeper in trivia. In any given year, the agency grinds out hundreds of orders in minuscule matters relating to, for instance, a San Francisco retailer's false advertising of television sets, a New York furrier's mislabeling of weasel for mink or, for that matter, the price of frozen fruit pies in Salt Lake City. In the same year, the commission's actions of consequence, such as the cement industry cases, can be counted on the fingers of one hand. The basic orientation of the FTC staff to concern with trivia can be demonstrated at will.

One zealous staff man was in a department store where he spotted a display of "Red Fox" brand overalls. His reaction was instant indignation: one of the laws the FTC administers, the Fur Products Labeling Act, says that fur garments cannot be identified with a particular animal unless the garment actually is made from the fur of that animal. Obviously, the overalls were not made of red fox fur. A law violation! A formal charge was prepared by the staff and debated by the commission. It probably would have been issued publicly, except that the Georgia maker of the overalls screamed so loudly that the FTC chairman flew back to Washington from a California vacation and quashed the case.

The FTC did issue a complaint against the country's biggest bubble gum manufacturer, formally charging it not with trying to monopolize the bubble gum market but with attempting to monopolize the baseball picture cards that kids got when they spent a nickel for a pack of gum. An examiner held the company, Topps Chewing Gum, Incorporated, guilty. But the commission by a split vote overruled the examiner, finding other bubble gum makers had competed successfully with football cards, Beatle cards and "Spook Theater" cards.

The FTC also brought deceptive trade practice charges against a television commercial in which a football star of the New York Giants tried to help sell Rapid Shave shaving cream. The sixty-second commercial showed the football player, "a man with a problem just like yours . . . a beard as tough as sandpaper," and then it showed in a separate picture a razor shaving clean a piece of sandpaper lathered with Rapid Shave. But, FTC investigators discovered, the sandpaper wasn't sandpaper at all. Rather, it was a TV mock-up consisting of a piece of Plexiglas on which sand had been sprinkled. The FTC spent five years on that case, which went all the way to the United States Supreme Court. An examiner took testimony which showed that Rapid Shave could shave sandpaper, if it was fine sandpaper, but the type depicted on TV had to be soaked eighty minutes before it could be shaved. But he said the inadequacies of television would have made real sandpaper look to viewers like mere colored paper, that Colgate-Palmolive Company (Rapid Shave's maker) hadn't committed any material sin and that the case should be dismissed. The commission overruled him and the Supreme Court in 1965 upheld the commissioner's finding of guilt.[5]

The Federal Trade Commission spent sixteen years getting the "liver" out of Carter's Little Liver Pills. That epic adventure in the trivia of consumer protection began in 1943. Just why the commission decided to issue a complaint in that particular year—when the nation was fighting World War II and when Carter's Little Liver Pills already had been a household laxative for seventy years—remains a mystery.

On May 28, 1943, the FTC issued a formal complaint, sixteen pages long, challenging the "liver" in Carter's Little Liver Pills because, the commission alleged, the remedy contained no ingredient of therapeutic value to the liver. Moreover, the complaint charged that Carter Products, Incorporated, was misleading the public when it advertised that its pills would clear away "dark clouds of listlessness," that they would "keep one smiling and happy." Hearings before an examiner did not begin until six months later, in November. They ran on for two whole years, not continuously, but off-again, on-again for a grand total of 149 sessions. By the time the examiner closed the case (for the first time) in November of 1945 the hearing record was fifteen thousand pages long, not including 2209 exhibits that had been introduced in evidence.

Understandably, the examiner needed seven more months to write his decision. It was 267 pages long and it concluded that Carter's should be found guilty of misleading the public over the last seventy-plus years. And there the case rested for six years. The examiner's decision remained pending until the commission on March 28, 1951, issued its decision, which accepted his conclusion.

Next step. The company appealed and the Court of Appeals said the examiner had denied Carter's Little Liver Pills a fair trial because Carter's lawyers had not been given all the opportunity they deserved to cross-examine three of the FTC's expert witnesses, by name Doctors Case, Bollman and Lockwood. The Supreme Court agreed and sent the whole case back to the FTC. Back to the examiner it went but by now Dr. Lockwood was no longer available for further cross-examination; he had died. A substitute was found, and his new testimony, plus the additional testimony of the fortunately surviving Doctors Case and Bollman, filled almost five hundred pages. In March, 1955, the examiner once more closed the case and once more decided that Carter's was guilty as originally (now twelve years earlier) charged.

The commission now had before it for decision some twenty thousand pages of testimony and papers going back to 1943 (in the two sets of hearings, minus only the deceased Dr. Lockwood's testimony), plus exhibits, many of them highly technical. The commission in October of 1956 issued its decision: fifty pages in which it formally held that Carter's Little Liver Pills did not help anyone who felt "blue, down in the dumps or bogged down." The huge collection of complicated medical technical data did give pause to the commission, which wrote: "Inasmuch as the laxation afforded by an irritant laxative or cathartic is not a normal physiological method of evacuation and is not based on any principle having relation to natural bowel motility, it is not true that the preparation represents a fundamental principle of nature." The "liver" must go from Carter's Little Liver Pills, the Federal Trade Commission ruled again.

Again to the Court of Appeals, which shuddered at the "record of monumental proportion," and decided that Carter's must by now have had a fair hearing. The court upheld the FTC, bowing to its judgment in weighing this "huge mass of medical testimony." The end of the case came on November 9, 1959, when the Supreme Court refused to hear any more of it.[6]

These demonstrations of the Federal Trade Commission's pre-occupation with trivia are not offered to embarrass an agency of government. The FTC is not proud of them either. They are offered to illustrate the contrast between what Congress intended longer than a half-century ago and what is. The FTC is not the intended agent of economic enlightenment and the fault rests as much, and perhaps more, with Congress than with the agency. The paradox of the FTC is that it cannot succeed in policing consumer protection throughout the nation because its resources are ridiculously small. It has only about a dozen field offices throughout the entire nation. In contrast, the Justice Department's law-enforcement resources include the investigative talents of the Federal Bureau of Investigation, which has almost as many agents in New York City as the total work force of the FTC nation-wide, plus the prosecutorial facilities of United States Attorneys in every state.[7]

Meanwhile, the problems of industrial concentration to which the FTC was supposed to address itself have today grown larger than ever before. It is ironic indeed that the FTC remains the nation's chief source of economic intelligence about industrial concentration. "Merger activity in 1967 experienced the sharpest increase in modern industrial history," the commission's Bureau of Economics reported. During 1967, large manufacturing and mining corporations acquired 155 other corporations with total assets of $8 billion. From 1948 through 1967, the nation's two hundred largest corporations acquired 476 other companies with aggregate assets of $22.5 billion, the FTC reported.[8] Merger activity and the growth of industrial concentration increased at a more rapid rate in 1968 than 1967, according to preliminary FTC statistics.

But the commission's annual reports on industrial concentration are mere fact-finding exercises. The commission gathers the facts and does little about them. The agency brought the leading test case against conglomerate mergers when it acted against Procter & Gamble's acquisition of Clorox. But that single, successful thrust did not by any means blunt the merger trend, as the FTC's statistics suggests, because neither the commission nor the Justice Department followed up by attacking with fistfuls of antitrust cases. Thus, the nation's fifty largest corporations have more than one-third of the nation's total manufacturing assets, the five hundred largest control more than two-thirds of such total assets, and antitrust is a "charade," according to Harvard economist John Kenneth Galbraith.[9]

A very large question that remains unanswered relates to the industrial and consumer consequences of increasing economic concentration through the medium of conglomerate mergers. Out of such mergers there are developing huge new industrial complexes that resemble in some respects the utility holding companies that were put together in the 1920's, not for reasons of industrial production efficiency, but for the financial satisfaction of their managements. Some of the conglomerate empires today represent unions of totally diverse elements, such as coal mining and whiskey making, or broadcasting and baseball. They seem not to be motivated by production efficiency but by the desires of managements, utilizing inflated stock prices to acquire other companies, to buy corporate security, power and ever rising per-share profits. Will conglomerate empires also collapse in some future year of recession or depression? Do the conglomerates represent inefficient combinations of production facilities that tend to increase the prices consumers pay for their goods and services? The FTC began to probe these questions, but not until the conglomerate trend was far advanced in 1968.

Industrial concentration poses another and still larger set of questions. They are, basically, questions that existed in more modest form in 1914 and that President Wilson seems to have had in mind when he proposed the Federal Trade Commission. They have never been answered and today they are as large as General Motors Corporation, General Electric Company, United States Steel Corporation and other huge corporations that dominate highly concentrated industries. The fundamental question is whether such huge concentrations of industrial wealth are too large to be efficient producers of the lowest priced and the best possible consumer goods and services. Is there a point in size at which mass production ceases to be more efficient and becomes less efficient? Does a huge company so dominate an industry that the biggest giant's prices become the prices charged by all producers? Is follow-the-leader pricing, in other words, the equivalent of price-fixing? What are the social consequences of a huge company's domination of a labor market, of its pace-setting settlements with unions, of its selection of television programs it will or will not sponsor, of its financial capacity to give or withhold contributions to political campaigns on the national, state and local levels?

Some of these are questions to which the Justice Department addressed itself, in the context of antitrust suits against trusts and corporations, in times past. Others are questions which the FTC itself raised, within the confines of the case against Procter & Gamble Company. But no office of government has addressed itself to the subject as a whole. Some academic economists have spoken to the questions, in whole or in part, and they disagree on the answers. But no private economist has available the investigative and subpoena powers which are the FTC's real resources.

The FTC of the 1960's did relatively little to explore real problems, all the while raising ever higher the banner of consumer protectionism that may be an appropriate symbol for another branch of government, but not for the FTC. What was said of the commission's failings in the 1920's by outsiders was said again in the sixties: "The challenge facing the Federal Trade Commission today [is] to recognize what is essential, to comprehend what is happening, to question and to act. New laws and new programs will be of little avail unless the FTC also revolutionizes its recruitment policies to begin attracting the finest talent in the land and purges its own house of the continuing and devastating impact of political patronage, cronyism and that 'tired blood' which infects the commission's staff."[10]

It seemed a bit late in the day.

PART FIVE

Reformers and Reforms

Past, Present and Future

"It seems to me," Mr. Dooley once commented, "that th' on'y thing to do is to keep polyticians an' businessmen apart. They seem to have a bad infloonce on each other. Whiniver I see an aldherman an' a banker walkin' down th' sthreet together I know th' Recordin' Angel will have to ordher another bottle iv ink."[1]

Finley Peter Dunne's Mr. Dooley offered that commentary on things as they seemed in 1906. More than half a century later, it seems that nothing has changed, except that much of the influence that aldermen once exercised over bankers and other local businessmen now is exercised by Washington over large national corporations. That exception is significant.

Federal regulation of interstate commerce is today undergoing changes which raise new constitutional and consumer questions that cannot yet be answered with certainty. Regulation of the most vital avenues of commerce, as it exists today, was Washington's original effort to promote the general welfare. It took its original form, consisting of the dispersal of government power among many agencies independent of the President, from constitutional necessity and from the writings of the muckrakers who had exposed the bad influences that state regulators and businessmen had on each other. It took its substance from the Populist revolt against the trusts and big business. It has not worked.

The public effects of dishonest abuses and honest mistakes of local aldermen and state legislators are self-limiting. The impact of chicanery and error committed in Washington reaches across the land. The central government is an inherently inefficient promoter of the general welfare because the Constitution purposefully divided its powers among three branches. Expert agencies that were arms of Congress, and thus independent of the President, were meant to overcome inefficiency and preserve constitutional doctrine. It is no coincidence that Presidents consistently have found fault with the agencies, that Congress, with rare exceptions, has accepted them and their works and that the Supreme Court has tried to defend the constitutional independence of the agencies and foster expertise in their works.

And now the search for efficiency moves on, generating great new currents of change in the exercise of the federal power to regulate producers for the benefit of consumers. Even as Congress votes new powers for the regulators, their old powers, like grains of sand, are being eroded and carried in the ill-charted stream of presidential power to the White House and the executive branch departments. Responsibility, the initial element of power, moves first; authority comes after. The shift of responsibility carries with it new attitudes. Presidents, Democratic and Republican, now tend to view big business not as a threat to the public welfare but as an opportunity to foster industrial stability through concentration and thereby to obtain greater public security in matters of wages and prices. The managers of America's largest corporations seem no less willing to sacrifice their competitive freedom to the President than to the regulators. Congress formally approves, or raises only weak objections to, the shift of power; it seems to share Presidents' conclusions that competition is destabilizing and antitrust law is outmoded. The Supreme Court has but infrequent opportunity to speak to the separation of powers doctrine.

The shift of responsibility, attitude and authority from the regulators to the President is by no means complete. Old agencies remain and new forms for the exercise of regulatory power still are taking shape. Yet, the history of presidential displeasure with the independent agencies can be traced back almost to the turn of the century. Presidents, even through Lyndon B. Johnson, did not object to the creation by Congress of new agencies, all the members of which they could appoint. They objected to older agencies they could not control through the appointment process, and some Presidents, thus frustrated, seemingly accepted the independence of the agencies and recommended to Congress ways of improving their efficiency. Theodore Roosevelt was the first President to find significant fault with the bureaucracy. Presumably his concern included the Interstate Commerce Commission, the only major independent agency at the time, when in 1905 he appointed the Keep Commission to "improve methods . . . to avoid conflict and duplication" in the bureaucracy. The commission, which was named for its chairman, a long-forgotten Assistant Secretary of the

Treasury, Charles H. Keep, studied the federal bureaucracy of 1905 for two years and in 1907 President Roosevelt reported to Congress, with rather immoderate optimism, that his commission had "made very satisfactory progress. Antiquated practices and bureaucratic ways have been abolished."[2]

The Keep Commission in fact accomplished rather little, because Congress did not think well of its reforms and because the departments and agencies failed to adopt some of its recommendations. Gifford Pinchot, the conservationist and close friend of President Roosevelt who was a member of the Keep Commission, later commented that it was unrealistic to expect the commission to eliminate "all the going stupidities and wastes of time and money" in the federal establishment of 1905.

There were some reform attempts, though none comparable in ambitiousness of purpose, during the Administrations that began with President Taft and ended with President Hoover. President Wilson, on taking office, clearly had faith in the concept of the independent regulatory agency since he sponsored the creation of two of them, the Federal Reserve Board and the Federal Trade Commission. President Wilson's doubts came later, when he considered ways to obtain a measure of control over the independent Federal Reserve Board he had helped create. Some of the other Presidents who sat during the years between World War I and the Great Depression also sought control of the regulators, but none overtly challenged the system of independent agencies. The reform proposals of modern significance began with Franklin D. Roosevelt and they have continued through each succeeding Administration.

President Roosevelt's attitude toward federal regulation of industry underwent a significant transformation during the years he was in the White House. During his first term of office, from 1933 to 1937, he sponsored the creation of more new regulatory agencies than any President before him and he attempted to control the old agencies. Perhaps because the Supreme Court thwarted his attempt, Roosevelt, during his second term from 1937 to 1941, concentrated on reform. He never repudiated the system of independent regulatory agencies. Whether he finally still believed that the system could be made to work satisfactorily is not known; World War II wholly preoccupied the President and deferred both executive and legislative consideration of all domestic matters that could wait.

Soon after his inauguration in 1937, Roosevelt sent Congress recommendations for increasing efficiency of the federal establishment in general, remarking that four of his predecessors had made "repeated but not wholly successful efforts" along the same lines. Two years later, in 1939, the President focused his reform efforts specifically on the regulatory agencies. He directed his Attorney General, Frank Murphy, to investigate the agencies "with a view to detecting any existing deficiencies and pointing the way to improvement." President Roosevelt's directive led eventually to enactment by Congress, in 1946, of the first statute that recognized the independent regulatory agencies as an entity of government and applied uniformly to all of them.

In 1939 Attorney General Murphy appointed a committee, which was headed by Dean Acheson and which in 1941 finished its work and reported back to Robert Houghwout Jackson, who by then was FDR's Attorney General. The Acheson Committee found so much wrong that it drafted legislation to improve the administration of all regulatory law.[3] World War II intervened, but in 1946 Congress passed the Administrative Procedure Act, the most sweeping effort yet at reforming the regulators but still a law that even then was recognized as only a beginning. The Administrative Procedure Act dealt only with procedure. It changed nothing in the Interstate Commerce Act, the Federal Trade Commission Act or any other of the regulators' enabling statutes. The act tried to make agency procedures more fair and more uniform; it required the agencies to keep the public informed of their rules, to encourage more public participation in the rule-making process and to adopt uniform procedures for hearings.

The Administrative Procedure Act was the product of good intentions, like all other regulatory law, but it also had unexpected side effects. The act forced the regulatory agencies to adopt more of the ways of courts and thereby slowed them down. It allowed more industries and companies to participate in formal agency hearings and permitted each party to have its full say. Thus it encouraged the delays for which the agencies are now famous, the arguments that go on for months and the case records thousands of pages long. Moreover, the act tended to isolate the regulators more from the executive and legislative branches by recognizing them as an independent entity in government and institutionalizing them in the form, though not the substance, of the courts.

So, if the Administrative Procedure Act solved some problems, it helped create more and, a year after President Truman in 1946 signed that act into law, he was appointing a new committee, the first Hoover Commission, named for its chairman, former President Herbert Hoover. Truman asked Herbert Hoover to "recommend organizational changes that would tend toward economy, efficiency and improved service" in the executive branch and the regulatory agencies. The Hoover Commission studied the regulators long and well. It had many criticisms, such as this of the Federal Trade Commission: "Its operations, programs and administrative methods have often been inadequate and its procedures cumbersome. It has largely become absorbed in petty matters rather than basic problems." The same had been said about the FTC in 1924. Of the regulatory agencies in general, the Hoover Commission said: "Administration by a plural executive is universally regarded as inefficient. This has been true in connection with these commissions. We recommend that all administrative responsibility be vested in the chairman of the commission."

President Truman prepared no less than twenty-five reorganization plans, based upon the Hoover Commission recommendations, proposing a grand realignment of bureaus, offices and chairs throughout the executive branch. His proposal, concerning the regulatory agencies, was that the President name the agency chairmen; his purpose, Mr. Truman said, was to "fix responsibility for day-to-day administration" in the chairmen and to increase "effectiveness and economy."

Congress went along with most of the Truman proposals. But, as things turned out, the presidential power to appoint regulatory agency chairmen—which Congress approved except for the ICC—intensified the politics of regulation more than it increased effectiveness and economy.

President Eisenhower appointed the second Hoover Commission, which didn't study the regulators as long or as well as had the first. The Eisenhower Administration, during its early years, also sponsored substantial reductions in the regulatory agencies' budgets that had no relevance to their workloads. But President Eisenhower attempted to be constructive in a new way: apparently concluding that years of presidential attempts to reform the regulators had come to nought, he would give them a chance to reform themselves. Under White House auspices, all the regulators met in conference and were joined by eminent professors of administrative law and practicing lawyers in what was called the Administrative Conference of the United States—a gathering that took its inspiration from the Judicial Conference of the United States, a body headed by the Chief Justice of the United States that had been successful in leading the way to improvements in administration of the federal court system. The Administrative Conference was a temporary affair, but the Eisenhower Administration also established in the Justice Department a permanent Office of Administrative Procedure, a day-in, day-out helpmate for the regulators. The Eisenhower Administration did something more; it created an Attorney General's National Committee to Study the Antitrust Laws which for the first time focused national attention on the growing conflict between regulatory law and antitrust law. For its efforts, the committee was roundly denounced on Capitol Hill; it was accused, for instance, of tarring the Robinson-Patman Act "with the same brush" of unconstitutionality with which the Supreme Court of 1935 had thrown out the National Industrial Recovery Act.

During the years that Dwight Eisenhower was in the White House, Congress also began to take a more active interest in the agencies. The Senate Commerce Committee held its hearings on "the deteriorating railroad situation." Those hearings led in turn to the Senate staff study of National Transportation Policy that was a landmark examination of the patchwork development of transport law and of conflicts among the agencies that administer the statutes.[4] The 1961 report remains a study and nothing more because Congress did little with the recommendations of its own study group.

The second event of note on Capitol Hill during the 1950's was the investigation of the regulatory agencies that was conducted by the House Legislative Oversight Subcommittee, a unit of the House Commerce Committee. The investigation was prompted by a House resolution that was introduced in 1957 by the late Sam Rayburn, the veteran Democratic Speaker of the House.

In the course of the Legislative Oversight Subcommittee's investigations, during the late 1950's and early 1960's, there was no major regulatory agency where real or alleged scandal was not involved. At the FCC, a half-dozen television station awards, in addition to the Miami Channel 10 case, were bounced back by the courts after the Oversight Subcommittee hearings disclosed improper off-the-record pleas to commission members. The courts returned to the Civil Aeronautics Board an important New York–San Francisco route case decision because of alleged off-the-record pleas. The Securities and Exchange Commission and the Federal Trade Commission were tarred and Sherman Adams was forced to resign as President Eisenhower's chief of staff because of allegations that Adams had contacted the two agencies to seek preferential treatment for Bernard Goldfine. An Interstate Commerce Commission member, Hugh W. Cross, resigned after investigators asked him whether he had used his position to influence the award by some railroads of a contract to bus passengers between train stations in Chicago.

No permanent reforms should have been expected to result from those congressional investigations and none did. Codes of ethics were dusted off and again forgotten. President Eisenhower replaced the disgraced regulators with "better" men. President Kennedy appointed what he thought were still better men; some were, and some were not. President Johnson's apointees generally were of the traditional, political variety. The House Legislative Oversight Subcommittee, which made all the headlines, faded into the white marble obscurity of the basement of the new Rayburn House Office Building after the Democrats took possession of the White House in 1961.

The Administration of John F. Kennedy was a high-water mark of reform activity. During his brief time in office, President Kennedy was not wholly consistent in addressing himself to each regulatory agency and all of the problems. His proposals did not succeed and his Administration ended inconclusively. But Kennedy was the first President in history who proposed to Congress not only ways of improving the agencies but also condemned the Interstate Commerce Commission's failures to serve the public interest and proposed to reverse seventy-five years of history by stripping the agency of much of its authority to prevent railroads from cutting their rates. He was defeated by Congress and the railroad industry.

President Kennedy brought to the White House a remarkable interest in federal regulation of industry and distrust of much of it. His unique interest apparently reflected the influence of his father, Joseph P. Kennedy, whom President Roosevelt in the 1930's named first to the Securities and Exchange Commission and later to the Maritime Commission.

As an interesting footnote, it must be added that the elder Kennedy's continuing interest in the regulatory process seemingly did not rub off on another son, Robert. After John Kennedy was inaugurated, his brother took office as Attorney General and, upon arriving at the Justice Department Building, Robert Kennedy discovered the Office of Administrative Procedure occupying prestigious space immediately across the corridor from the Attorney General's office. The office, set up during the Eisenhower Administration to help find solutions to regulatory agency problems, had been housed next door to the Attorney General so that it would not get lost in the huge department. But Attorney General Kennedy ordered it out to make way for his public relations staff. The office was moved first into a corridor and then out of the Justice Department Building, into an old commercial building on Pennsylvania Avenue. The Attorney General's words spoken in meetings with department careerists, as well as his actions, left the distinct impression that he knew little about regulatory law. Later, as Attorney General and particularly as senator, Robert Kennedy began to show some of the interest of President Kennedy in reforming the regulators.

After he won election in November, 1960, John Kennedy sent James M. Landis to Washington to take a hard, quick look at the regulatory agencies. Mr. Landis, a long-time associate of Joseph Kennedy, originally had come to Washington in the early New Deal days, and had served on the SEC with the elder Kennedy and later had become chairman of the Civil Aeronautics Board. In December of 1960, after working long hours in a small rented office, James Landis delivered his report to the President-elect.[5] The Landis report was not a long, dull volume drafted by a committee; it was a short, outspoken volume of criticism by a man who was qualified to criticize.

President Kennedy acted on much of James Landis' advice, and then went beyond it. He sent to Congress a special message on the agencies, declaring they were shot through with "delays . . . incompetence."[6] He sponsored reorganization plans for each agency, which permitted the commissioners and board members to expedite their work by delegating decisions of lesser importance to their staffs. He asked the chairman of each agency to file monthly progress reports with the White House. And he called a new Administrative Conference of the United States to seek long-term answers to the structural inefficiency of multimember agencies.

President Kennedy's truly remarkable undertaking was his attack on the ICC. It was only a beginning. He did not follow up at all on Landis' criticism of the Robinson-Patman Act, for instance, presumably because he didn't live long enough and he didn't possess sufficient political influence with Congress while he did live. It would appear that he felt transportation problems to be most pressing, so he began there. He appointed a task force to study national aviation goals, which raised doubts about the CAB's service to the consumer.[7] And he sent to Congress his 1962 Special Transportation Message, which implicitly said the ICC's regulation of freight rates was a fraud on the consumer and explicitly said the ICC's power to hold railroad rates up should be repealed.[8]

President Johnson seemed to cast his lot with the reformers early in his Administration, by signing into law on August 30, 1964, a bill to confer permanency on the Administrative Conference of the United States. The conference would become a congress of the regulators, a forum where the regulators and scholars in the field of administrative law and government would come together periodically to seek the reforms that so long had been needed. The conference would have a permanent secretariat; the Office of Administrative Procedure would be recalled from limbo to form its nucleus. There would be a chairman, appointed by the President with the advice and consent of the Senate—a regulator to preside over the regulators as the Chief Justice of the United States presides over the Judicial Conference of the United States. The headless fourth branch at last would gain a head. "A goal long sought by those who wish to improve the operation of the administrative process," intoned a senator. But President Johnson seemed to lack the enthusiasm for reform of his predecessor. It took Lyndon Johnson longer than three years to appoint a chairman and thus to activate the Administrative Conference. On October 14, 1967, he named as chairman Jerre S. Williams, a law professor at the University of Texas at Austin. The President apparently acted then only because his long delay was giving rise to criticism, and the critics included Robert Kennedy.[9]

President Johnson also signed into law, on July 4, 1966, the Freedom of Information Act. It was an amendment to the Administrative Procedure Act of 1946 which, among other things, had provided for public access to the regulatory agencies' official records, with certain exceptions. The exceptions had proved so large that Congress in 1966 passed a new law. But it also contained nine specific exemptions and, as a Senate subcommittee in 1968 observed, its usefulness to the public was uncertain.[10]

The history of reform since 1904 has been uneven and disappointing. It has been written largely by stronger Presidents who, frustrated by the Supreme Court in their efforts to gain meaningful control of the agencies, have accepted their independence and permanence and proposed to Congress ways of improving them. Their reform proposals also being frustrated, partially or totally, succeeding Presidents have offered still more ambitious and inventive reforms. Congress, however reluctantly, has begun to accept more of the reforms, giving the President power to designate the chairmen of the agencies, allowing his Budget Bureau to clear the appropriations and legislative requests.

The ascending tempo of reform, the slow submission of Congress and the gradual accretion of presidential responsibility are threads in the larger fabric of recent economic, political and constitutional history. The independent regulatory agencies were and are particularized responses of government to the needs and desires of the people. Population, industrial production and consumer affluence have continued to grow, most dramatically since World War II, and federal concern has expanded into areas of the public health, education and welfare that had been left to the states and individuals. As the total size and responsibility of the federal establishment have grown, the inherent inefficiency of government powers divided among three coequal branches and a splintered fourth branch has become much more burdensome. The desirability and perhaps necessity of fixing responsibility, securing greater coordination and establishing some consensus on priorities have become more obvious.

Larger public concerns began to bring forth new governmental responses as long ago as the 1930's. The national trauma of the Great Depression produced the National Industrial Recovery Act of 1933, by which Congress delegated to the President almost the whole of its power to regulate commerce, and President Roosevelt began to fix wages and prices and, through establishment of the National Recovery Administration codes, squelch competition before the Supreme Court declared the act unconstitutional. Congress thereupon delegated some of the powers over wages, prices and competition to new and old independent regulatory agencies, and the Supreme Court concurred. But the nation's fears of depression were not stilled and its deep desires for economic stability and personal security were its first order of domestic business as World War II drew to a close.

The vehicle of its desires was the Employment Act of 1946 which, despite its uninspired name, summed up America's determination henceforth to secure economic stability and material abundance. President Truman's words on signing it on February 20, 1946, were not wholly unlike the hopes spoken by President Wilson in 1914, when he signed the Federal Trade Commission Act, or even those of President Roosevelt in 1934, when he signed the Securities Exchange Act. President Truman said the new law "gives expression to a demand of the people for positive attack upon the problems of mass unemployment and ruinous depression . . . of speculative booms and business failures. It is not the government's duty to supplant private enterprise [but] to create conditions in which the businessman and job seeker have a chance to succeed."

It was not the purpose of the act that was so novel to American history; it was the method by which government sought to achieve that purpose. The law for the first time in history placed upon the President the responsibility for full employment and full purchasing power. It created on the White House staff a Council of Economic Advisers, which was directed to appraise national economic development and advise the President on means to achieve the goals of "maximum employment, production and purchasing power." It directed the President, in turn, to report to Congress annually on the state of the nation's economic progress.

Congress with the Employment Act did not delegate to the President its power to regulate commerce; neither the President nor the Council of Economic Advisers was empowered, as the independent agencies had been, to write rules and decisions with the force of law. It transferred responsibility; it did not transfer authority. The law was not all that President Truman had asked. The legal powers of the President were essentially still those of recommending and vetoing the acts of Congress. Every recent occupant of the White House has complained, as an aide to President Kennedy once said, that the President is charged with "greater responsibility . . . than he has authority to fill those responsibilities."[11]

The complaint remains valid. Yet, the distinction between responsibility and authority always has been less than crystal-clear and the ambiguity in the years since 1946 has tended slowly but certainly to be resolved, with or without act of Congress, by enlargement of the authority of the President. The trappings of office are indicative of the trend. The Council of Economic Advisers has become a super economic planning bureau and the President has become the economic as well as the political chief of state. The Economic Report he annually sends to Congress, as required by the 1946 Employment Act, today is a companion document to his State of the Union message, which is required by the Constitution.

The precise forms that more complete presidential authority ultimately may take remain less than clear. But certainly the forms will take their shape from presidential experimentation, which has been underway since the Truman Administration.

Presidents and their economic advisers, informally and on a rising scale, have intervened directly in the competitive economics of particular industries and corporations. Inasmuch as the overriding economic problem of the post–World War II era turned out to be inflation rather than depression, Presidents have used their powers of economic persuasion principally against proposed price and wage increases. President Kennedy, armed only with the power of persuasion, confronted United States Steel Corporation and forced it to rescind a price increase. President Johnson similarly confronted the steel industry and he forced Chrysler Corporation to roll back a price increase it already had made by convincing General Motors Corporation it should keep its automobile prices at acceptably lower levels. Presidents similarly have intervened in aluminum, copper and many other pricing matters. It is true that the power of persuasion on occasion has been augmented. President Kennedy called out the Federal Bureau of Investigation and apparently threatened antitrust action and President Johnson ordered military contracts withdrawn from companies that increased prices.[12] Whatever the weight of the threats, General Motors no longer proposes price changes without first checking informally at the White House, and presumably other large corporations do also.[13] Presidents in addition have intervened to try to reduce wage increases in the automobile, steel, railroad and other industries; they have not succeeded as well as in the pricing area, perhaps because unions cannot effectively be threatened with antitrust suits and contract withdrawals. President Nixon promised to dispense with the formal wage and price guidelines of his Democratic predecessors. But Nixon of course did not repudiate presidential responsibility for fiscal and monetary policy as means nor for full employment and purchasing power as ends. Like Johnson, Nixon also used government purchasing power to try to roll back price increases posted by the plywood and other industries.

Presidents and their economic advisers also have used their powers of persuasion for a variety of other governmental purposes. They informally have asked General Motors to help the nation's balance of payments problem, by building in the U.S. small autos that can compete with foreign imports. They have asked GM and many other large corporations to make positive efforts to hire the Negro unemployed and to help improve housing in the nation's urban ghettos.

The moral righteousness of the presidential interventions is not questioned, nor is his legal authority. The Employment Act did not specifically sanction the economic advisers' wage and price guidelines nor the Presidents' interventions. But the guidelines and interventions do not have the force of law; companies and unions in legal theory can ignore them.

On the other hand, presidential experimentation in the exercise of informal authority necessarily has brought the White House into conflict, in spirit and in fact, with the independent regulatory agencies. Presidents, in attempting to ensure full employment and purchasing power through the management of fiscal policy and tax rates, have collided head-on with the Federal Reserve Board, when it has decided that monetary policy requirements of the moment are higher interest rates and tighter money. Presidents have forced roll backs in steel, auto and other prices at the same time the Interstate Commerce Commission and Civil Aeronautics Board have authorized transportation rate increases. They have intervened to open jobs to Negroes, although that task was assigned to the Equal Employment Opportunity Commission.

Presidents have attempted to reach certain accommodations with the agencies. President Johnson, for instance, appointed a consumer assistant to the White House staff and a consumer counsel to the staff of the Attorney General and these individuals put in formal appearances before some of the agencies to argue that the ICC should not permit a rate increase or the FTC should police advertising misrepresentations by ghetto merchants. But the White House attempts to accommodate to the agencies quite apparently produced no satisfactory results. For the Council of Economic Advisers' annual reports to the President have become a source of continuing criticism of the agencies and their works. The council, as a result of the Big John case, became critical of the ICC's regulation of railroad freight rates. More recently, it has said that "regulated industries are vitally important [and] the markets and technologies of these industries are subject to the forces of persistent change, which requires that existing policies be continually reexamined." Regulation, if it is "vigilant," can "stabilize or reduce the cost of living and the costs of business," the Council added, but instead it has led to "protective efforts" unrelated to consumer protection.[14]

Congress has not addressed itself in any comprehensive fashion to the conflicts of presidential responsibility and regulatory agency authority and perhaps it never will. It more likely will formalize presidential authority in bits and pieces of legislative delegation. Congress has not yet acceded to Presidents' requests that it delegate limited fiscal authority to raise and lower tax rates on individual and corporate incomes for the purpose of expanding or contracting purchasing power and employment. But Congress has been delegating to the President larger pieces of power applicable to other areas of private commerce. First, it has begun to delegate to the great departments of the executive branch types of regulatory responsibility and authority that once were thought to be within the exclusive competence and constitutional jurisdiction of the independent agencies. Second, Congress has resorted to a more novel type of delegation by creating government-industry consortiums in which the President has a direct voice.

Congress throughout history has, of course, delegated to the President and his executive branch the authority to see to the faithful execution of laws written by Congress pursuant to the domestic powers assigned it by the Constitution. Such delegation has been constitutionally permissible when Congress has written finite law and left little to the discretion of the administrators in the executive branch. Such law traditionally has been enforced through actions brought against individuals and corporations by the executive branch and decided by the judicial branch. As the nation and the body of federal statute law have grown more complex, a large layer of administrative law has been inserted between the laws of Congress and the decisions of the federal courts. It consists of regulations which are written by cabinet members and their subordinates who serve at the President's pleasure and which have the force of law. The Treasury Department, for instance, writes tax regulations; the Department of Health, Education, and Welfare has regulations governing Social Security benefits and the Interior Department has regulations covering importation of oil. The writing and the enforcement of all such regulations are subject to the due process provisions of the Administrative Procedure Act. Decisions reached by executive branch officers under their regulations may be appealed to the courts.

Administrative law as written and enforced by the executive branch, in growing volume since the 1930's, is a presumably necessary and not unconstitutional invention of big government. Congress has not delegated its power to fix tax rates, Social Security payments and the like. It has delegated authority which reaches widely to the private privileges and obligations of millions of Americans but which is narrow in the range of discretion left to the President's officers. Administrative law, as practiced by the executive branch since the 1930's, thus is distinct from the delegation to the independent agencies of almost unlimited discretionary authority to fix rates and prices and engage in economic planning for private industry.

The distinction between executive branch and independent agency regulation, however, has become less distinct in recent years. Since the passage of the Employment Act enlarging presidential responsibility, Congress has been delegating to the executive branch authority to write regulations involving exercises of discretion quite akin to the discretionary powers of the independent agencies. The Kefauver-Harris Drug Amendments of 1962 enlarged the authority of the Food and Drug Administration to regulate the pharmaceutical industry for the protection of drug consumers; FDA is an executive branch agency which is part of the new Department of Health, Education, and Welfare. Congress has enlarged the authority of executive branch departments also, for example, to regulate commodities exchanges and to police labor union constitutions and bylaws for unfair discrimination against minority members.

But the most significant enlargement of executive branch responsibility and authority, in an area once thought within the exclusive competence and constitutional jurisdiction of the independent regulatory agencies, occurred with the creation of the Department of Transportation in 1966.

The authority of the Secretary of Transportation still falls far short of his responsibility. But the evolution of this department demonstrates the force of currents of change within the powers of government. Congress in 1940 had written its national transportation policy, assigning to one of its arms, the Interstate Commerce Commission, the responsibility and seemingly the authority to coordinate all federal transportation regulation and promotion. The ICC did not and could not fulfill the responsibility assigned. In 1950, President Truman created the position of Under Secretary of Commerce for Transportation, saying his purpose was to give central leadership to "the development of over-all transportation policy." The Under Secretary accomplished almost nothing and Congress in 1966, at the request of President Johnson, abolished the position and created the Department of Transportation, headed by a full secretary of cabinet rank. In so doing, Congress implicitly transferred from the legislative branch to the executive branch the responsibility to coordinate federal transportation programs. It also transferred certain amounts of authority. It transferred to the new department the authority of the Interstate Commerce Commission and the Civil Aeronautics Board to write regulations with the force of law governing safety requirements in the railroad, trucking and airline industries. When Congress enacted the National Traffic and Motor Vehicle Safety Act of 1966, it delegated to the department the authority to regulate automobile manufacturers, to the extent of requiring them to install safety devices in their products and to disclose to consumers statements itemizing auto prices.

The authority of the Secretary of Transportation to regulate automobile, truck, railroad and airline safety is not the equivalent of the power to engage in economic planning on the scale of the ICC and CAB. Congress has given the Secretary no authority to regulate transportation rates and he has no real power over spending and development of the federal highways and airways systems. But the Bureau of Public Roads and the Federal Aviation Administration are part of the Transportation Department and certainly strong Secretaries and Presidents to come will escalate their power to control these subordinate units in the cause of transportation co-ordination.

Shortly before he left office in 1969, President Johnson was handed a task force report recommending establishment of a Department of Communications. The task force, led by former Under Secretary of State Eugene Rostow, recognized an urgent need to coordinate federal communications policies and improve communications planning. It therefore proposed to charge these responsibilities to the President, whose Secretary of Communications would assume also some of the authority of the Federal Communications Commission.

Congress and the Constitution, not to mention the ICC, CAB and FCC, surely would resist the transfer to the executive branch of the authority to regulate rates and prices and otherwise engage in economic planning for private industry. The resistance, however, could fall to the necessities of efficiency, coordination and priority. The agencies may not fall; Congress has no taste for abolishing its creations. But the agencies would be shells, left with little real power. The manner of the transfer of their authority to the President cannot be predicted in detail, but it is likely that the authority of the regulators will be made part of a still greater authority of the President to control prices and wages in general. The informal price and wage guidelines with which Presidents Kennedy and Johnson sought full employment and purchasing power without undue inflation or recession were not successful. President Nixon dispensed with the guidelines but not the objectives. Their attainment ultimately may well require a permanent program of price and wage controls, patterned on the powers Congress delegated to the President during World War II and the Korean conflict.

If, on the other hand, congressional and constitutional resistance will not permit wholesale transfer to the President and his executive branch of all the powers to regulate private industry now vested in the independent agencies, alternatives are available. One, for which the United States presumably is not ready, is nationalization of those private industries which are most vital to consumers. Nationalization of private industry may or may not be more efficient than regulation of private industry. The democracies of western Europe have gone on from regulation to nationalization. If, in America, Congress at some future time decides to nationalize the railroads and other industries and place their control directly in the hands of the President, the Constitution quite apparently would not resist.[15] It does not bar the taking of private property for public use, but merely guarantees that owners shall not be deprived of their property without due process of law and just compensation.

A second alternative to presidential regulation of private industry is the government-owned corporation, created by act of Congress. The Tennessee Valley Authority is an example. If Congress nowadays feels that the creation of more TVA's would too closely approach nationalization, it clearly is not distrustful of a third alternative in the form of government-industry consortiums, which also enjoy contemporary popularity in western Europe. The consortium is a halfway measure between nationalization of industry and its operation by the President, on the one hand, and regulation of industry by independent agency, on the other. The technique was employed by Congress in the Communications Satellite Act of 1962.

Commercial telephone, television and other communications by way of satellites, orbiting as high as 21,000 miles above the earth, represented a technological breakthrough which could have been regulated by an independent agency, just as the Federal Communications Commission for many years had regulated the companies providing international communications by way of short-wave radio and submarine cable. Satellite communications could have been regulated by the old FCC, or Congress could have created a new independent agency as it created the Atomic Energy Commission in 1946 to promote and regulate civilian uses of atomic energy. Instead, Congress in 1962 created a government-industry joint venture, which became known as the Communications Satellite Corporation. Comsat is regulated by the FCC and owned by American Telephone and Telegraph Company and other companies that were in the business of transmitting overseas communications by radio and cable. The public also, by terms of the 1962 act, may own Comsat stock. But the joint venture represents an advance in the art of regulation because Congress conferred on it a monopoly of international commercial communications that originated or terminated in the United States and that are transmitted by way of satellite. Congress also absolved Comsat of certain antitrust law responsibilities. And it prescribed the capital structure of the corporation, empowered the President to designate its incorporators and gave him permanent authority to name three of Comsat's fifteen directors.

The government-industry partnership concept has proved increasingly appealing, at the White House and in Congress, for a variety of purposes. A government-sanctioned industrial monopoly, in which the President has an amount of continuing authority, has been advocated for such diverse purposes as the development of a supersonic commercial airliner, the operation of the nation's fleet of railroad passenger equipment and the rebuilding of America's inner-city slums.

It is important, in considering the future of the federal government's efforts to regulate industry on behalf of the consumer, to distinguish among the various elements of the present conflict between the responsibility of the President and the still large authority of the independent agencies. The President and his Council of Economic Advisers, his Secretary of Transportation and his consumer counsels seek lower rates and prices, the coordination of federal programs and the establishment of priorities for government spending, including subsidy spending. The independent agencies resist the President on all fronts. But the President and the regulators are not in disagreement on how best to achieve their different ends. They share the conclusion that government regulation of private industry can best be achieved through big business, industrial concentration, diminution of competition and repeal of the antitrust laws.

Comsat and other government-industry consortiums by their nature cannot exist without repeal of the antitrust laws. Informal presidential regulation of prices and wages requires no formal repeal, but Presidents and their economic advisers have found, as the independent agencies discovered long ago, that regulation works best where competition is least. It is patently impossible for the President to attempt to impose wage and price guidelines on industries, say, of tomato planters or auto body repair shops, consisting of thousands of competitors all over the land. It is entirely practical for him to impose the guidelines, as well as requirements to hire Negroes and assist in the balance of payments problem, on General Motors Corporation.

Congress time and again has repealed the Sherman and Clayton Antitrust Acts for the benefit of the independent agencies and the industries they regulate. Antitrust law has been repealed informally by the absence of vigorous enforcement by the Department of Justice. The antitrust division cannot file antitrust suits without the written authority of the Attorney General and the Attorney General does not authorize suits without checking the White House. Antitrust law is not dead but a Sherman Act suit to divide General Motors into a half-dozen competing manufacturers was prepared in the antitrust division several years ago and was never filed.[16]

The vigor of antitrust enforcement has declined for a number of reasons. The Defense Department feels it needs the biggest of big business for military production requirements. The State Department prefers big business to assist in the accomplishment of foreign policy objectives, including the amelioration of balance of payments problems. Labor unions, once supporters of any liberal cause, seem in their maturity to feel that their stability and security are best served by concentrations of industrial wealth in giant corporations from which workers can more easily and surely win their wage demands. Big government, in all its manifestations, seems invariably to foster big business and to repudiate competition and the antitrust laws.

Liberal economists of the Galbraith school hold that antitrust law is and should be dead because giant corporations and their technostructures are necessary to contemporary America's desires for economic stability, corporate security and consumer protection. The few remaining legislators of the old Populist school wonder and grope. "Antitrust is sick and nobody seems greatly concerned," Senator Philip A. Hart, the Michigan Democrat who headed the Senate antitrust subcommittee, has said. "What our corporate executives desire is not competition but security. In Professor Galbraith, they have found their apologist; in the Federal government, I fear they have found an accomplice."[17]

Most legislators and certainly most Americans vote with the liberal economists for individual and corporate security, big business and centralization of governmental power in the office of the President. If those ends and means tend to conflict with economic freedom, competition as enforced by antitrust laws and separation of government powers, so be it. The Supreme Court, still the constitutional judge of the exercise of power by the other two branches, has had but one significant opportunity to speak directly to the rise in recent years of presidential responsibility and authority. That was in 1952, when President Truman ordered the seizure of the nation's steel mills to prevent a nation-wide strike. The court held that the President had usurped unconstitutionally the powers of Congress. "The power of Congress to adopt such public policies as those proclaimed by the order is beyond question," said Justice Black in the opinion of the court. But Congress has "exclusive constitutional authority" to make such laws.[18]

Justice Frankfurter, in his concurring opinion, added this view of presidential power: "It is absurd to see a dictator in a representative product of the sturdy democratic traditions of the Mississippi Valley. The accretion of dangerous power does not come in a day. It does come, however slowly, from the generative force of unchecked disregard of the restrictions that fence in even the most disinterested assertion of authority."[19]

But the Supreme Court's discipline of presidential power in 1952 did not speak broadly to the rise of that power and the decline of congressional power since 1946. The Truman Administration, in defending the constitutionality of its seizure, did not cite the Employment Act nor any other statute. It rested its case largely on what it termed the inherent powers of the Presidency.

Perhaps the Supreme Court will find in the Constitution ways of speaking more broadly and meaningfully through cases and controversies to matters of presidential power, big government, competitive freedom and individualism. It still searches. The court reread the Constitution in 1968 and conferred upon individual citizens, "who assert only the status of Federal taxpayers," the right to challenge in federal courts the constitutionality of federal spending programs.[20] The Supreme Court in 1923 had found in the Constitution no such right of taxpayers. The Johnson Administration, represented by the Solicitor General, argued in 1968 that the Constitution still conferred no such right; that a taxpayer's interest in a spending program is too minute to matter and that the judicial branch must defer to the other two branches in such policy matters.

But time and the Supreme Court had changed since 1923. Chief Justice Warren, writing the court's opinion, noted the growth of federal taxes and spending. Justice Douglas, in a concurring opinion, said, "We have a Constitution designed to keep government out of private domains. But the fences have often been broken down." The Constitution alone "is not adequate to protect the individual against the growing bureaucracy in the legislative and executive branches. He faces a formidable opponent in government [and] is almost certain to be plowed under, unless he has a well-organized active political group to speak for him." The church, the press and labor unions have been such groups, Justice Douglas continued, but when they are lacking, "individual liberty withers."[21]

The Supreme Court thereby gave the individual a voice to speak against big government. But, as Chief Justice Warren added, the force of the voice will depend upon whether taxpayers can formulate cases alleging that their tax money is being spent in violation of specific constitutional protections against abuses of legislative power and upon how the Supreme Court in the future decides such allegations.

The most that can be said is that new experiments in governmental power and old searches for constitutional meanings will continue.

A Proposal for Reform

Given the present state of domestic economic affairs, probably the worst that Americans can expect in the immediate future is higher taxes, higher prices, more traffic jams, more blackouts and more old movies on television. Highway contractors, those members of Congress who own TV stations and the Washington lawyers who know a way through the mazes of government will get richer. Negroes who expect equal job opportunities will grow more frustrated and the rest of us will become more confused.

The efforts to adapt big government and big business to the Constitution will continue apace. The regulators will meet together in the Administrative Conference of the United States to attempt to reform themselves. There may be an American Ombudsman, that officer of government invented by Scandinavian Socialists so that frustrated citizens have a place to register their complaints against the bureaucracy. The Supreme Court will continue to search the Constitution for words that give new meaning and vitality to individualism and economic freedom. Contrariwise, there will be efforts to adapt the Constitution to big government and big business. Rexford Guy Tugwell has written no fewer than thirty-two drafts of a new Constitution. Tugwell as a young man was one of President Franklin Roosevelt's New Deal brain trusters and as an older man he has felt "an uneasy sense of something wrong" in the relationship of the old Constitution and the new reality of economic and social responsibility and authority vested in the central government.[1]

All these efforts to adapt reality to the Constitution or to write a new Constitution more in keeping with reality are unlikely anytime soon to assuage public frustrations, remedy old conflicts in federal programs and bureaus or discipline total federal spending to some system of priorities. Consequently, Congress will continue to shift to the President, his Council of Economic Advisers and his executive branch departments more responsibility for governmental efficiency and economic security and Congress will delegate piecemeal to the

President and those who serve at his pleasure more authority to fulfill his responsibilities. It seems unlikely that a President anytime soon will emerge as the dictator whom Justice Frankfurter in 1952 said could come forth from the accumulation of presidential power, no matter how disinterestedly that authority was gained. America was sufficiently bothered by the precedent of Franklin D. Roosevelt's four terms so that it ratified the Twenty-second Amendment in 1951 to bar a future President from more than two full terms in office.

If the near-term threat of dictatorship in America may thus be dismissed, certain other risks cannot. It remains to be seen whether the President, his economic advisers and his great departments can succeed where Congress and its regulatory agencies have failed. The executive branch, by and large, is not now as defenseless as are the regulators against pressures brought by special-interest segments of the population and against commitment to special private causes. The pressures bear on the great departments, some of which tend in time to become advocates of broad special-interest groups. The Department of Labor is regarded by all concerned as the voice of organized labor; the Department of Commerce is the accepted advocate of business; the Department of Agriculture is the spokesman for as well as subsidizer of farmers. But these departments are advocates of very large special-interest groups which, because they are not of a single view on matters of competition, subsidy and so forth, expose department officers to varying points of view. And, most importantly, their advocacies are not unduly objectionable to the public at large because cabinet secretaries are subject to the discipline of the President whose constituency embraces all the people.

If the President and his executive branch are now reasonably secure against the pressures and commitments that have plagued the regulators, they may not remain so. The experience of the democracies of western Europe suggests that increased centralization of power within government generates its own pressures and problems. Big business and big labor are capable of generating big political pressures that do not necessarily assist efficient government planning. Issues of mechanization, full employment and higher wages in industries such as transportation, communications, steel and automobiles that have been cartelized or nationalized tend to be resolved more by political than economic means, and if they are not resolved, big labor is capable of general strikes that paralyze a nation. Government, industry and labor relationships in the United States do not yet parallel those in Europe. But neither is America as far from Europe as it once was. General Motors says industry and government should work "not as adversaries, but as allies," and government no longer disagrees.[2]

The alternatives to a continuation of the present trend of public frustration and government inefficiency resolved through growing centralization of authority in the President are not simple. But neither are alternatives an unexplored miasma. President Kennedy proposed an alternative in the transportation area when he called not for the transfer but for the repeal of much of the Interstate Commerce Commission's authority to regulate rates. He was inconsistent in that he proposed to rely "more on competition" and antitrust law concerning railroad rates but he used the informal persuasive powers of his office, rather than antitrust law, to prevent steel and other price increases. Perhaps he did not, in his own mind, act inconsistently; his means varied but the ends he sought were lower prices. John Kennedy was, obviously, a pragmatist.

His contribution was to state the problem and offer an alternative solution. "We must begin," he said, to resolve the conflicts and inefficiencies in transportation programs or face the certainty of "even more difficult and costly solutions in the not-too-distant future."[3] Some of those who served President Kennedy, such as Newton Minow, added the thought that agencies such as the Federal Communications Commission should be abolished and their responsibility and authority redistributed among the three constitutional branches of government. Taken as a whole, the Kennedy era was tentative and groping, but it rejected the cynicism that the only thing history teaches is that it teaches nothing. Certainly the need for greater efficiency in the administration of each federal program and for establishment of some scheme of priority among programs, applicable to federal spending and manpower resources, are greater now than when Kennedy spoke. At the end of its time, the Johnson Administration counted no fewer than 435 federal social and economic programs, compared, it said, with 45 at the time President Kennedy came to office.[4]

Big government and its counterparts in industry and labor will not disappear; they were responses to the demands of the people in an era of industrialization and urbanization, for economic security and abundance. Blind condemnation of bigness, no less than blind affirmation, is of no help. If the needs of governmental efficiency and priority are to be met, and balanced anew with doctrines of economic freedom and individualism, bigness must be disciplined through a redistribution of powers among the three constitutional branches; a re-evaluation of the relationship between the federal government and the states and a reaffirmation of antitrust law as the best and only means this nation has discovered to assure economic freedom and economic individualism. The Constitution is not out-moded as a charter of government and of liberty. The competitive free enterprise system, enforced by antitrust laws, is not incapaci-tated as the most efficient means men have found to assure con-sumers the lowest prices, the greatest technological progress and the best allocation of resources.

The independent regulatory agencies as they presently exist, should be abolished, and the powers of each should be carefully re-examined. Those promises and powers in their laws which do not conflict with competitive principles and antitrust statutes should be distributed among the three branches; those that do conflict should be repealed. In redistributing those powers which are retained, consideration must be given to the question of whether some tasks, assumed by Washington in pursuit of the general welfare of the entire nation, can more effectively be performed by state and local governments, alone or in a new form of partnership with the federal government. Washington must treat all who are subject to its laws and beneficiaries of its programs with equality and uniformity. That fundamental constitutional requirement inhibits effectiveness of centralized planning in a nation as large, populous and variegated as is the United States. The transportation requirements of New York are not the same as those of Nashville and Tucson. The Federal Trade Commission admittedly has not been able to effec-tively police the retail advertising of all merchants on every Main Street and one FCC member has said, "Federal efforts alone can never be successful."[5] If Washington delegates or shares its tasks, it must also share its tax revenues. The most promising method is block grants to the states; Washington would, for example, grant to each state a proportionate sum for transportation purposes and allow the state to decide where and how to spend the money. Federal authority and money cannot be shared in areas of exclusive federal jurisdiction, such as navigable waters and airways. But federal funds, shared or not, should not be used to subsidize private corporations.

In the redistribution of powers among the executive, legislative and judicial branches of the federal government, each branch would be charged with larger economic responsibility and authority.

The authority of the President must in some degree be commensurate with his responsibility and both must be disciplined. Unlimited responsibility without some amount of authority invites irresponsibility and invasion in matters of private rights involving prices and wages. If Congress insists that the President bear responsibility for full employment and full purchasing power, then he must have a voice in authority for making monetary policy, which now is vested in the Federal Reserve Board. Perhaps efficiency also requires that he have the authority to raise and lower income tax rates within a limited range prescribed by Congress. But his authority should be confined to power that is narrow in its range of discretion and uniform in its application. He should not, formally or informally, exercise authority over prices charged by private corporations or wages negotiated by labor unions. Nor should his Council of Economic Advisers promulgate price and wage guidelines. The role of the council should be to advise the President, in the exercise of his authority and in his recommendations to Congress, and to coordinate the enforcement and administration of law by the great departments of the executive branch.

Congress is the least efficient, and most democratic, of the three branches. It is a committee of more than five hundred and its composition is more or less constantly changing. It has devised a permanent supporting structure, consisting of professional committee staffs, the legislative research services of the Library of Congress and the executive branch monitoring functions of the General Accounting Office. But Congress apparently is inherently incapable of itself regulating the nation's commerce or else it would not have created the independent regulatory agencies and, more recently, enacted the Employment Act and created the Council of Economic Advisers. Having charged the President with responsibility, and having now begun to enlarge the authority of the executive branch,

Congress should have no great difficulty in removing the regulators and reapportioning their powers.

Congress doubtless will remain the least efficient branch, but certainly it can be strengthened. Members of the most democratic branch should receive at least $100,000 annually, plus expenses, for their services. They should not need private incomes; the repeal of the regulators' powers over industrial pricing and entry into the business will remove from the lawmakers' reach the temptation to use public office for private gain. Congress could further be strengthened if the Constitution were amended to provide four-year terms for members of the House of Representatives, as President Johnson suggested. The proposal for terms longer than two years has merit and if it is adopted consideration also should be given to limiting a representative or senator to no more than two, or perhaps three, consecutive terms. What is good for the President may be good also for members of Congress. Moreover, a limitation on length of service would eliminate, or alleviate, an objectionable feature of congressional committee organization: the seniority system which permits elder legislators to unduly dominate the work of Congress.

The judicial branch long has been the third of three, insofar as size and money are concerned. Lower federal courts perennially are weighted down by dockets of cases awaiting trial and their work loads would be greatly increased by abolition of independent agencies whose formal decisions take the place of federal district court decisions and which are appealable directly to a federal circuit court of appeals. Congress has recognized the problem of overloaded dockets to the extent of creating some new federal judgeships and a few federal district courts of specialized jurisdiction, such as the United States Court of Claims and the United States Court of Customs and Patent Appeals. If the regulatory agencies are abolished, it must create more. It could reconstitute the National Labor Relations Board as a labor court. It should create at least one additional specialized court, to be known as the commerce court, to decide antitrust cases as well as enforcement actions in such matters as food and drug labeling, fraud in the sales of securities and transportation industry safety violations. These specialized courts would decide cases brought by the executive branch or by private citizens, or by the executive branch on behalf of private citizens, as the Justice Department now brings suits to open employment opportunities to Negroes. The commerce court might be constituted from out of the Federal Trade Commission. But the judges of all such courts would have lifetime tenure and be subject to the discipline of the Supreme Court; they would not have the power to both make law and decide it, as the regulatory agencies now do.

There is no constitutional solution to the problem of the regulators other than to abolish them, as they now stand, and redistribute those powers which constitutionally may be exercised by the three branches. The Constitution created a government of the people and the people gave their sovereignty only to officers whom they elected and judges to whom they gave lifetime tenure.

Regulators are extensions of the legislative branch but it would be totally inconsistent and wholly impractical to elect regulators to four-year or other terms. Congress created the agencies for the very purpose of removing the regulation of commerce from politics and substituting independent expertise for political partisanship. There is no reason to believe that popular election of regulators would not further intensify the politics of regulation and deny expertise and independence.

To confer upon the regulators, as they now exist, lifetime tenure also would be inconsistent and impractical. The Constitution, in granting tenure to judges, denied them the power to decide issues other than those brought before them in cases and controversies. Judges cannot reach out to make law where they feel law should be made; it was the purpose of regulation by independent agency to do precisely that. Judges do, of course, make law, but it is subordinate to and contained by statute law written by Congress. To confer upon the regulators something less than lifetime tenure, say terms of ten or twenty years, might make them more efficient but it also would be an unsatisfactory compromise. It would deny them lifetime tenure, which is the only real badge of independence, and it would make them more arbitrary in the exercise of powers which are essentially political, and which for that reason are constitutionally apportioned to the legislative, and most democratic, branch.

To transfer the regulators and their powers intact to the executive branch would confer upon the President powers which, as the Supreme Court has said, would be so discretionary in form and so arbitrary in effect as to be unconstitutional.

Abolition of the agencies, it must be emphasized, does not mean abandonment of specific federal promises of the lowest possible rates and prices and the greatest abundance of goods and services or repeal of the general promise of economic stability and security. It does mean restructuring of some parts of government and of industry for the purpose of improving the likelihood those promises can be fulfilled and economic freedom will not be lost.

Reaffirmation of competition as a national policy and refurbishment of antitrust law as the means of enforcing that policy are absolutely essential prerequisites to abolition of the regulatory agencies. The writing and enforcement of antitrust law never has been and never will be a pure science, economic or political. Antitrust is, as regulation attempted to be, a political policy addressed to industrial economics. The policy of antitrust is to foster competition; the policy of regulation, formal or informal, is to suppress competition. There are and will continue to be valid exceptions to the rule of competition. Natural monopolies, in the form of local electric, water and transit companies, are exceptions that will continue to be regulated under state authority. But all the exceptions that by law or habit have been created in Washington should be re-examined.

The preferences of the Defense and State Departments for big business and their implied distrust of competition rest on premises of national interest and national defense that, at best, have little relationship to the consumer interest; the Krupp steel mills of prewar Germany served similar national interests. The preferences of the regulatory agencies rest on efforts to make regulation more efficient and these efforts, as they have turned out, also bear little relationship to the consumer interest. So far as the preferences of the President and his Council of Economic Advisers are concerned, these also rest on the needs of efficiency in the attempt to secure lower prices and to foster economic stability.

The purported justification underlying all these various preferences for industrial concentration rest basically on the economic assumption that concentration is more efficient than competition as a means of securing lower production costs and, consequently, lower prices or more rapid technological advance. It is assumed that the bigger business is, the larger will be its capability of reducing production costs, lowering prices and/or engaging in research and development. The Federal Trade Commission has not addressed itself to the question of whether in fact prices decline and technology advances in direct ratio to business bigness. But the preponderance of evidence produced by economic studies at a number of universities demonstrates rather conclusively that bigness results in lower prices and greater innovation up to a point, and bigness beyond that point results in potentially monopolistic profits, rising prices and an abatement of inventive genius in corporate research and development laboratories.[6]

It is not clear whether the point at which bigness breeds inefficiency may be reached when a corporation has $1 billion or $20 billion or $100 billion of assets. The point unquestionably varies among different industries.

Antitrust law is a useful, if not perfect, instrument for enlarging the store of knowledge concerning the public effects of industrial concentration. It can be made more useful. Enforcement by the Justice Department should be coordinated with the work of the Council of Economic Advisers. The informal efforts of the President to regulate prices and wages through the prestige or inherent powers of office would be abandoned and those ends pursued through formal antitrust actions, coordinated with fiscal and monetary policy by the Council of Economic Advisers, filed by the Justice Department and decided by the commerce court. The formal exceptions to antitrust law enacted by Congress for the benefit of the regulatory agencies should be repealed.

Antitrust law does not seek to minimize the consumer benefits of mass production; it seeks to maximize those benefits by fostering a maximum amount of competition among a reasonable number of corporations. The antitrust division of the Justice Department sought not to break up General Motors Corporation into one hundred companies, but into a half-dozen competing automobile manufacturers. The law avoids the pitfalls of regulation of industrial prices and practices by dealing with the structures of industries. It aims to foster the greatest possible amount of competition among mass producers by attempting to ensure that older companies do not dominate or monopolize an industry to the extent of frightening off potential new entrants; by barring mergers of substantial competitors; by banning price-fixing conspiracies among competitors and by guarding against the great variety of agreements with suppliers and with retailers by which producers can discriminate against competition.

The Sherman Act still is a forceful deterrent to price-fixing, and the Clayton Act, as amended by Congress in 1950 with the Celler-Kefauver Anti-Merger Law, effectively prevents horizontal mergers of direct competitors and vertical mergers of producers with their suppliers or retail customers. Indeed, the only substantial price-fixing and the only substantial mergers of direct or related competitors that remain are in the regulated industries. Federally regulated industries are not monopolies and they should be subject to the full range of antitrust remedies and they should not be the beneficiaries of federal subsidies.

Conglomerate mergers, the new vogue among regulated as well as unregulated industrialists, sometimes involve the union of disparate companies but more often are a large corporation's method of entering a related line of business which it could have entered through expansion of its own facilities. The big soap manufacturer entering the household bleach business by acquiring a bleach company is the standard example. Conglomerate mergers of this sort, in addition to sometimes involving stock transactions of questionable financial integrity, are anti-competitive in that the acquiring company is eliminated as a potential competitor. By this line of reasoning, all conglomerate mergers are potentially anti-competitive where the merger partners are large companies, each financially capable of entering the other's industry through internal expansion and thus of increasing the number of competitors in each industry.

The Sherman and Clayton Acts as written are legally adequate laws but enforcement has been inadequate. Active participation by the Council of Economic Advisers in formulation of antitrust policies and suits should result in greater enforcement effort. But, pending the council's participation, Congress can act to reinvigorate enforcement. The antitrust division of the Justice Department needs more money and manpower. The division in recent years has had an annual budget of about $7 million, which is less than half the budget of a single large regulatory agency and one-tenth the amount the government has paid in airline subsidies in a single year. After giving it more money and manpower, Congress should curtail the division's frequent consent decree settlements of antitrust suits it has brought. It has been allowed to compromise suits on the theory that, being understaffed, it thus could bring more suits. Suits should go to trial and, in price-fixing suits, businessmen no longer should be allowed to plead no-contest and thus avoid trial where the trial record can be used by private parties and by the states as the basis for triple-damage suits against the price-fixers.

Congress should further augment enforcement by enacting an absolute ban on all mergers in the future involving significant competitors—direct, indirect or potential. A significant merger could be defined as one in which one of the merger partners has annual sales or assets in excess of $100 million. Pending clarification by the Council of Economic Advisers of the points in various industries at which mass-production economies no longer yield lower prices and greater product innovation, the absolute bar would permit mergers of smaller companies and ban automatically those of larger corporations. The acquiring company in a conglomerate merger would be required to prove it is not a potential entrant, through internal expansion, in another industry. The only other exceptions to the ban would be where the acquired company was failing and would go out of business except for the merger or where the acquired company was privately held by an owner who died and, for that reason, might otherwise go out of business. But the burden of proving entitlement to these exceptions should also be placed on the parties to a merger proposal.

Antitrust law does not and should not in any way bar business bigness achieved through internal sales success and inventiveness, rather than by merger. It does not and should not prevent any corporation from entering another line of business through internal expansion, instead of merger. Industry is and will continue to be free to capitalize on economies of large-scale production and on the capabilities of managerial talents. Internal growth and expansion predictably will not result in monopoly, if a large and successful company's business remains open to new competitors.

Almost all industries in America today which are dominated by very large corporations with near-monopolistic powers—regulated industries such as the railroads and non-regulated industries such as steel and automobiles—are in fact the results of mergers which took place many years ago and which were not challenged at the time. Mergers of competitors, actual and potential, are and will be banned; in all fairness, mergers of years past that permit industry domination today should also be undone. Antitrust laws as they now exist can be applied to old mergers because Congress has applied no statute of limitations to these laws.[7] Some economists, including a recent Assistant Attorney General in charge of the antitrust division, have suggested that Congress reach existing industrial concentrations by enacting a new law which would make it illegal for a dominant corporation to hold "unreasonable market power" in its industry.[8]

When competition is reaffirmed and antitrust law is refurbished, there will be no need of regulators. The agencies should be abolished on a first-in, first-out basis.

The transportation area demands first attention, as President Kennedy indicated. The antitrust law exemptions that permit railroads, truck lines and barge lines to fix rates should be repealed. The Interstate Commerce Commission's controls on entry into these industries, through its power to license common carriers, and its power to approve mergers also should be repealed. Railroad and other transportation industry executives who persist in fixing prices should be subject to the criminal penalties of the Sherman Act. Antitrust law would take the place of regulatory law and there no longer would be any function for the ICC or its National Transportation Policy mandate, which is impossible of fulfillment.

The authority of the Civil Aeronautics Board to fix domestic airline fares, control entry into the industry and approve mergers should similarly be repealed. Commercial airlines are no longer an infant industry and they should by law be declared ineligible for subsidies. If these actions are taken, and antitrust law is thereby substituted for regulatory law, there will be no reason or excuse for a Civil Aeronautics Board.

The elimination of rate-fixing conferences, subsidies and controls on entry will not be so easily accomplished in areas of overseas air and ocean transportation. The democracies of western Europe, which have ownership interests in their international airlines and shipping companies and which are the mainstays of the International Air Transport Association and other rate-fixing conferences, will resist United States withdrawal. Nonetheless the United States supplies far more passengers and freight than any other nation and it should use its influence to re-establish competition on international air and sea traffic lanes.

Pan American World Airways and other U.S. companies operating international air services are not now receiving federal subsidies and they, like domestic airlines, should no longer be eligible for subsidies. To end the need for federal subsidization of construction of commercial ships, American shipping companies should be given the freedom they now are denied to build ships in foreign shipyards. To end the need for ship operating subsidies, U.S. ship lines must meet foreign-flag competition the same way other United States producers are expected to compete on the international market. Higher American wages and other operating costs must be offset by superior American technology and automation. American shipbuilders, ship operators and maritime labor for too long have lobbied in Washington intensively and successfully for subsidies with the fundamental argument that America needs its ships for national defense emergencies. Automated ships designed in America and built in foreign yards will be under American control for defense emergencies.

Coordination of the remaining federal programs involving domestic transportation will lie within the responsibility and authority of the Department of Transportation. It already has authority as well as responsibility in matters of rail, highway and aviation safety that formerly was vested in the ICC and CAB. Regulation of automobile safety was vested in the department in 1966. Regulation of safety matters in international ocean transportation should be transferred to the department; the Federal Maritime Administration, its authority to subsidize ship construction and operation having been repealed, can thus be totally abolished.

Aviation safety, on domestic and international air routes, will continue to be an important matter of Transportation Department concern. The public interest requires continued operation by the Federal Aviation Administration of the nation's air traffic control system and certification by FAA of new types of aircraft. FAA is part of the Transportation Department; its spending must be coordinated with actual levels of air traffic and with total federal spending. Airlines and other civilian users of the FAA's air traffic control and navigation system should pay their full share of the costs of operating and improving the system, through establishment of airways user charges. Federal spending to develop a supersonic commercial airliner should end. The SST should not be built until private enterprise can develop a reliably safe and commercially sound airplane and perhaps an SST should not be built even then, if the public nuisance of sonic booms cannot be substantially reduced.

Improvement of the nation's rivers, harbors and coastal waterways for navigation, flood control and generation of electricity also must remain a federal concern because these navigable waterways belong to no single state and are in exclusive federal domain. But the works of the Army Corps of Engineers must be transferred to either the Transportation Department or the Department of the Interior. Inasmuch as federal promotion of barge line transportation will be inappropriate in a new era of transportation competition, perhaps the other purposes of waterways improvements will be paramount and the works of the Engineers therefore should be transferred to the Interior Department. Control of floods, dredging of harbors and control of beach erosion and pollution certainly are proper federal concerns, but barge lines and other private interests that gain special advantage from such programs must pay appropriate user charges for the benefits received.

Federal spending for improvement of surface transportation within the United States cannot quickly be curtailed. If construction of the Interstate Highway System were stopped prior to its planned completion in 1972, millions of motorists would write irate letters to their congressmen. Federal highway construction already has gone so far that federal subsidies probably are essential to save what is left of the nation's urban and intercity surface transportation facilities. Federal spending for highways and common-carrier forms of transportation will continue to grow until 1972. But coordination, through the Transportation Department, can begin before then. The Highway Trust Fund, which defies coordination, should be eliminated and highway spending controlled by annual appropriations; highway user charges larger than those presently collected should be required of all truck lines. The federal government then should adopt a block grant program for transportation, giving to each state annually a proportionate sum, based upon population, to be allocated for urban and intercity highways, rail facilities, subways or buses. The Transportation Department would have authority to make certain that the grants are used efficiently and honestly, but state governments would have final authority to decide how and where the money is expended.

Communications services, like transportation services, involve a combination of intrastate, interstate and international responsibilities and demand new and enlightened approaches. Domestic telephone and telegraph companies are natural local monopolies whose rates and practices will continue to be regulated by the states. Long-distance telephone and telegraph services, both interstate and international, also have been monopolistic in nature and have been regulated by the Federal Communications Commission. Technology, however, has blurred the distinction the FCC has attempted to maintain between voice (or telephone) services and written communications (or telegraph) services, and technology is further blurring distinctions between wire, cable and radio as methods of carrying all types of communications. It seems entirely likely that, given free rein, communications satellites offer a relatively cheap new method of transmitting very large volumes of interstate and international communications and of opening both domestic and overseas long-distance communications to a new era of competition. If this potential of communications satellites were realized, competition and antitrust law could be substituted for regulation of long-distance services and the land-based, local telephone and other connecting services would continue to be regulated by the states.

Enlarged use of communications satellites would of course require assignment of more radio frequencies and complicate the already large problem of frequency allocation. The existing problem of allocating frequency space among users of industrial radio services, public police and fire departments and similar users and commercial broadcasters demands more comprehensive and enlightened government study and action. The responsibility for study and the authority to allocate frequency space should be transferred from the Federal Communications Commission to the executive branch. Allocation authority could be shifted to the Commerce Department, where it originated, but would better be pinpointed by transfer to the Transportation Department, which then would be the Department of Transportation and Communications.

In re-evaluating present and projected radio spectrum usage, the executive department should immediately add to the space available for satellite and other communications by moving all television broadcasting into the ultra high frequency channels, and thus freeing the very high frequency channels for other uses. The move will inconvenience television receiver owners, but no more than they already have been inconvenienced. It will put all commercial TV broadcasters on an equal footing, increase competition in the industry, eliminate the most onerous features and politics of the FCC's 1952 master plan and perhaps even bring back to life more television networks.

Further, the executive department and Congress should reconsider the 1962 Communications Satellite Act. Reconsideration might well lead to the conclusion that competition, rather than a monopolistic government-industry consortium, is appropriate for international as well as domestic communications. They clearly should reject the proposal, made late in 1968 by a presidential committee headed by a State Department official, of a still larger government-sponsored monopoly that would own all U.S.-held submarine cable and other facilities, including satellites, for international communications.[9] In addition, Congress and the executive branch should endorse competition by encouraging the development of cable-television and pay-television services within the United States. And the Federal Communications Commission should be abolished.

Re-examination of federal responsibility and authority in the area of energy resources also is long overdue. The inability of the Atomic Energy Commission to promote civilian uses of atomic energy, to the extent hoped, suggests that Congress again should relax governmental controls over private use and take new measures to foster industrial competition. Civilian control of atomic energy should remain, but control should be transferred to the Department of the Interior. The department could regulate safety and other aspects of private industrial usage of atomic energy. Inasmuch as the primary private use apparently will continue to involve atomic generation of electricity, it is entirely appropriate that the Secretary of the Interior become the coordinating agent of all federal programs concerning energy resources. The Federal Power Commission's authority to license the construction of hydroelectric dams on navigable waterways should be transferred to the Secretary and Congress must fix standards he is to follow in deciding whether contested dam sites are to be developed by private investor-owned utilities or by public authorities. His decisions would be appealable to the new commerce court. Federal regulation of interstate transmission of natural gas and of gas producers should be abandoned; neither transmission nor production is a natural monopoly and competition should be required in both areas through the application of antitrust law to entry into the business, to merger proposals and to rate-fixing.

Regulation of electric and gas utilities, which are local distribution monopolies, should remain with the states.

Federal supervision of national banks and federal insurance of deposits in national and state banks are essentially safety functions which should be consolidated in the Treasury Department. The Office of Comptroller of the Currency, already in the department, could be renamed the Federal Banking Administration. The administrator would assume the Comptroller's authority to examine and supervise national banks. The bank regulatory authority of the Federal Reserve Board would be transferred to the administrator and the function and authority of the Federal Deposit Insurance Corporation also would be consolidated in the new office of the administrator.

The Federal Reserve Board, thus relieved of its responsibility and authority to examine and regulate member banks of the Federal Reserve System, would become solely an agent of monetary policy, adjusting the nation's supply of money and credit to its needs of the moment. The Federal Reserve System of member commercial banks would remain intact but the board should be abolished as an independent agency. It should be reformed as a part of the executive branch and must be, if the responsibility which has been charged to the President by Congress for full employment and purchasing power is to be fulfilled.[10] Conservative bankers assert that the Federal Reserve Board's independence is a healthy brake on the soft money and easy credit policies of some liberal Presidents. But the Federal Reserve Board has not proved itself unerring in economic wisdom either and divided responsibility and authority lead to conflict and invite irresponsibility. The President, not the board, is accountable to the intended beneficiaries of full employment and purchasing power. Authority for monetary policy should be vested in a multimember board, but the board should be part of the executive branch. Its members should be confirmed by the Senate and should serve at the pleasure of the President. It could be composed of the chairman of the Council of Economic Advisers, who also would be chairman of the new Federal Reserve Board; the Secretary of the Treasury; and the administrator of the new Federal Banking Administration.

Reform, over the long term, also should include an end to the dual system of national and state banks. Chartering of commercial

banks by the federal government and the states has led to conflicting standards of competition. Chartering of new banks, which
means control of entry into the business, should be left to the states
alone. State law on branch banking already controls national as well
as state banks and should remain. Banks are not in fact interstate
businesses and should not be allowed to spread themselves across
state lines. More competition among banks is desirable and antitrust
law should apply to bank mergers and, to the extent possible, to
other competitive matters in the banking industry.

A banking industry consisting entirely of state-chartered and state-
regulated banks need not be inconsistent with a central banking
system headed by the reconstituted Federal Reserve Board. State
banks as well as national banks presently are members of the
Federal Reserve System.

Federal jurisdiction in matters of consumer protection from false
advertising, securities frauds, flammable fabrics and the like should
be re-evaluated and new balances struck between federal and state
authority and government regulation and free competition. Federal
efforts to police hundreds of thousands of retailers and other
businessmen who deal directly with consumers should be re-examined and abandoned where Washington cannot succeed. Those
policing functions which the federal government can best perform,
such as guarding against false advertising on national television and
stock manipulation on national securities exchanges, should be
transferred to a new Consumer Affairs Division in the Justice
Department. The division would police consumer frauds and misrepresentations by filing suits in the new commerce court. Policing
of lesser frauds and misrepresentations would be left to the states
and to individuals. To assist, the federal government should provide
funds in the form of state grants which would be distributed to
Better Business Bureaus and similar organizations and would be
used to expand the embryonic program, now administered by the
federal Office of Economic Opportunity, to provide legal services to
consumers who cannot afford a lawyer's fees.

The Federal Trade Commission's authority to police misleading
advertising, flammable fabrics and mislabeled furs thus would be
redistributed between the Consumer Affairs Division and the states.
The FTC's authority to enforce the Clayton Antitrust Act would be
consolidated with the same authority already existing in the anti-

trust division of the Justice Department. The Robinson-Patman Act amendment to the Clayton Act, which the antitrust division has almost never used, would be repealed. Hopefully, federal exemptions from antitrust laws which permit states to enact fair-trade laws also would be repealed. And the Federal Trade Commission would be abolished and made over into a part of the judicial branch.

The Securities and Exchange Commission would similarly be taken apart and abolished as it now exists. Authority to investigate fraud in the sale of securities and manipulation of stock market prices would be transferred to the Consumer Affairs Division. Its authority to control entry into the stock market business and to regulate stock exchange commission rates would be repealed. Entry would be free and mergers and commission rates would be subject to antitrust laws. Antitrust law thus reaffirmed would be employed to bar forevermore member firms of the New York Stock Exchange and other exchanges from fixing commission rates and to bestow on investors the benefits of commission rate competition. The new federal program of grants to the states for the purpose of strengthening Better Business Bureaus and other consumer protection agencies might well be expanded to also strengthen the securities regulatory agencies of New York, California and other states.

The labyrinth of federal bureaucracies that regulate labor and management relations ought to be reformed. Federal laws guaranteeing workers' right to organize, those proscribing unfair union and management practices and those written to assure democratic procedures in unions' internal affairs should be administered by the Labor Department through suits filed in the new labor court. The National Labor Relations Board can be reconstituted as the court. The Labor Department already polices unions' internal affairs, through suits filed in federal district courts. It also should assume the functions now vested in the NLRB, including the supervision of union representation elections among employees.

Federal programs now assigned to the National Mediation Board and the Federal Mediation and Conciliation Service should first be combined and then reviewed by Congress and the Labor Department. Federal mediation clearly has not been successful in transportation. Its collateral effect of stagnating labor-management bargaining, leading ultimately to compulsory arbitration, is surely undesirable. Greater reliance for mediation and conciliation might be placed on state agencies which already exist for those purposes.

Labor's basic right to organize and bargain for wages and other benefits is not an abuse of antitrust laws but organized labor should not enjoy total immunity from those laws. Unions ought not to be used as price-fixing mechanisms, either by barbers, musicians and other self-employed persons or by agreement of workers with employers. Antitrust law does and should apply to conspiracies of unions with employers for the purpose of damaging competitive employers or unions.

The Equal Employment Opportunity Commission should be abolished because it is an inefficient means of opening job opportunities to Negroes and other minority groups. Its responsibility should be transferred either to the Labor Department or to the civil rights division of the Justice Department. Suits to require employers and unions to fulfill their obligations under the 1964 Civil Rights Act would be filed in the new labor court, as they now are filed by the Justice Department in federal district courts.

The reform of the regulators will not be quick or easy. More and perhaps better answers may be found in the course of abolishing the independent regulatory agencies and subjecting their promises and powers to the discipline of constitutional doctrine and of the competitive system reinforced by antitrust laws. If those promises and powers are not so disciplined, governmental efficiency, coordination and priority will be pursued by other means. Greater economic stability and consumer security will be found, but at greater expense of economic as well as individual freedom.

Appendix

Congress has delegated to more than one hundred federal administrative agencies and offices the authority to write regulations which apply with the force of law to private obligations and privileges. This listing includes only the major agencies and offices that are concerned with economic affairs. It does not include those agencies, such as the Subversive Activities Control Board, that are concerned with areas of private obligation or privilege which have no economic relevance. It also does not include those executive branch offices, such as the Council of Economic Advisers or the antitrust division of the Justice Department, to which Congress has not delegated authority to adopt regulations that carry the force of law.

This listing divides the major economic-type agencies and offices between those that are independent of the President and those which are part of the executive branch. Any such categorization of course is made with less than finality; the constitutional line between independence and subordination has moved from time to time in history and independence at all times has been a matter of degree.

The agencies and offices are listed alphabetically, with the year in which each was created in its present form and with its major responsibilities. A more complete and detailed catalogue may be found in the United States Government Organization Manual, an official publication revised annually.

INDEPENDENT AGENCIES

Atomic Energy Commission	1946	Promotes and regulates civilian use of atomic energy.
Civil Aeronautics Board	1938	Promotes and subsidizes air transportation and regulates airline passenger fares and freight rates.

Equal Employment Opportunity Commission	1964	Investigates charges of racial and other discrimination by employers and labor unions.
Federal Coal Mine Safety Board of Review	1952	Hears appeals from orders issued under the Federal Coal Mine Safety Act.
Federal Communications Commission	1934	Regulates civilian radio and television communication, excepting rates, and interstate and international communication by wire, cable and radio, including rates.
Federal Deposit Insurance Corporation	1933	Insures deposits of eligible commercial banks and supervises certain insured banks.
Federal Home Loan Bank Board	1932	Provides credit reserve for savings and home-financing institutions.
Federal Maritime Commission	1936	Regulates fares, rates and practices of steamship companies engaged in United States foreign commerce.
Federal Power Commission	1930	Regulates rates and practices in interstate sale at wholesale of electric energy and regulates transportation and sale of natural gas.
Federal Reserve System	1913	The board of governors determines monetary and credit policy for the system and regulates member commercial banks.
Federal Trade Commission	1914	Administers certain anti-trust statutes as well as laws concerning advertising misrepresentation, flammable fabrics, packaging, and labeling of certain products.
Interstate Commerce Commission	1887	Regulates rates, fares and practices of railroads, truck

		and bus lines, oil pipelines, domestic water carriers and freight forwarders.
National Labor Relations Board	1935	Conducts union representation elections and regulates unfair labor practices of employers and unions.
National Mediation Board	1926	Conducts union representation elections and mediates labor-management disputes in the railroad and airline industries.
Securities and Exchange Commission	1934	Requires disclosure of material facts by issuers of securities making public offerings and by certain companies whose securities are publicly traded; regulates rates and practices of stock exchanges and over-the-counter securities dealers; regulates certain practices of mutual funds, investment advisers and public utility holding companies.
Tax Court of the United States	1924	Adjudicates cases involving deficiencies or overpayments in income, estate and certain other Federal tax matters; regulates settlement of certain classes of such controversies.
United States Tariff Commission	1916	Investigates tariff and certain other foreign trade matters.

EXECUTIVE BRANCH AGENCIES AND OFFICES

DEPARTMENT OF AGRICULTURE

Commodity Credit Corporation	1933	Finances farm price support and production stabilization programs.

Commodity Exchange Authority	1922	Regulates trading and pricing on commodity exchanges.
Packers and Stockyards Administration	1916	Regulates fair business practices in livestock and meat marketing.
Rural Electrification Administration	1935	Administers loan programs for rural electrification and telephone service.

DEPARTMENT OF COMMERCE

| Maritime Administration | 1936 | Promotes the merchant marine and subsidizes construction and operation of certain merchant ships. |
| Patent Office | 1836 | Administers patent and trademark laws. |

DEPARTMENT OF DEFENSE

| Army Corps of Engineers | 1824 | Constructs and maintains rivers and harbors improvements. |

DEPARTMENT OF HEALTH, EDUCATION AND WELFARE

| Food and Drug Administration | 1931 | Administers laws concerning purity, safety and accurate labeling of certain foods and drugs. |
| Social Security Administration | 1933 | Administers Federal retirement, survivors and disability insurance programs. |

DEPARTMENT OF THE INTERIOR

| Oil Import Administration | 1959 | Regulates importation of crude oil, fuel oil and petroleum products into the United States. |

DEPARTMENT OF LABOR

| Bureau of Employment Security | 1933 | Administers the national system of public employment services and Federal |

		unemployment compensation programs.
Labor-Management Services Administration	1963	Administers the law requiring reporting and disclosure by certain employe welfare and pension plans.

DEPARTMENT OF TRANSPORTATION

Federal Aviation Administration	1958	Certifies airworthiness of aircraft, licenses pilots and operates air traffic control system.
Federal Highway Administration	1966	Administers highway safety programs and includes the Bureau of Public Roads which administers Federal-aid highway construction programs.
Federal Railroad Administration	1966	Administers high-speed railroad development program and the railroad and oil pipeline safety programs formerly administered by the ICC.
National Transportation Safety Board	1966	Investigates aviation and surface transportation accidents to determine probable cause.
United States Coast Guard	1915	Maintains sea search and rescue services and aids to navigation; regulates seaworthiness of vessels and licenses merchant marine personnel.

DEPARTMENT OF THE TREASURY

Comptroller of the Currency	1863	Regulates national banks.
Internal Revenue Service	1862	Administers Federal income, alcohol, tobacco and other tax programs.

The following are offices which are part of the executive branch but that are not within the departments:

Office of Economic Opportunity	1964	Administers Federal poverty and youth job programs.
Renegotiation Board	1951	Renegotiates national defense contracts to eliminate excess profits. (Although independent in form, members of the board serve at the pleasure of the President.)
Small Business Administration	1953	Makes loans to and otherwise promotes small business.

Notes

Chapter 1: Consumers, Bureaucracies and Big Brother

1. Special Message on Protecting the Consumer Interest, March 14, 1962.
2. To Protect the Consumer Interest, a Message to Congress, February 6, 1968.
3. *Statistical Abstract of the United States,* 87th ed. (Washington, D.C.: Bureau of the Census, U.S. Department of Commerce, 1966). Other consumer expenditure figures also are from this source.
4. *Utah Pie Co.* v. *Continental Baking Co.,* 386 U.S. 685, 689 (1967).
5. *Baltimore and Ohio Railroad Co.* v. *U.S.,* 386 U.S. 372, 478 (1967).
6. A history of the legislative efforts that led to enactment of the Act to Regulate Commerce of 1887 may be found in *Interstate Commerce Commission Activities 1887–1937* (Washington, D.C.: Government Printing Office, 1937).
7. See the appendix for a relatively complete listing of the administrative bodies upon which Congress has conferred authority to decide private obligations and privileges exclusive of presidential direction. This listing attempts to cover all such bodies with responsibilities in the economic sphere. There are, in addition, a number of bodies that exercise powers in specialized, noneconomic areas. Examples are the Subversive Activities Control Board and the Board of Immigration Appeals. The decisions of all such bodies carry the force of law and they are appealable to the courts; appeals usually are taken directly to a United States circuit court of appeals.
8. *Federal Trade Commission* v. *Ruberoid Co.,* 343 U.S. 470, 488 (1952), dissenting opinion of Justice Jackson.
9. Message on Transportation, April 4, 1962.

Chapter 2: Regulation and the Spirit of the Constitution

1. Thurman W. Arnold, in an address titled "Antitrust, Then and Now —a Reminiscence," New York, N.Y., January 24, 1968.
2. Testimony of Sam H. Flint before the House Interstate and Foreign Commerce Committee on H.R. 5401, March 26, 1965. See also the press release of the United States Chamber of Commerce concerning the testimony. Mr. Flint testified as chairman of the Chamber's transportation subcommittee.

3. *Northern Pacific Railway Co.* v. *U.S.,* 356 U.S. 1, 4 (1958).
4. *Charles River Bridge* v. *Warren Bridge,* 11 Peters 420 (1837).
5. *Munn* v. *Illinois,* 94 U.S. 113, decided in 1876.
6. See *German Alliance Insurance Co.* v. *Kansas,* 233 U.S. 389 (1914).
7. The Supreme Court in 1824 handed down a leading decision on the constitutional issue arising where states and the federal government legislated in the same areas of the law. State legislatures had granted many exclusive franchises for operation of steamboats in particular waters. Congress also had passed a law providing for federal franchises for steamboats in the coastal trades. A suit was brought to determine whether a New York State statute or federal law governed the franchising of steamboats operating in New York harbor. Daniel Webster argued before the Supreme Court that federal law must prevail and the court agreed. It ruled, first, that the power of Congress to regulate commerce included the right to franchise steamboats in New York harbor and, second, that when federal and state law collide state law must fall. *Gibbons* v. *Ogden,* 9 Wheat. 1 (1824).
8. *Myers* v. *U.S.,* 272 U.S. 52 (1926).
9. *Schechter Poultry Corp.* v. *U.S.,* 295 U.S. 495 (1935).
10. *Humphrey's Executor* v. *U.S.,* 295 U.S. 602 (1935).
11. *Youngstown Sheet & Tube Co.* v. *Sawyer,* 343 U.S. 579 (1952).
12. *Weiner* v. *U.S.,* 357 U.S. 349 (1958).
13. *The Federalist,* No. 48.

Chapter 3: People and Paraphernalia

1. *Federal Trade Commission* v. *R. F. Keppel and Bros. Inc.,* 291 U.S. 304, 314 (1934). The court's statement in part is taken from *Report of Senate Committee on Interstate Commerce,* No. 597, June 13, 1914, 63rd Cong., 2nd Sess., p. 9.
2. For a discussion of the role of hearing examiners in the federal government, see John W. Macy, Jr., "The APA and the Hearing Examiner: Products of a Viable Political Society," *Federal Bar Journal,* Vol. 27, No. 4 (Fall, 1967).

Chapter 4: The Regulators and the President

1. As quoted in Henry J. Friendly, *The Federal Administrative Agencies* (Cambridge: Harvard University Press, 1962), p. 29.
2. The Wilson threat is attributed to Senator Carter Glass. See Marver H. Bernstein, *Regulating Business by Independent Commission* (Princeton, N.J.: Princeton University Press, 1955), p. 110.
3. *Ibid.,* p. 132.

4. Herbert E. Cushman, *The Independent Regulatory Commissions* (New York: Oxford University Press, 1941), pp. 249–250.

5. *Ibid.,* pp. 681, 685.

6. *Ibid.,* p. 682.

7. The source of the information concerning the White House intervention was an interview conducted on July 21, 1965, in Washington. For details concerning the publicly announced vote of the SEC on August 8, 1945, to abolish floor trading, and the commission's reversal on August 28, 1945, see *Report of Special Study of Securities Markets of the Securities and Exchange Commission,* printed as House Document No. 95, 88th Cong., 1st Sess. (1963), Pt. 2, pp. 229–232.

8. Hearings before the Antitrust and Monopoly Subcommittee of the Senate Judiciary Committee pursuant to S. Res. 61, 84th Cong., 1st Sess., Pt. 1 (1955), pp. 377–426.

9. See *Report of the Special Subcommittee on Legislative Oversight of the House Interstate and Foreign Commerce Committee,* 85th Cong., 2nd Sess., House Report No. 2711 (1959), pp. 41–50.

10. Sherman Adams, *First-Hand Report, The Story of the Eisenhower Administration* (New York: Harper & Brothers, 1961), p. 445.

11. James M. Landis, *Report on Regulatory Agencies to the President-Elect,* printed for use of the Senate Committee on the Judiciary, 86th Cong., 2nd Sess. (1960).

12. The White House, Remarks of the President, on meeting with heads of independent regulatory agencies, Cabinet Room, December 3, 1963.

13. Landis, *op. cit.,* p. 11.

14. F. D. Hall, president of Eastern Air Lines, in remarks before the Aero Club, Washington, D.C., May 26, 1964.

15. Quoted in "Banks Fear Tightening of U.S. Control Could Follow Current Turmoil," *Wall Street Journal,* April 12, 1965, Eastern Edition, p. 1.

16. Quoted in Joseph P. Harris, *The Advice and Consent of the Senate,* (Berkeley: University of California Press, 1953), p. 277.

17. Hearings on Monopoly Problems in Regulated Industries, Antitrust Subcommittee of the House Judiciary Committee, 84th Cong., 2nd Sess., Pt. 1 (1956), p. 153.

Chapter 5: The Regulators and Congress

1. Hearings before the House Committee on Interstate and Foreign Commerce on H.R. 14, 87th Cong., 1st Sess. (1961), pp. 88–89.

2. See Jerry Landauer, "Political Fund-Raising: A Murky World," *Wall Street Journal,* June 28, 1967, Eastern Edition, p. 14.

3. See Harris, *op. cit.*, p. 276.
4. *Ibid.*, pp. 178–194.
5. An outstanding example is the late Representative Albert Thomas, a Democrat of Texas, who for many years prior to his death in 1966 was chairman of the Independent Offices Subcommittee of the House Appropriations Committee. As such, he was the most influential single member of Congress in matters of CAB appropriations for airline subsidies and agency operations. According to a CAB staff official, Houston, which Thomas represented, for years enjoyed a greater quantity of airline service, in terms of airlines authorized to serve the city and flight frequencies, than any other city, relative to its size. Thomas, the CAB aide said, probably made no overt appeals to the CAB but the agency accorded Houston excellent service simply because of the position he occupied.
6. *Broadcasting*, a weekly trade magazine published in Washington, annually compiles from FCC public records the radio and television station interests of members of Congress.
7. See Bernard Schwartz, *The Professor and the Commissions* (New York: Alfred A. Knopf, 1959), p. 96.
8. Figures on Senator Magnuson's purchases and sales of stocks in companies holding licenses for the KIRO radio and television stations in Seattle are taken from records of the stations maintained by the FCC in Washington.

Chapter 6: The Regulators and the Regulated

1. *Wall Street Journal,* April 21, 1966, Eastern Edition, p. 2.
2. Civil Aeronautics Board, Press Release No. 60–28, November 17, 1960, and attached minutes of a CAB meeting held November 16, 1960, Washington, D.C.
3. See "Business-Backed Political Groups Seeking to Elect Friendly Candidates, Offset Labor," *Wall Street Journal,* October 17, 1968, Eastern Edition, p. 4.
4. *Ibid.*
5. *Ibid.*
6. Louis J. Hector, *Problems of the CAB and the Independent Regulatory Commissions,* a Memorandum to the President, dated September 10, 1959, Washington, D.C.
7. Newton N. Minow, letter to the President, May 31, 1963, Washington, D.C.
8. Howard Morgan, letter to the President, January 23, 1963, Washington, D.C.

Chapter 7: The Question of Competition

1. *Dr. Miles Medical Co.* v. *Park & Sons Co.*, 220 U.S. 373 (1911).
2. *Schwegmann Bros.* v. *Calvert Distillers Corp.*, 341 U.S. 384 (1951).
3. For an account of the legislative history of the Robinson-Patman Act, see Corwin D. Edwards, *The Price Discrimination Law* (Washington, D.C.: The Brookings Institution, 1959), pp. 21–53. The role of the lawyer-lobbyist is described at p. 22.
4. *FTC* v. *Ruberoid Co.*, 343 U.S. 470, 483 (1952), the dissenting opinion of Justice Jackson.
5. *Ibid.*, at 483.
6. Landis, *Report on Regulatory Agencies to the President-Elect.*
7. Joseph E. Sheehy, Director, Bureau of Restraint of Trade, Federal Trade Commission, before the Antitrust Law Section of the American Bar Association, Washington, D.C., April 15, 1966.
8. *Automatic Canteen Co.* v. *FTC*, 346 U.S. 61, 63 (1953).
9. Frederick M. Rowe, in "The Robinson-Patman Act—Thirty Years Thereafter," an address to the Antitrust Law Section of the American Bar Association, Washington, D.C., April 15, 1966.
10. See Paul Rand Dixon, Chairman, Federal Trade Commission, in "Self-Restraint: The Strength of Democracy," a speech delivered before the Better Business Bureau, Kansas City, Mo., March 30, 1966.
11. For a lucid description of the first two decades of FTC and court enforcement of the Robinson-Patman Act, see Frederick M. Rowe, "The Evolution of the Robinson-Patman Act: A Twenty Year Perspective," *Columbia Law Review*, Vol. 57, No. 8 (December, 1957).
12. *FTC* v. *Morton Salt Co.*, 343 U.S. 683 (1948).
13. *Standard Oil Co.* v. *FTC*, 340 U.S. 231 (1951).
14. *Automatic Canteen Co.* v. *FTC*, *op. cit.*
15. See, for example, *FTC* v. *Ruberoid Co.*
16. *FTC* v. *The Borden Co.*, 383 U.S. 637 (1966).
17. *Utah Pie Co.* v. *Continental Baking Co.*, 386 U.S. 685 (1967). Utah Pie Co.'s victory in 1967 was less than complete. The Supreme Court remanded the case but the Tenth Circuit Court of Appeals ruled that Utah Pie's evidence was insufficient for purposes of awarding damages and remanded to the district court for a new trial on the damage issue. Utah Pie asked the Supreme Court to review the Tenth Circuit's remand order but the High Court declined, No. 367, October Term, 1968, Cert. denied October 14, 1968. Utah Pie's fate in victory seemed to be the "endless litigation" Justice Jackson earlier spoke of as the fate of a company that lost a Robinson-Patman case before the Supreme Court.

18. Simon N. Whitney, *Antitrust Policies—American Experience in Twenty Industries*, Vol. I (New York: The Twentieth Century Fund, 1958), p. 133.
19. Edwards, *op. cit.* See pp. 630–637 for Professor Edwards' conclusions concerning the economic consequences of the Robinson-Patman Act.
20. For a discussion of the development of rate conferences, see an Interstate Commerce Commission decision titled *Western Traffic Association-Agreement*, 276 ICC 183, October 3, 1949.
21. Interstate Commerce Commission, Twelfth Annual Report, 1898.
22. *Georgia* v. *Pennsylvania Railroad Co.*, 324 U.S. 439 (1945).
23. See Hearings Before the Committee on Interstate and Foreign Commerce, on HR 4700 and HR 4701, Transportation Act—1963, 88th Cong., 1st Sess., Pt. 2. The exchange between Chairman Harris and Mr. Heineman appears on p. 851.
24. *Ibid.,* p. 884.
25. *Ibid.,* p. 738. Similar sentiments were stated frequently throughout the hundreds of pages of ICC testimony before the House Committee in 1962 and 1963.
26. William H. Tucker, Interstate Commerce Commission, in "Changing Commission Concepts," a speech delivered before the Boston Chamber of Commerce, Boston, Mass., February 14, 1963.
27. *Economic Report of the President Together with Annual Report of the Council of Economic Advisers,* transmitted to Congress January 27, 1966, pp. 126–127.
28. A number of antitrust experts seem to agree on the estimate. See Pogue, *The Rationale of Exemptions from Antitrust*, 19 American Bar Association, Antitrust Section, 313 (1961). See also, Carl Kaysen and Donald F. Turner, *Antitrust Policy* (Cambridge, Harvard University Press, 1959).

Chapter 8: Services and Prices

1. See *Selected Reports of the Administrative Conference of the United States,* printed for use of the Committee on the Judiciary, Senate Document No. 24, 88th Cong., 1st Sess., Report on Licensing of Domestic Air Transportation, p. 324.

The CAB in general has apportioned routes among airlines on a regional basis. Although it has avoided direct route competition, as many as three airlines have been authorized to compete on heavily traveled, usually profitable routes such as the New York–West Coast transcontinental route. On a very few other such routes, such as New York–Washington, more than three lines hold authorizations but their certificates usually contain various operating restrictions and in practice only two or three airlines actively compete.

2. See *McLean Trucking Co. v. U.S.*, 321 U.S. 67 (1944).
3. See *Seaboard Air Line Railroad Co. v. U.S.*, Per Curiam, 382 U.S. 154 (1965).
4. The Justice Department initially opposed the merger but later supported it. The reason or reasons for the department's change in position remain unclear. Stuart Saunders, who was board chairman of Pennsylvania Railroad and a long-time Democrat and friend of President Johnson, has suggested that the President directed the department to change its position. See *Time*, January 26, 1968, p. 71A. On the other hand, the department's public position in support of the merger rested largely on the fact that the ICC had conditioned its merger approval on the eventual acquisition by the merged company of the ailing New York, New Haven & Hartford Railroad. The department, as well as the ICC, was of the opinion that acquisition by the Penn Central was the only practical means of attempting to assure the survival of the New Haven's commuter service into New York City.
5. *Baltimore & Ohio Railroad Co. v. U.S.*, 386 U.S. 372, 478 (1967).
6. *Ibid.*, at 441.
7. Penn-Central Merger and N&W Inclusion Cases, 389 U.S. 486, 492 (1968).
8. *Northern Securities Co. v. U.S.*, 193 U.S. 197 (1904).
9. See William H. Orrick, Jr., writing in *The Antitrust Bulletin*, Vol. X, Nos. 5 and 6 (September–December, 1965), p. 674.
10. *U.S. v. Philadelphia National Bank*, 374 U.S. 321 (1963).
11. *U.S. v. First National Bank of Lexington*, 376 U.S. 665 (1964).
12. *U.S. v. First City National Bank of Houston*, 386 U.S. 361 (1967).
13. For a discussion of the effect of low-priced nonscheduled airline competition on fare levels of the scheduled airline industry, see the brief of the CAB Bureau of Economic Regulation, filed with Examiner Robert L. Park in Supplemental Air Service Proceeding, CAB Docket 13795, *et al.*, March 19, 1965.
14. *Ibid.*
15. The rise and later decline of regional stock exchanges is discussed at length in *Special Study of the Securities Markets*, Securities and Exchange Commission, printed as House Document No. 95, 88th Cong., 1st Sess. See Pt. 2, pp. 911–961.
16. *Ibid.*, Pt. 2, p. 958.
17. *Ibid.*, Pt. 2, p. 295.
18. Orrick, *op. cit.*, p. 677.
19. *Silver v. New York Stock Exchange*, 373 U.S. 341 (1963).

20. See the exchange of letters between Chairman Manuel F. Cohen of the SEC and Senator A. Willis Robertson, *Congressional Record,* August 2, 1965, p. 18309.

21. *Kaplan* v. *Lehman Brothers,* 389 U.S. 954 (1967), Cert. denied.

22. Charles A. Webb, in "Ratemaking Innovations and the Transportation of Energy," an address before the Energy Transportation Conference, St. Louis, Mo., November 12, 1963.

23. *Arrow Transportation Co.* v. *Southern Railway Co.,* 372 U.S. 658 (1963).

24. *ICC* v. *Cincinnati, New Orleans & Texas Pacific Railway Co.,* 379 U.S. 642 (1965).

25. D. W. Brosnan, Southern Railway Co., Washington, D.C., in a preface to an undated reprint prepared by Southern Railway of his statement before the House Interstate and Foreign Commerce Committee on HR 11583, July 13, 1962.

26. *Economic Report of the President Together with Annual Report of the Council of Economic Advisers,* transmitted to Congress January 27, 1966, pp. 126–127.

27. Merton J. Peck, *Competitive Policy for Transportation?* (Washington, D.C.: The Brookings Institution, 1965). Reprinted from *Perspectives on Antitrust Policy* (Princeton, N.J.: Princeton University Press, 1965).

Chapter 9: Introduction to a Labyrinth

1. Source of estimates of private sector expenditures on transportation is Transportation Association of America, Washington, D.C. Figures on federal government transportation expenditures for more recent years, are taken from the annual budget of the United States. For years prior to 1960, figures generally were supplied by individual agencies. For excellent compilations of expenditures prior to 1960, see *National Transportation Policy,* a report to the Senate Commerce Committee by a Special Study Group on Transportation headed by John P. Doyle, Committee Print, 87th Cong., 1st Sess., January 3, 1961. This study henceforth is cited as the Doyle Report.

2. See *Subsidy and Subsidy-Effect Programs of the United States Government,* Materials Prepared for the Joint Economic Committee, 89th Cong., 1st Sess. (1965), p. 3. This document traces the history of merchant marine, airline and other federal subsidy programs.

Chapter 10: Engineering Waterways

1. Doyle Report, *op. cit.,* pp. 167, 175.

2. Maj. Gen. Jackson Graham, director of Civil Works, Army Corps of Engineers, in an address at Little Rock, Arkansas, July 7, 1965.

3. *Ibid.*
4. Doyle Report, *op. cit.*, pp. 95–96, which calls the Arkansas River project "an outstanding example of lack of coordination." Discussion of this project also is based on information contained in *Arkansas River and Tributaries*, a pamphlet published by the U.S. Army Engineer District, Little Rock.
5. Doyle Report, *op. cit.*, p. 95.
6. *Proposed Program for Maritime Administration Research*, Vol. I: Summary. Prepared by the Maritime Research Advisory Committee, National Academy of Science–National Research Council, Washington, D.C. (1960).

Chapter 11: Railways

1. The source of the $900 million estimate is the House Committee on Interstate and Foreign Commerce, Report No. 393, 79th Cong., 1st Sess., March 26, 1945. Total acreage received by the railroads under the Land Grant Acts, the value of the lands and the total payments to the government in the form of reduced railroad rates all remain matters of controversy. A principal collection of basic data may be found in U.S. Federal Coordinator of Transportation, *Public Aids to Transportation* (Washington, D.C., 1940).
2. Association of American Railroads, Washington, D.C., booklet titled *Quiz on Railroads and Railroading*, Item N. 181.
3. The idea that railroad profits should be no more than a fair return on investment was reflected even in the original 1887 Act to Regulate Commerce. The idea became much more formalized with the 1913 Valuation Act, in which Congress directed the ICC to ascertain the value of each piece of railroad property and equipment; it was under this law that the ICC began to devote huge amounts of time and money to fixing valuations. However, it was the 1920 act that made valuation the keystone of regulation by providing for recapture of rail earnings in excess of what the ICC considered to be a fair return on investment. For a description of this almost forgotten chapter of ICC history, see *Interstate Commerce Commission Activities 1887–1937*, a history published by the ICC in 1937, chap. VIII.
4. As noted earlier, the Supreme Court in 1968 affirmed the validity of the 1940 law by stating that the policy of Congress continued to be the encouragement of railroad mergers. Penn-Central Merger and N&W Inclusion Cases, 389 U.S. 486 (1968).
5. For a discussion of the legislative history of the 1935 Motor Carrier Act and the 1940 Transportation Act, see Doyle Report, *op. cit.* See particularly pp. 130–134 for the more important exemptions from

ICC regulation accorded truck transportation of agricultural commodities.

6. Long-term transportation trends are discussed at length in the Doyle Report, *op. cit.*, chap. 1 of Pt. II. See also *Intercity Ton-Miles*, ICC Statement No. 6103, a study prepared by the ICC Bureau of Transport Economics and Statistics (April, 1961). Pertinent statistics also are published annually by the Association of American Railroads and the American Trucking Associations, both of Washington, D.C.

7. *ICC Practitioners' Journal*, Vol. XXVI, No. 10 (September, 1959), pp. 1143–1145, quoted in part in Doyle Report, *op. cit.*, pp. 122–124.

8. The ICC's Division 2, when it in 1963 approved the full amount of the Big John grain rate cuts proposed by Southern Railway, formally held that barge and truck rates should reflect the federal costs of providing their rights of way. The idea was rejected by the full commission when it, later in 1963, refused to approve the full amount of the Big John reductions. Although the Big John rates eventually were put into effect, nothing came of the Division 2 idea.

Chapter 12: Highways

1. Doyle Report, *op. cit.*, pp. 166, 173. Federal expenditures on highways also are taken from a Bureau of Public Roads publication titled *Federal-Aid Highway Program in 50th Year*, dated September 19, 1965.

2. The government trust fund, as a device for segregating specified federal tax monies from general Treasury receipts and earmarking such monies for particular spending programs, is increasingly popular among special-interest groups. The device assures that tax monies paid by an industry or group will not be used to finance general government spending, such as in the defense or welfare areas, and will not be diverted to particular programs the special interests may oppose. The airline industry, for example, has advocated creation of an Airport Development Trust Fund. Income would come from a 2 percent tax on domestic airline tickets, paid by passengers, and disbursements would be earmarked for $6 billion of new airport construction. See, Stuart G. Tipton, president of the Air Transport Association, in an address before the Cleveland Traffic Club, Cleveland, Ohio, April 24, 1968.

3. E. H. Holmes, director of planning, Bureau of Public Roads, in an address delivered at Sacramento, California, January 28, 1964.

4. See "Freeway Planning Struggle in Washington May Determine Shape of Nation's Urban Highway System," *New York Times*, January 28, 1968, p. 44.

5. "State Highway Officials Oppose Federal Rule for Hearings on New Roads," *New York Times*, November 19, 1968, p. 29.
6. A leading case was brought by Negroes living in North Nashville, Tennessee, to prevent the construction of a highway that would cut their community in two. Federal courts dismissed the action and the Supreme Court declined review. *Nashville I-40 Committee* v. *Ellington*, 390 U.S. 921 (1968), Cert. denied.
7. Message on Transportation, transmitted to Congress March 2, 1966.

Chapter 13: Airways

1. See *Subsidy and Subsidy-Effect Programs of the United States Government, op. cit.*, for a discussion of the development of airline subsidies. See also the annual reports submitted to Congress by the Civil Aeronautics Board.
2. Judge Friendly traces the CAB's case-by-case development of the domestic airlines' route structures and concludes that the board's inability to develop and adhere to intelligible standards of convenience and necessity in the issuance of competitive certificates has imposed higher costs on the traveling public, and needless and serious losses on airline investors." *The Federal Administrative Agencies, op. cit.*, p. 74. See also Landis, *Report on Regulatory Agencies to the President-Elect, op. cit.*, p. 42.
3. *Ibid.*, p. 42.
4. *Report of Task Force on National Aviation Goals*, subtitled Project Horizon, a report to the President (September, 1961), p. 9.
5. The Civil Aeronautics Board repeatedly investigated Howard Hughes's management of Trans World Airlines. He finally relinquished control of TWA in 1966 by selling his stock interest at a very large profit.
6. Knut Hammarskjold, director general of the International Air Transport Association, in an address before the Wings Club, New York City, December 14, 1966.
7. *Report of Task Force on National Aviation Goals, op. cit.*, p. 9.

Chapter 14: The Resultant Chaos

1. Civil Aeronautics Board, Order No. E-22186, in the matter of Military Standby Fares, May 20, 1965.
2. See *Transportation Facts and Trends*, 4th ed. (April, 1967), p. 15. Published annually by the Transportation Association of America, Washington, D.C.
3. *Ibid.*, p. 8.

4. Doyle Report, *op. cit.*, p. 282. Statistics also were supplied by Pennsylvania–Reading Seashore Lines, Philadelphia.
5. See Interstate Commerce Commission, Railroad Passenger Train Deficit, Docket No. 31954, a report dated May 18, 1959.
6. See Penn–Central Merger and N&W Inclusion Cases, 389 U.S. 486 (1968).
7. Civil Aeronautics Board, statement of the chairman to the Senate Appropriations Subcommittee concerning the fiscal 1966 budget, May 12, 1965.
8. Interstate Commerce Commission, statement of the chairman before the Surface Transportation Subcommittee, Senate Commerce Committee, on the "Decline of the Nation's Common Carrier Industry," August 30, 1961.
9. J. D. Braman, *Nation's Cities,* February, 1968. Mr. Braman was mayor of Seattle and chairman of the Committee on Transportation and Communications, National League of Cities.
10. George M. Smerk, *Traffic Quarterly,* January, 1967.
11. Interstate Commerce Commission, report and recommended order of John S. Messer in No. 34733, titled Adequacies–Passenger Service –Southern Pacific Co. between California and Louisiana, April 22, 1968.

Chapter 15: The Regulation of Energy

1. Federal Power Commission, Forty-second Annual Report, for the fiscal year ended June 30, 1962, transmitted to Congress January 9, 1963; p. 55.
2. National Power Survey, a Report by the Federal Power Commission, October, 1964, Pt. 1, p. 1.
3. "Blackout Peril. FPC Worries Utilities Are Moving Too Slowly To Bar Power Failures," *Wall Street Journal,* November 8, 1968, Eastern Edition, p. 1.
4. "A Big Blackout Could Happen Again," *Washington Star,* June 26, 1968, p. 2.
5. *Wisconsin* v. *FPC*, 347 U.S. 672 (1954).
6. *Special Message on Regulatory Agencies,* transmitted to Congress April 13, 1961.
7. Landis, *Report on Regulatory Agencies to the President-elect, op. cit.*
8. Permian Basin Area Rate Cases, 390 U.S. 747 (1968).
9. *Ibid.,* the dissenting opinion of Justice Douglas at 829, 843.
10. Joseph C. Swidler, "The Future Shape of Public Utility Regulation," an address before the Chicago Law Club, Chicago, Illinois, February 4, 1965.

11. Statistics on natural gas production and reserves are published annually by the American Gas Association, New York.
12. John A. Ward III, Sun Oil Company, in "Why the Public Will Be Hurt by FPC Area Price Regulation of Independent Producers of Natural Gas," an address delivered before the Federal Power Bar Association, Washington, D.C., May 12, 1965.
13. For a discussion of the Atomic Energy Commission's accomplishments and shortcomings, from a congressional point of view, see Senator Clinton P. Anderson, "Atoms for Peace: The Dream, The Reality," *New York Times Magazine*, April 30, 1968.
14. See Department of Justice, a statement of Assistant Attorney General Donald P. Turner before the congressional Joint Committee on Atomic Energy, Washington, D.C., April 30, 1968.

Chapter 16: The Master Plan for Television

1. Address before the National Association of Broadcasters, May 9, 1961, Washington, D.C.
2. Minow resigned from the FCC on June 1, 1963, to return to private law practice in Chicago. Subsequently, he served as special counsel to Curtis Publishing Company. He severed his connections with Curtis late in 1967 and later appeared as Chicago counsel for Columbia Broadcasting System.
3. The Federal Communications Commission from time to time has temporarily halted grants of new licenses for commercial radio stations but these periods of cessation have not altered the basic competitive structure of the radio broadcasting industry. One freeze on new grants was in effect from 1962 until 1964, while the FCC prepared new regulations to encourage the operation of new stations in so-called "white" areas of the nation without primary local radio service. Another freeze, perhaps of greater significance to future grants, was ordered in July of 1968. The FCC again was concerned about remaining "white" areas, but it also wanted to study whether there was a "significant national need" for additional AM radio stations.
4. See *An Economic Analysis of Community Antenna Television Systems and the Television Broadcasting Industry*, a report requested by and submitted to the FCC by Martin H. Seiden, February, 1965. The figures are as of December, 1964.
5. *Ibid.*, p. 83.
6. *Ibid.*, p. 10.
7. See the dissenting opinion of Commissioner Robert Jones, to the

Sixth Report and Order on Television Allocations, FCC, April 11, 1952.

8. For a discussion of the economic importance to television stations of network affiliation, see *Network Broadcasting*, a report of the FCC Network Study Staff headed by Roscoe L. Barrow. Printed as a report of the House Committee on Interstate and Foreign Commerce, 85th Cong., 2nd Sess., January, 1958. For a summary, see p. 5.

9. See Staff Report to the Special Subcommittee on Legislative Oversight of the House Committee on Interstate and Foreign Commerce, 86th Cong., 2nd Sess., December, 1960, pp. 26–27. The FCC's policy against trafficking was upheld by the U.S. Court of Appeals for the District of Columbia, *Crowder* v. *FCC*, Cert. denied, November 25, 1968.

10. Details of the Mack case are taken principally from the Initial Decision of Judge Horace Stern, released by the Federal Communications Commission on December 1, 1958. Judge Stern sat as a special FCC hearing examiner, In re Applications of WKAT, Inc., L. B. Wilson, Inc., North Dade Video, Inc. and Public Service Television, Inc., FCC Docket No. 9321 and Nos. 10825–10827.

11. The source of this detail is Schwartz, *The Professor and the Commissions, op. cit.*, p. 196.

12. Seiden, *op. cit.*, p. 1, 27.

13. *U.S.* v. *Southwestern Cable Co.*, 392 U.S. 157, 173.

14. The California pay-TV system, which as proposed would have been the most ambitious subscription television venture in the nation, was organized by Subscription Television, Inc., of which Sylvester L. Weaver, Jr., was president.

15. Radio and television station licenses must be renewed every three years. The FCC renewal process consists of a review of each station's programming, primarily to ascertain that it will air some amount of local news, commentary and public service information along with entertainment programming and national network shows. In fact, renewals are routinely granted by the FCC staff and the commission has never refused to renew the license of a major station on a finding that its programming failed to meet public interest obligations. The renewal process has been criticized from time to time but has remained unchanged. See *Wall Street Journal*, June 3, 1968, Eastern Edition, for an account of the criticisms of two minority FCC commissioners, Nicholas Johnson and Kenneth A. Cox.

16. Comments filed by the NAM Committee on Manufacturers Radio

Use, December 4, 1962, with the FCC in the matter of Inquiry into the Problem of Additional Frequency Space for Land Mobile Services, RM 370.

17. See "U.S. Running Short of Radio Waves for Urban Communications," *New York Times,* July 28, 1968, p. 55.

18. *Radio Spectrum Utilization, a Program for the Administration of the Radio Spectrum.* Report of the Joint Technical Advisory Committee of the Institute of Electrical and Electronics Engineers and Electronic Industries Association (1964). See pp. 6–16.

19. Major portions of the story of the Johnson family's acquisitions of broadcasting properties appeared in the *Wall Street Journal.* See "The Johnson Family Wealth," March 23, 1964. A second article, headed "Johnson and the FCC," appeared March 24, 1964. Both Eastern Edition, p. 1.

20. Supplemental Report of the Committee on Rules and Administration pursuant to S. Res. 212 and S. Res. 367, Senate Report No. 388, 89th Cong., 1st Sess., 1965.

Chapter 17: The Regulation of Banking and Investment

1. See *Investigation into Crown Savings Bank Failure,* a staff report to the House Committee on Banking and Currency, Subcommittee Print, 89th Cong., 2nd Sess., February 21, 1966.

2. J. L. Robertson, in an address before the Independent Bankers Association, Minneapolis, Minnesota, April 11, 1964.

3. See, for example, an address prepared for delivery by James W. Davant, Atlanta, Georgia, November 12, 1968. Mr. Davant, managing partner in Paine, Webber, Jackson & Curtis, spoke as chairman of the Association of Stock Exchange Firms to rebut Justice Department proposals presented to the SEC for lower commission rates for small investors.

4. See *Staff Report on Organization, Management and Regulation of Conduct of Members of the American Stock Exchange,* prepared by the Division of Trading and Exchanges and the Special Study of Securities Markets, Securities and Exchange Commission, 1962.

5. *Ibid.,* pp. 53, 54.

6. *Report of Special Study of Securities Market of The Securities and Exchange Commission, op. cit.*

7. Quoted in "Pending CPA Rulings Expected to Clarify Firms' Profit Reports," *Wall Street Journal,* May 12, 1966, Eastern Edition, p. 1.

8. *Report of Special Study of Securities Markets of The Securities and Exchange Commission, op. cit.,* Pt. 4, p. 708. See Pt. 4, pp. 692–728, for an evaluation and recommendations concerning the performance

of the SEC in regulating stock exchanges and the National Association of Securities Dealers.

9. *Ibid.,* Pt. 1, p. xvi. The comments are made in the special study staff's letter of transmittal to the commission.

Chapter 18: The Labor Market

1. *Soloner* v. *Gartner,* 390 U.S. 1040 (1968), Cert. denied.
2. Statistics on work stoppages are compiled annually by the Bureau of Labor Statistics, Department of Labor.
3. *Report of the Presidential Railroad Commission,* submitted to President Kennedy in February, 1962.
4. *White Collar Employment in 100 Major New York City Corporations,* a survey published by the Equal Employment Opportunity Commission, January 1968.
5. Ulric Haynes, Jr., *Harvard Business Review,* Vol. 46, No. 3 (May–June, 1968), p. 113.
6. *Report of the National Advisory Commission on Civil Disorders* (New York: Bantam Books, 1968), p. 203.

Chapter 19: The Regulation of Trade

1. *FTC* v. *Ruberoid Co.,* 343 U.S. 470, at 488.
2. For a discussion of the origins of the FTC written when legislative history was fresh, see Gerard C. Henderson, *The Federal Trade Commission* (New Haven: Yale University Press, 1924).
3. *Ibid.,* p. 339.
4. *FTC* v. *Procter & Gamble Co.,* 386 U.S. 568 (1967).
5. *FTC* v. *Colgate-Palmolive Co.,* 380 U.S. 374 (1965).
6. The Carter's Little Liver Pills case is perhaps the most labored in the history of administrative law. See the final circuit court of appeals decision, *Carter Products, Inc.* v. *FTC,* 268 F. 2d 461 (1959).
7. The Federal Trade Commission generally has encouraged, or has not resisted, the assignment to it by Congress of an ever growing responsibility for enforcement of laws that require investigative and policing actions. For a well-reasoned exception to this trend, see the Separate Statement of Commissioner Philip Elman, submitted with the FTC majority view, on the proposed authorization to seek temporary injunctions. Letter to the Senate Commerce Committee on S. 3065, 90th Cong., 2nd Sess., forwarded by the FTC on March 27, 1968.
8. FTC press release, titled "Merger Activity Set New Record Last Year," March, 1968.
9. Planning, Regulation and Competition, Hearing before subcommit-

tees of the Senate Select Committee on Small Business, 90th Cong., 1st Sess., June 29, 1967, pp. 5, 7. The percentages of manufacturing concentration are as of 1962.

10. Statement on Consumer Problems and the Federal Trade Commission, delivered before the FTC, November 12, 1968, by Members of FTC Investigation Project. The self-styled project was a private effort of a group of young lawyers headed by John Schulz, Assistant Professor of Law at the University of Southern California. The project was sponsored in part by the *Yale Law Journal.*

Chapter 20: Past, Present and Future

1. Finley Peter Dunne, *Dissertations by Mr. Dooley* (New York: Harper and Brothers, 1906), p. 275.
2. See Harold T. Pinkett, "The Keep Commission, 1905–1909: A Rooseveltian Effort for Administrative Reform," *Journal of American History*, September, 1965, p. 297.
3. See *Final Report of the Attorney General's Committee on Administrative Procedure* (1941).
4. Doyle Report, *op. cit.*
5. Landis, *Report on Regulatory Agencies to the President-elect, op. cit.*
6. Special Message on Regulatory Agencies, April 13, 1961.
7. Report of Task Force on National Aviation Goals, September, 1961.
8. Message on Transportation, April 4, 1962.
9. See Robert F. Kennedy, "Government Injustice to Business," *Nation's Business*, Vol. 55, No. 6 (June, 1967), p. 70.
10. *Freedom of Information Act*, a report by the Senate Subcommittee on Administrative Practice and Procedure, May, 1968, 90th Cong., 2nd Sess.
11. Gordan Murray, Bureau of the Budget, in "Balancing the Books on Transportation," an address delivered at the National Transportation Institute, Chicago, Illinois, January 19, 1965.
12. See "Government, Steel Industry Escalate War over Prices," *Wall Street Journal*, August 2, 1968, Eastern Edition, p. 3.
13. "GM Checks Price Boosts with White House, It Says," *Wall Street Journal*, May 2, 1968, Eastern Edition, p. 2.
14. *Economic Report of the President Together with Annual Report of the Council of Economic Advisers*, transmitted to Congress January, 1967, pp. 115–117.
15. See *Youngstown Sheet & Tube Co. v. Sawyer*, 343 U.S. 579 (1952).
16. See "A Proposed Suit Aimed at Breaking Up GM Poses Perils for LBJ," *Wall Street Journal*, October 31, 1967, Eastern Edition, p. 1.

17. Philip A. Hart, remarks to the Antitrust Section, American Bar Association, Shoreham Hotel, Washington, D.C., April 4, 1968.
18. *Youngstown Sheet & Tube Co.* v. *Sawyer, op. cit.*, at 588.
19. *Ibid.*, at 593, 594.
20. *Flast* v. *Cohen*, 392 U.S. 83, 102 (1968).
21. *Ibid.*, at 111.

Chapter 21: A Proposal for Reform

1. "U.S. Constitution: A New Scrutiny," *New York Times*, March 10, 1968, p. 69.
2. James Roche, chairman of the board, General Motors Corporation, in an address before the Illinois Manufacturers Association, Chicago, Illinois, December 12, 1968.
3. Message on Transportation, April 4, 1962.
4. "Great Society: What It Was, Where It Is," *New York Times*, December 9, 1968, p. 1.
5. James M. Nicholson, member of the Federal Trade Commission, in remarks before the Allied Daily Newspapers of Washington, Vancouver, Washington, May 24, 1968.
6. See Kaysen and Turner, *Antitrust Policy, op. cit.* See also Joe S. Bain, *Barriers to New Competition* (Cambridge: Harvard University Press, 1956).
7. See *U.S.* v. *E. I. du Pont de Nemours & Co.*, 353 U.S. 586 (1957).
8. Kaysen and Turner, *Antitrust Policy, op. cit.*, pp. 266–272, for their draft of a new antitrust law.
9. See "New Policy Urged in Communication," *New York Times*, December 9, 1968, p. 1.
10. M. J. Rossant, writing in the *New York Times*, March 20, 1967, p. 34, also concludes that the Federal Reserve Board's independence of the President is undemocratic and inefficient. Rossant, then a member of the editorial board of the *Times*, argued that the President should have authority to match his responsibility for monetary policy but did not advocate a method by which authority would be granted. Comments on the Rossant editorial page article appeared in the *Times*'s Letters to the Editor columns on March 23 and April 4, 1967.

James J. Saxon, former Comptroller of the Currency, also has criticized the Board's independence. See "More Political Control over Reserve Board Is Urged by Saxon, Citing Its Planning Role," *Wall Street Journal*, June 16, 1967, Eastern Edition, p. 18.

bus industry, 149, 182, 271; military fares, 172–73
business: big, and stability, 266, 284; concentration and Federal Trade Commission, 251 ff.; entry limited, 105–8; protectionism and price regulation, 84 ff.; radio use, 217–19. See also industry; specific subject.

cable companies, 203, 302
campaign contributions, 52, 56, 76 ff.
canals, 134, 145
Capital Cities Television Corporation, 62–63
cartelization, 97 ff., 117
Carter's Little Liver Pills, 257–59
Cary, William, 70, 239–40
CATV (cable television), 214–16
Celler, Emanuel, 81, 88
Celler-Kefauver Act, 255–56, 295
cement and concrete industry, 255
chain stores, 87
Charles River Bridge v. Warren Bridge, 21–22
Civil Aeronautics Board (CAB), 31, 69, 71, 133, 271, 280; appointments, 41, 48, 49, 50; competition limitation, 107–8; congressional relationships, 60; highways, 179–80; hospitality issue, 74–75; industrial pressures, 81–82; nonscheduled airlines, 115–16; planning, 161 ff., 172, 173; Presidential intervention, 277; promotion by, 173
Civil Rights Act of 1964, 244, 248–49, 306
Clayton Act, 86–87, 88, 108, 112, 254, 255, 284, 296
coal industry, 57
Coast Line–Seaboard merger, 109
commercial banking, 10, 11, 106, 111–14, 231–35
commissions. See regulatory agencies; specific names, subjects.
Committee of American Steamship Lines (CASL), 144
Communications Department, 281
Communications Satellite Act, 282, 302
commuter services, 176 ff., 181 ff.
competition, 17 ff., 83 ff.; allocation of natural resources, 18; antitrust

laws, 105, 285; conglomerate mergers, 296; consumer protection, 21; destabilizing, 260; entry limitation, 105–8; limitation of, 104 ff.; mergers, 108 ff., 296; pricing, 9 ff., 20, 84 ff., 115; reaffirmation and reform, 294 ff.; shipbuilding, 142
competitive free enterprise, 5, 290
Congress: agency relationships, 34–35, 53 ff.; appropriations, 34, 60, 137, 153; atomic energy, 201; aviation, 161; banking, 232; broadcasting investments of members, 61–68; campaign contributions, 56, 76 ff., 114; canals, 134; commercial communications, 203; committees, see specific House and Senate committees; competition, 108; highways, 134, 153 ff.; jurisdictional disputes, 171; labor, 242 ff.; mergers, 109, 111 ff.; power industries, 187 ff.; railroads, 147 ff., 181 ff.; reform of regulatory agencies, 265 ff.; regulatory power: 7, 15, 19, 21; delegation, 7, 15, 25, 266, 274–75, 278 ff., 287–88; rewards to from regulators, 61; securities business, 236, 238–39, 240; seniority, 292; subcommittees, see also specific names, 60–61; subsidies, 140 ff.; tenure of appointed officers, 23–25; terms and salaries, 292; trade, 251 ff.; trucking, 149; water transportation, 149, 150. See also specific agency, subject.
Connally, John B., 221, 226
consortiums, 282–84
Constitution: adaptation to big business and big government, 287 ff.; Bill of Rights, 19, 26; Fifth Amendment, 19, 23; private property, and power to regulate, 19; separation of powers, 23, 265, 274; varying interpretations of, 7, 25–26. See also Supreme Court, rulings.
consumer: laws, scope and growth, 3 ff.; natural gas prices, 196–98; price-fixing, 84 ff., 92; regulation and, 81–82, 93–94; transportation charges, 6, 114–15, 127–28, 131. See also specific industry.
Cook, Donald C., 74

telegraph industry, 14, 203, 301; entry limited, 105

telephone industry, 4, 14, 72, 93, 203, 300; entry limited, 105, 106, 107

television industry, 4, 71, 72, 203–28; Albany Channel 10 case, 62–63; all-channel receivers, 213; CATV (cable television), 214–16; channel allocations, 204 ff., 217 ff., 301–2; commercials, deceptive, 257; congressional intervention in behalf of, 54–55; congressional participation in, 61–68; educational, 207, 213; entry limitation, 105, 107; Johnson enterprise, 222 ff.; Miami Channel 10 case, 210–12; networks, 72, 208–9; ownership, 30, 61 ff.; pay- (subscription) TV, 214, 215–16; planning, 204 ff.; VHF and UHF allocations, 206–10, 301–2

Tennessee Valley Authority, 43, 123, 187 ff., 282

tenure of appointed officers, 23–25, 29, 36 ff.

textile industry, 79

tobacco industry, congressional intervention in behalf of, 55–56

Tobey, Charles W., 99

trade associations, 72–73. *See also* specific industries.

trade regulation. *See* Federal Trade Commission; specific subject.

transportation, 4, 5–6, 148–49; authorities, metropolitan, 185; capacity and resources, 174; labor relations, 243, 246–48; laws, study of development of, 270; planning, 131–35, 171–86, 280–81; private, 150, 175, 176 ff.; Under Secretary of, 280. *See also* specific agencies, industries, subjects.

Transportation Act of 1920, 146 ff.

Transportation Department, 133–34, 185, 280–81, 299, 302

trucking industry, 6, 79–80, 94 ff., 121, 149–51; entry limitations, 105, 106; mass transit and, 176 ff.

Truman, Harry S., 25, 41, 46–47, 49, 50, 57 ff., 66, 99, 100, 153, 269, 275, 276, 280, 281, 285

Tugwell, Rexford Guy, 21

UHF and VHF allocations, 206–10, 301–2

unions, 4, 244 ff., 305–6

United States Shipping Board, 40, 140–41

United States Wholesale Grocers Association, 87

urban: highways and expressways, 156–59; mass transit, 176 ff., 181 ff.

Veterans Broadcasting Company, 62–63

Wagner Act, 244

War Claims Commission, 25

water transportation, 133–34, 136–44, 149, 150. *See also* specific agency, subject.

waterways, development and use of, 133, 134, 136–40, 145, 151, 173, 300; hydroelectric projects on, 187, 189–90, 300, 302

Western Trunkline Committee, 95–97

Whiteside, Thurman, 211–12

Wilson, Woodrow, 24, 37, 40, 140, 252–53, 267, 275

yak fat case, 95–97

Zwerdling, Joseph, 194–95

Designed by Robert Freese
Set in 10 point Caledonia Type
Composed, printed and bound by American Book–Stratford Press, Inc.
HARPER & ROW, PUBLISHERS, INCORPORATED